COYOTE
WISDOM

Coyote Wisdom

Edited by

J. Frank Dobie,
Mody C. Boatright, Harry H. Ransoı

Publications of the Texas Folklore Society Number XIV

University of North Texas Press
Denton, Texas

Contents

Coyote Wisdom

Pertinences and Patrons

By THE EDITOR

THE Texas Folk-Lore Society is no longer a one-hoss shay, so far as its editorial staff is concerned. The volume preceding this, *Straight Texas,* had as associate editor Mody C. Boatright, author of *Tall Tales from Texas Cow Camps.* Now Harry Ransom, assistant professor of English in the University of Texas, has been added to the staff. The older an editor grows, even before he grows so very old, the more inclined he is to throw off on others. Boatright and Ransom are mighty good fellows to throw off on. In addition to doing much of the editorial work, they have read proof and made the index of this book. Marcelle Lively Hamer, treasurer of the Society, designed the typography. For various illustrations especial thanks are expressed to Mark Storm, of Houston, brother to the writer Dan Storm. For further help in illustrating, which includes musical scores, thanks are expressed also to Winfred Gustafson and Jack Pence, and to Miss Miriam Landrum for transcribing one of the scores.

In his charming book, *The Charm of Birds,* Viscount Grey of Fallodon says, "No one ever said to me, 'I heard the first willow-warbler today,' or, 'I wonder how many hundred times that chaffinch has repeated his song this morning'; and I grew up without identifying even such common songs as these." Very few people realize on more than a mere fraction of the potentialities for positive living that life offers. An enormous amount of negative existence comes from a lack of awareness of things that surround the

Coyote Wisdom

liver — though one has also to forget a lot of them in order to keep from going crazy.

One of the functions of the Texas Folk-Lore Society is to bring into the realm of awareness the components of Texas and Southwestern life. Our institutions of so-called higher learning, which should be leaders in making people live their own lives more abundantly, are for the most part manned by human beings who in the first place are not observant at all and who in the second place eschew all relevancy to their environment — all beyond an academic circumference that encloses more of the unnatural than of the natural. Every orthodox English teacher, for instance, has been made aware of Reynard the Fox in English and other European literature; only a few realize that Coyote, perhaps the most characteristic animal of the West, the Southwest and Mexico, is the subject for more living tales and myths than the European Fox ever was. Coyote is the hero of this book. His significance in the culture of America is such that only sheer ignorance or stupid pedantry will rule him out of the realm of things worth being aware of.

The Texas Folk-Lore Society never derives enough income from the dues of its members to make publication of the annual books possible. The deficit is largely made up by Patrons and Life Members. A Patron, who is a Life Member, becomes such by paying into the treasury of the Texas Folk-Lore Society $50 or more. The sum is being advanced to $100. Think of it, there was a time when life-membership was only $5! The persons named below have paid $50 or more.

Blaffer, R. L., Houston
Dobie, Mrs. R. J., Beeville
Dougherty, James R., Beeville
Farrell, J. E., Fort Worth
Green, John E., Houston

Pertinences and Patrons

Hill, George A., Jr., Houston
Hogg, Miss Ima, Houston
Marcus, Stanley, Dallas
Miller, Roy, Corpus Christi
O'Connor, Mrs. Thomas, Victoria
Parten, J. R., Houston
Philpott, W. A., Dallas
Randall, Mrs. W. S., Dallas
Sandburg, Carl, Harbert, Michigan
Spoonts, Mrs. Lorrine Jones, Corpus Christi
Walsh, C. C., Dallas
Wharton, Clarence R., Houston

The Little Animals of Mexico

By Dan Storm

El Coyote, the Doves, and the Dogs

LISTEN, and hear how El Coyote was one day stepping through the woods slow in the shadows and swift in the sunlight, looking ahead and listening behind, and smelling in all directions as well as down to the ground and up to the branchy ceiling of the forest. In the brush at the edge of every clearing that lay in his way too wide or difficult to circle, he lingered to hold brief council with his allies—his eyes, his ears, his nose and also his magic and diabolical spirit. Then across through the treeless grass he would pass with his ears flat against his head and his tail almost dragging, his impish eyes moving rapidly, as he went running low on his feather feet.

Many were the smells and voices that came riding to him on the wind from all the *creatures* of the forest of wings, of hoofs, and of claws. And now his ears picked out from the other sounds the notes tranquil and sweet of that song which travels soft but clear through the leafy branches of the waving trees deep from the loving breast of a mother dove.

This Dove was high in a tree so big around that two men embracing it from opposite sides could not have touched the ends of each other's fingers. She was sitting on the edge of her nest singing to her baby *palomitas*. While she was singing her lullaby and admiring her little doves, she heard a voice coming from the ground below.

The Little Animals of Mexico

She looked down and there stood El Coyote looking up at her with a grin too pleasant to be friendly.

"Hola. Good day, Friend Dove. *Cómo le va?* How are you?"

The Dove, very innocent, felt no fear, for El Coyote was too far down to harm her. He could not jump up to the branch that supported her nest, and he had no wings.

"What beautiful children you have," said the Coyote, not giving the Dove time to answer. " How many do you have?"

"They are three," said the Dove.

"Three," repeated the coyote, shaking his head slowly. "That is too many for you. Give me one."

"No," said the dove.

"Give me only the one who is most ugly in the face," said the Coyote, raising his eyebrows and moving his hand in a circle in front of his face.

"There is not one of the three who is not beautiful in the face," said the mother Dove.

"Give me one," said the Coyote, dropping the smile from his face and music from his voice, "or I will knock down this tree and eat all three of your children."

Now, indeed, was the Dove frightened, for she realized that the Coyote was an animal very devilish who could do many things that seemed impossible.

So, rather than see all her children be eaten up by the Coyote, she, much against her will, took one of the little doves out of the nest and dropped it over the side. The Coyote below caught it in his mouth and made a quick sound.

"*Klopt -klopt. Muy bueno,*" he said. "Very good. Many thanks. Give me another!"

"I will not," cried the Dove. "I should never have given you that one, poor little thing," and the mother Dove began to weep.

» 9 «

Coyote Wisdom

"Just as you like," the Coyote called up, extending his arms in a manner very magnanimous, making a gesture of great tolerance and generosity. "But if you do not give me another, I will surely knock down this tree and eat all your children and you, also."

The Dove said nothing and hid her face in fear.

"All right," called the Coyote. "Here I come knocking down the tree."

The Dove could not help looking down to see what the Coyote was going to do. And what did she see? Around and round the tree the Coyote ran more rapidly than a whirling riata. So fast he ran, it seemed he would surely overtake his tail.

As the Dove watched, it seemed that truly enough the tree was falling; poor thing, she did not know she was getting dizzy from watching the Coyote circle the tree trunk.

"Don't! don't!" she cried. "Stop! stop! Do not knock down the tree, I beg you. I will give you another." So saying, she sacrified one more of her little *palomitas* to the Coyote. Then, imagine to yourself only, this scoundrel, so audacious and without shame, asking for another dovelet, the last of the three.

But the mother Dove did not heed the last demand of this bandit Coyote so insolent and devilish. Crying in sorrow, she refused to part with her last darling. Finally the Coyote saw that further success was impossible and went his way laughing loudly at the foolishness of the Dove and at his own wicked wiles, which he thought were great jokes.

The Dove sat mourning in her nest: "U, u, u, ooh - alas." She was very young, this Dove. This was her first nest. But she had learned her lesson. She began very soon to teach this little girl dove who was left in the nest always to keep a good watch for Coyote but never to listen to him;

and never to bargain with those without principle and character.

And so it happened a year later this little Dove had grown up and had a nest up in a tree at the back of a house standing near some hills at the edge of a wide valley. Here lived the *ranchero* with his horses, his cattle, his chickens and his two dogs, large and very swift. They were white with red spots and loud of bark and long of teeth.

These dogs were very good friends of the dove; and because the *ranchero* had trained them to come when he imitated the dove's song, they always answered her call.

At this certain time the same Coyote who the year before had so cruelly tricked this Dove's mother was looking from behind a nearby tree listening to the barking of the dogs up on the hill away from the house and to the soft song of the *paloma* singing thus to her bird children so tender, young, and featherless.

"Another foolish Dove," thought the Coyote. "The dogs are away. This is my chance." So up to the tree behind the house he boldly strode. Beside the doorway of the house, half sitting and half lying, slept the *ranchero* in the sun, his *sombrero* down over his face.

"Good day, Friend Dove," said the Coyote, standing directly under the nest and with the trunk of the tree between himself and the house. "Very beautiful children you have there in that nest."

"Think you so?" said the Dove.

"Yes," said the Coyote. "They are beautiful because they resemble you. Ha-ha, yes, yes."

The Dove gave no answer, and then the Coyote said, "How many do you have?"

"They are seven in all," said the Dove, "four men and three women."

"Ooo!" sang the Coyote, flinging his hand back over his

head in a gesture to express absurdity. "They are too many. It is better that you gave me one."

"Why should I give you one?" asked the Dove.

"Because if you do not, then I shall knock down this tree and eat all of them at my leisure."

"Hurry up, then," said the Dove. "Go ahead and knock it down. *Tumbalo.*"

Imagine the amazement of the Coyote upon receiving such an answer. But wise and magical devil that he is, the Coyote could have soon thought up something to say, but the Dove would not give him time to think. His tongue jumped about in his mouth hunting words, and finding none, remained still. He tried to summon his thoughts rapidly to his aid with the result that his ideas in anxious haste became confused and began running together inside his head.

While Coyote stood thus speechless and with his mouth open—a very unusual pose for this fellow—under the tree, the Dove cast a glance up at the sun.

"I believe it is mid-day," she said, "the hour of dinner for the dogs. I think I shall call them."

"*Pues,* call them if you like," said the Coyote, tilting his head back and to one side and lifting his shoulders up about his ears. "It is of no importance to me."

You see El Coyote thought that the Dove was playing his own game. To him the idea of the Dove calling the dogs was absurd; he thought she was resorting to his own bully and bluff.

For a moment the Dove listened toward the hills, not far from the house, where the dogs were hunting. They were barking from time to time; and then for a time they would be silent. The *ranchero* was still asleep by his doorway, his face on his knees and his *sombrero* on the back of his neck, his arms clasped over his shins. Under the tree below the nest stood the Coyote waiting for the time to get ripe for him to run in a circle under the tree round and round the trunk so as to make the dove dizzy enough to lose her sense or fall out of the nest. Little did he know that all the running he was ever to do again would be in a fairly straight line.

For a moment the dogs on the hill stopped barking, and in this moment the Dove in her nest was seen to take a deep breath of air. With all her might she sent her soft but sonorous call echoing up to the hills: "*Tu - - Tu.*"

The Coyote said, "Here I go knocking the tree down." But hardly had the words left his mouth when he heard the brush break at the foot of the hill, and saw the two dogs red and white come bounding into the clear toward the house, their tongues lashing their teeth.

In the same moment that they saw the Coyote the dogs loosed a terrible yelling: "Yo! Yo! Yo! Yo! No, Yo, No, Yo. No-Yo."

With the big fellows nearly upon him and both claiming him as their prize, the Coyote had no choice of direction and took straight across the level desert valley, as the oncoming dogs had cut off his retreat to the hills.

Far faster now he flew than ever he had flown around trunk of tree, dodging among the cactus, magueys, and boulders too tall to leap, and darting under low mesquite limbs, while behind him in the cloud of dust he was raising he heard the dogs arguing at the top of their voices, as they raced each other, lessening at every leap the distance between their diversion and his health. Frantically he called upon his powers to rally to his aid in this hour of uneven odds. He realized now that two can run faster than one. Sharply his frantic eyes swept the hills across the valley. Straight ahead he could see something that looked very good to him if it were only closer—something dark and round. His brains told him that this was a cave, and told him also that with every *momento* that passed the dogs were coming closer to the settlement of their loud argument.

Coyote in his terrible race realized that the dogs were well matched for speed and would reach him at the same time. They would thereupon divide him and re-divide him. As Coyote had these thoughts the dark spot on the hillside became only slightly larger—not at all in proportion to the growing loudness of the clamoring of the dogs in the dust behind. How could the dogs follow him so closely through all the dust he was kicking up? Harder he struck the ground with his feet and farther he leapt in his mad running. Would the cave never near? The ground rose upward before his face as the bottom of the hill presented itself. Up, up, he dashed straight toward the cave with the dogs almost upon him, exploding like cannons in his ears. Before him black and round appeared the cave as the breath of the dogs blew hot upon him from behind. Gathering all his strength for a final leap into the cave, Coyote heard the dogs become silent and knew that they had opened their mouths wide behind him, but not to bark. Diving like a flying frog into the mouth of the cave, he felt an idea very terrible quickly haunt his brain, as the dog jaws came together behind: *click-klop*, uprooting some of the tip-end hairs of his tail.

The terrible thought that had possessed El Coyote upon the moment of his flying dive into the cave was that the mouth of the cave might be large enough to let the dogs enter also. But good luck had touched him this day. The cave door was just big enough to admit him, and it was made of solid stone. The dogs stuck their noses in and sniffed and growled but soon saw that they were cheated and began running back and forth in front of the cave grumbling and yelling: *"Ni tu, ni yo! Ni tu, ni yo! Escapa'o! Escapa'o!"*

Then they ran down the hill, their voices growing fainter

and fainter; but Coyote inside the cave so welcome and benign, sitting with his back tight against the far wall, blowing as if he were trying with all his might to bring some dying embers in a fire to life as quickly as possible, knew dog tricks well enough to know that it would not be best to stick his nose out of the cave for hours yet.

Bueno! There he sat safe and sound, and quickly his courage returned. Victorious again. The dogs would never get him now.

Directly he began laughing at the dogs, and talking to the various members of his body about the episode so exciting.

"*Patos,*" he said, looking at his four feet one at a time, "what did you do?"

"We," spoke the feet, "what did we do? We carried you away. We kicked up dust to blind the bad dogs. We jumped over the cactus and rocks. And we sent you flying into this cave."

"Good, very good," said the Coyote to each of the statements of the four feet. "You fellows did well."

He then addressed his ears. "And, Ears, what was your part in this affair?"

"I listened to the right," said the right ear.

"And I to the left," said the left ear.

"We both listened behind to know how close the dogs were so that the feet would know how fast to carry you," said both of the ears at the same time.

"*Múy bueno,* my Ears," said the Coyote. "Very good indeed. And, Eyes, what did you do in this contest with the enemy?"

"We did many things," said the eyes. "We picked the road for feet to run on. We saw the cactus and rocks that were too high to jump. We watched always for your safety. Yes, and it was we who saw this very cave. Yes, and we guided you to it."

Coyote Wisdom

"Splendid," said the Coyote. "Very truthful and very good remarks, my Eyes." And he became very proud of himself and turned loose a yell and a laugh of approval.

"You are very able allies, fitting companions for one like me. Who can defeat me? No one! Aha . . ."

So saying, in his satisfaction with himself, he reached over his shoulder and patted himself affectionately between the shoulder-blades. As he did this he chanced to see his tail back there.

"*Que hubo!* What ho, my old friend Tail! By the saints, I was about to forget you. Some of your hairs gone from the end of you, I see. You came very near to getting us caught. Did you not? No? Yes? Let me hear what you were doing in the midst of the battle. Come, come, where is your tongue? Give account of yourself."

Coyote should have known that the tail was the thing that balanced him and kept him straight when he jumped over rocks or cactus, and kept him from falling down in making a sharp turn; and in fact enabled him to jump straight into the mouth of the cave without hitting the sides. But he really thought his tail rather useless; and the tail knew he thought thus.

And what was the tail's answer? "I," said the tail, "what did I do? I was back there motioning the dogs to run faster and get you. I waved beckoningly to them all the way, and in the dust, I waved from side to side so they could see me in my whiteness and thus follow you the better. I showed them which way you were going."

"*Silencio!*" shouted Coyote, trembling in all his body with surprised rage.

"Traitor!" he roared, exploding the word from his mouth like a mouthful of poisoned water. "*Traidor y sinverguenza.* Yes, not only traitor but one utterly without shame. As if it were not bad enough to be an ingrate and an enemy within the ranks, you have no bridle on your tongue. Having betrayed, you now throw insults at your benefactor. After having plotted against the one who saved your life, you now become insolent."

El Coyote's voice rose with his wrath. "You do not merit being one of us, ingrate and unworthy one that you are." Thereupon, he arose and stood with his back toward the cave opening. Pointing first to his tail and then shaking his finger at the round piece of daylight that was the cave door, he threw all his wrath into a bellow that made the cave walls ring:

"Get out! Outside!"

And, imagine the barbarity, he began walking backwards step by step to the cave door, cursing his tail at every step and commanding it more fiercely to go outside. Figure then to yourself what anger must have been his, that— marvel of marvels unbelievable—he backed his tail outside the cave door into the shining daylight.

Outside, on either side of the cave, the dogs were waiting ready. And when they grabbed the tail, they caught the Coyote also. So you, having listened to this story, now realize that men have learned their ways of life from El Coyote.

"Get out! Outside!"

Coyote Wisdom

The Coyote and Juan's Maguey

This was a country fellow very poor named Juan. He had no other crops except one maguey plant. His *jacal* was the same size as the others in this same region; but, standing near this maguey plant, it looked like a child's house for dolls, because this maguey was the largest one in all the country. It held its blades curving over the roof in the manner of the branches of a tree.

Juan was very proud of this giant maguey, which gave him his living; he tended it with care and affection. He did not use a gourd and straw to suck out the *agua miel*, as this "honey water" is extracted from ordinary magueys. He bailed the honey water out from the hollow in the center of the great maguey with a gourd dipper and stored it in jars. The plant gave so much honey water that he had plenty to sell and plenty left over to make pulque to drink during the plant's period of resting.

And now after many mornings of good harvest from his great plant, came Juan just at sunup out of his house toward his maguey, gourd and jar in hand. He was singing a *cantina*, a bar-room song, that he had composed out of his own head—about this maguey of his, the greatest in the world.

Mi novia, mi maguey
Nunca falla, nunca falla,
Con su dulzura,
Nunca falla
Con el agua miel.

My sweetheart, my maguey
Never fails, never fails,
With its sweetness,
Never fails
With its honey water.

Hardly looking at all into the hollow among the great leaves in the trunk of the plant where the sweet liquid always collected without fail, he dipped his gourd down

The Little Animals of Mexico

and presently stopped his song and became somewhat sober. The hole was dry.

On his hands and knees Juan looked for tracks, and right away he saw them. They were of the little hands and feet of a Coyote.

"This thief must be caught," said Juan to himself. "He will continue this custom and tell all his *compadres* how sweet and delicious is this *agua miel*."

So all day Juan cut long poles with his *machete* and sharpened them on the ends and drove them into the ground very close to each other around the great plant. By dusk he had built a round corral almost as high as his head about the maguey. Close to the ground he made a little door just large enough for the Coyote to enter. He filled the hollow up with *agua miel* and put a little pulque in there also and walked away past his house toward the hill just as darkness was dropping little by little from the sky. Juan did this so that if the Coyote were watching him, the animal would think the man was nowhere around because he could not smell him.

Before the dark could all come, the moon showed its rounded section above the nearby hill top, and then the world got lighter and lighter until the whole round moon was very brilliant; and here in the moonlight came the Coyote trotting straight up to the maguey.

From the moon-shadows where he was hiding, Juan watched the Coyote stop in surprise when he saw the fence. But he must have been very thirsty for the *agua miel*, because he went around the corral till he saw the little door. Then he quickly entered.

And here came Juan, stooping low in a creeping run on his *guarache*-shod feet, fingering in his hand a stout stick. As he approached the corral, he could hear the coyote already saying "Slup, slup; gulp, gulp."

Coyote Wisdom

"Drink well, my fearless devil," Juan whispered, as he stepped close against the corral, leaning directly over the little door. "Drink well, shameless one. For it is your last drink." So saying, he drew a deep breath and tore the air, shrill and loud, with a *vaquero's* Indian yell.

From outside the corral Juan saw the Coyote jump backwards out of the hollow straight up into the air into the moonlight and begin running with his feet while still in the air. Down he came and went flying around and around the inside wall of the corral so fast that he could neither stop nor see the little door. Juan thought that this was the funniest thing he had ever seen in his life and fell immediately into an insane fit of laughter: 'Hua, hue, huee-haaa! What fright I gave him. Hua, hua, haee!"

Finally, while Juan was laughing so loudly and bragging about the terrible fright he had given the Coyote, this animal found the door and stuck his head through to come out.

" . . . LAUGHING AND BRAGGING . . . "

The Little Animals of Mexico

In this moment Juan raised his club—still laughing—to bring it down upon the Coyote's head; but there he stood, holding his club aloft in the air like a statue, paralyzed with laughing while the Coyote came through the hole in the corral and escaped, running past Juan's front door. Juan tried to throw his club at the Coyote just as he turned the corner of his house, but, no. All he could do was stand there laughing and saying, "What a fright I gave him!" Not until the Coyote was out of danger in the night was Juan able to stop his laughing and begin cursing, in his frenzy stamping on his *sombrero*.

Juan, at that time, threw upon himself the blame for failing to kill the Coyote, but if he has any more sense now than he had then, he knows that the Coyote, through certain powers as a magician, simply chose this method of casting him under a spell of witchcraft.

Mr. Coyote and the Two Sheep

Two Sheep, one thin and one very fat, were traveling through the country. When they rounded a turn in the trail, who should step out from behind a joshua tree and stand facing them but Mr. Coyote—grinning, with his hands on his hips, there in the middle of the road.

"Good day, Friend Sheep," said the Coyote, glancing up at the sun. "I have not yet had breakfast this morning."

"Do not eat me," said the Fat Sheep. "I am too fat. You might choke."

"Oh, do not eat me," said the Thin Sheep, "I am too thin. See how the bones are trying to come out of my hide."

"I am going to eat both of you, of course," said the Coyote. "Only I cannot decide which of you to eat first."

"Don't eat me first," spoke up the Fat Sheep. "Save me for afterwards."

Coyote Wisdom

"Do not eat me first," cried the Thin Sheep. "There is not enough of me to get started on."

"In order to decide this question," said the Coyote, "we will play a game."

He was going to divert himself with these two foolish creatures. Looking to the left and the right of the road, he saw that the land was level. Then with his toe he began drawing a line lengthwise of the road down the middle in the sand.

"Now, Fat Sheep," he said, "you take fifty steps straight out from this line to the left, and you, Thin Sheep, you take fifty steps straight out from this line to the right. I will stand here with one foot on either side of the line, and when I give you the signal with my *sombrero*, both of you start running as fast as you can to see which one of you can cross the line first right here in front of me. The winner will be eaten second and the loser first."

When the Coyote had finished giving his orders, the two Sheep began taking their steps very carefully out from the line, counting aloud: one-two-three, while the Coyote was drawing the line deeper in the sand with his toe there in the middle of the road.

When the two Sheep had finished taking their fifty steps and stood at equal distances in opposite directions from the road, the Coyote shouted final instructions for the race.

"When the *sombrero* comes down over the line, that is the signal to start running. Cross the line right close in front of me so that I can judge the winner and shout his name as soon as he crosses the line. If Fat Sheep crosses first, I will shout '*Gordo!*' If Thin Sheep crosses first, I will shout '*Flaco!*' So get ready to run your best, boys, for the first over the line will be the second dish for dinner."

Mr. Coyote raised his big *sombrero* at arm's length over his head. "Ready, Sheep! Watch the *sombrero* . . ."

The Little Animals of Mexico

Swoosh! And the *sombrero* came swinging down and the two sheep jumped, running furiously toward the line in front of the Coyote, who stood there straddling it, holding his *sombrero* behind him with both hands, grinning so that the ends of his Coyote mustache were up in his ears. Villain that he was, he was expecting to laugh loudly when the two Sheep in their blind haste would run into each other in their headlong rush to the line and crack their skulls open. This was to be his diversion. So he had not told the truth when he said that he would shout the winner's name. He was going to mention neither of their names, for he cared not who won the race.

Closer, closer came the hoof-beats of the two Sheep, running from opposite directions very evenly, and bigger became the Coyote's devil grin as he looked down at the line he was straddling. The Sheep were close now, and the Coyote was opening his mouth not with intention of judging the race but with the idea of laughing. The Sheep were almost about to cross the line now. Then, just one jump from the line, they swerved out of their course one step and both together came flying right at Mr. Coyote.

"THEY RAMMED THEIR HEADS AGAINST HIS RIBS"

Before he could move out of his tracks they had rammed their heads against his ribs from both sides at exactly the same moment, making him judge the race against his will, for their simultaneous charge at his ribs knocked him off the ground and forced a loud and truthful word squawking out of his mouth with all his air, "It's a tie."

By the time Don Coyote was able to regain his breath and get up off the line he had drawn in the middle of the road, the two sheep were such small specks on the landscape that it was impossible for him to tell which was Lean and which was Fat.

Señor Coyote Acts as Judge

At the foot of a high mountain one day lay that bandit of the *animalitos*, Señor Rattlesnake, basking in the sun. While he lay sleeping, a great stone somehow came loose high upon the mountainside and came rolling down and finally settled right on top of Mr. Rattlesnake, pinning him fast to his bed.

After the snake had remained a writhing prisoner under the stone for some hours and had begun to fear that no one would ever come to his rescue except an enemy, here came jolly Señor Conejo.

"Greetings, Mr. Snake," said Mr. Rabbit. "I see you are trying to crawl under that stone."

"Do not taunt me, please, Brother Rabbit," begged the Rattlesnake in a pitiful voice. "I am in terrible pain. Only roll this stone off of me, and I will see that you are well rewarded."

Now Mr. Rabbit knew well that the Rattlesnake was no friend of his; but he was a friendly fellow and hated to see even his worst enemy in distress.

"Very well," he said, and began immediately to push and dig his feet into the ground, first on one side of the big stone and then on the other. Finally, after much pushing and prying from the good Rabbit, the heavy stone rolled half over and Mr. Rattlesnake was free and there stood Señor Conejo very tired.

"Now," said the Rattlesnake, "in regard to your reward . . ."

"Oh, that will be all right," said the Rabbit.

"Yes," said the snake, "I think it will be all right enough."

"What do you mean?" asked the Rabbit.

"I mean," said the Rattlesnake, "that as a reward for your help to me you are to have the privilege of being my dinner."

"No, no!" cried the Rabbit, beginning to walk backwards. "Do not eat me, Hermano Vibora!"

"Yes, yes," said the Snake, following the Rabbit and keeping his snake eyes fixed firmly upon him. "I must have my dinner."

In this very moment appeared Señor Coyote.

"What goes on here?" he demanded. Both the Rabbit and the Snake began talking at the same time. Each was willing for Señor Coyote to act as judge.

"Thus it is," the Rabbit said. "I came here and found Señor Rattlesnake helpless under this stone, and I pushed it off of him. He promised me a reward, but I ask none. All I want is my life. What a reward he wants to give me! He wants to eat me up. That is to be my reward. Now does it seem to you . . . ?"

"Nonsense and foolishness," the Snake interrupted. "What Señor Conejo says is not the truth. I was under the stone, true enough, but I could have gotten out from under it any time. Señor Conejo was trying to roll the stone upon me so that it would crush me. Thus, I have the right to eat him."

Señor Coyote sat thinking with his chin in his hands, looking first to the Rabbit and then to the Snake. "Let us

Coyote Wisdom

see," he said slowly. Then he said, "My friends, we must settle this matter very correctly. Now in the first place both of you are agreed that Señor Vibora was under the stone. Is it not so?"

"Yes," said the Rattlesnake, "that is true."

"Yes," said the Rabbit, "that is correct."

"Very well," went on Señor Coyote. "I must know now just how everything was. Mr. Rattlesnake, will you please move over here next the stone and Señor Conejo and I will roll it back on top of you so that I may get an idea of just how everything was when Señor Rabbit arrived upon the the scene. Then, you see, I can decide the thing correctly."

The snake agreed, and the Rabbit and Señor Coyote rolled the stone back upon the snake's back.

"Now," said Señor Coyote, "is that the way you were, Brother Rattlesnake?"

SENOR COYOTE GETS AN IDEA

» 26 «

"Yes," said the Rattlesnake, squirming in discomfort. "Yes, this is the way I was."

"*Pues*, that is the way you will stay," said Señor Coyote. "Now you have your reward for trying to eat Mr. Rabbit after he had treated you with kindness."

Judging Between Lions

King Lion and Queen Lioness were sleeping in their cave in the mountains one night, when King *León* coughed and awoke. "How can I sleep?" he growled to Queen *Leona*. "Your nose smells so terrible it keeps me awake. I cannot sleep. Your nose smells too bad."

"You lie," said the Queen Leona; "it is your own nose you smell. Nothing more."

From this they began to quarrel louder and louder. At daybreak they were still shouting at each other, and then the Leona in real anger raised her clawed hand to strike her husband. Immediately the León became more pleasant of manner, at the same time putting his arms up about his face to defend himself.

"Patience, please, my dear wife," he said. "We will call together all the animals and creatures from the mountains, the plains, and the forests; and they shall decide which of us is the offensive one—today."

The Leona agreed, and King León sent word out over the land by his crows, who flew in all directions telling the creatures to come to the meeting at once, as a decision very important was to be made that same day.

Before long, from every direction they began coming in on the trails until by mid-day the Bear, the Burro, the Horse, the Goat, the Armadillo, the Buzzard, the Paisano, the Rattlesnake, the Fox, the Javelina, the Coyote—all had arrived. Oh, many, many, they came from afar and close by—these creatures of claw, of hoof, and of wing until all the creatures of the land from small to large stood assembled in front of the royal cave.

"*Bueno*," said Queen Leona in a loud voice, as her fierce eyes swept from one to the other of the gathering, "we are about to decide an important question. Señor Burro, step up here and see if you can tell us whether it is Señor León or I who has an ill-smelling nose."

Without hesitation Señor Burro stepped out from the crowd, and immediately bowed low to the Queen and smiled, for he was not without his gallantry and was very proud to win the favor of a fine lady like the Queen Leona. He went first to the Lion and smelt his nose and then to the Lioness. "Ah," he said, "this is easy to decide. You, Señor León, are the offensive one."

The queen laughed heartily as the Burro, very proud of himself, smiled at her and then at the rest of the animals.

"See only how smart is this fellow," she said to the Lion. But the Lion was not impressed much by the decision and was already making pieces of the unfortunate Burro.

"You will have to do better than that," the King Lion told the crowd, as he looked from one animal to the other. "Come here, Miss Sheep. I think you can settle this matter."

Little Señorita Sheep was a great admirer of the big León, and as she stepped out from the crowd it was plain to see what her decision would be. With a haughty glance at Señora Leona, she made only a pretense at smelling the noses of the king and queen and said, "It should be plain that Señora Leona is the disagreeable one."

Loud was the King's laugh, but quick was the Queen's leap upon the Sheep, who went the way of Señor Burro.

"I wonder if there is someone out in that gathering who has some brains," snarled the Lioness, shading her eyes with her paw and scanning the great crowd of creatures who were now beginning to show definite signs of becoming uneasy. Her eye found Señor Coyote trying to hide behind Señor Caballo, the Horse, and her manner brightened sweetly.

"Don Coyote," she sang out pleasantly, "come out from behind Mr. Horse where we can see you, handsome fellow. You are such a wit and such a very fair fellow, that you, I am sure, can decide this question in a simple and just way."

So saying, the queen gave Don Coyote her best smile and motioned him to the front.

Now Don Coyote liked the ladies, but he was not the one to fall into this kind of trap baited with flattery. Here was a man who was no fool. As he stepped forward through the crowd of creatures, every head turned to look eagerly into his face.

The crowd was silent and motionless as Don Coyote went first to smell the King's nose and then the Queen's nose. Then with an air of great fairness and impartiality, he spoke. "I think you both had better stop this quarreling," he said, walking back and forth in front of the King and Queen. "After a careful consideration of the situation I find that neither one of your noses smells any too sweet." And Señor Coyote turned his back upon the Leon and the Leona and started to walk back into the crowd, thinking that he would hear a burst of applause from all present for having solved things so cleverly; but, no, he had hardly taken a step before the Leon and the Leona came flying through the air landing upon the Coyote both at the same time, and began fighting each other in their haste to destroy him quickly.

Some sort of commotion was going on in the back of the crowd. "What is it, back there?" shouted the King.

"Señor Zorro, the fox, is trying to leave the meeting without permission," came a voice, and it was Mr. Rattlesnake speaking.

Coyote Wisdom

"What does this mean?" roared the King. "If you have anything to say for yourself, say it quickly."

Señor Zorro began to talk, but his words did not reach up to the King and Queen.

"Come up here in front where I can hear you," shouted the Lion.

"Yes, do come up here, Don Fox," called the Queen. And immediately a path began opening up in the crowd of animals, and here came little Mr. Fox walking up to the front with his big *sombrero* in his hand.

Before the King could begin scolding him, the Queen began to talk. "Señor Fox, I hear that of all the creatures in the world you are the sharpest of smell. They say you are a very gifted fellow in many ways. And so good looking, too. Please settle this thing here and now, once and for all." And she smiled upon him a smile even bigger than the one she had given Don Coyote.

Without a word Mr. Fox went up to the Lion and smelt his nose, sniffing loudly. Then he went and smelt the nose of the Lioness, sniffed the air several times, and smelt again. Then with his big straw hat held behind him with both hands and his head down, he began walking back and forth in front of the two mighty beasts upon whose capricious notions his life depended.

Then, as all the birds and brutes in the animal crowd watched him closely, he again went up to the Lioness and sniffed with all his lung power at her nose. Up to the Lion he went again and smelled at his nose, making a noise louder than a wild horse snorting. Shaking his head, he turned away and stood with his chin in his hands thinking. Thus he stood silent, shaking his head from time to time and scratching his head first with one hand and then the other. Every pair of eyes present was fixed directly upon the small body of Mr. Fox. They had all seen Don Coyote, the arch-trickster, come to failure. Would the cunning of the Fox fail likewise? So it looked. Señor Fox was at the end of his rope, bewildered, speechless.

Impatience overpowered the King and the Queen, and they shouted in one voice to the Fox, "Speak, man, speak! Have you lost your tongue?"

The crowd moved closer as the Fox began to speak. "Ahem," he coughed. "Ahem, I can hardly speak," he said, his voice coming in a low hoarse whisper out of his throat. "The truth is that I fell asleep out in the open as I lay down under a tree last night on my way home from the *cantina.* This morning my wife asked me where I had been. Ahem! When I opened my mouth to explain, I found I had lost my voice, such a terrible cold I had caught. So she drove me away from the house, thinking I was just sulking and did not want to answer. I am just now beginning to be able to talk just a little; but the truth is, Señor King León and Señora Queen Leona, your majesties—that my

"SPEAK, MAN! SPEAK!"

catarro is still so terrible that I am unable to smell anything at all!"

Señor Coyote and Señor Fox

In this certain country of which I am telling you there was a great rock very tall standing alone in the center of a plain. Looking at it from a distance, one would think that it was perhaps a church tower that had come straight up through the ground. But upon approaching closely to this strange thing, anyone could see that it was a great cliff higher than any church.

One day when Señor Zorro was traveling through this country he lay down to sleep in the shade close to the wall of this cliff and close to one corner. But Mister Fox never sleeps in the daytime with both eyes closed, and this is why he saw Señor Coyote before that very smart animal saw him. When he saw the Coyote's shadow appear around the edge of the cliff, the Fox sprang to his feet and started pushing against the wall of the cliff.

"Pues, mira no mas! just look!" exclaimed the Coyote. "After all the times you have escaped from me, here we are at last met again. Aha, do not try to climb the cliff, man. Stay for dinner. It is meal time for me."

"Cuidado!" yelled Mr. Fox, pushing against the face of the cliff and skidding his feet on the ground. "Look out! This cliff is falling. Help me hold it up. Hurry!"

Mr. Coyote looked up to the top of the high cliff, and as he was standing right almost against it, it did seem to be toppling slowly over.

"It is falling, sure enough," he gasped and with a leap was at Mr. Fox's side pushing against the cliff and grunting and pawing a hole in the ground to hold his feet.

"We can't continue this for a very long while," said the Coyote between puffing and blowing. "We will perhaps stay here until our bleached bones will be propped here holding up this rock."

"I tell you what we will do," said the Fox. "It is certain that we must hold this cliff up. We cannot try to run to safe ground, because we cannot outrun this cliff when it once really starts falling. It is only trying to topple now. You keep on bracing the rock up and I will run and get some help and also some food."

"Oh, no," said the Coyote quickly, "it is necessary for both of us to be here to hold up this cliff."

"You saw me holding it alone when you came up," Señor Fox gravely replied. "Surely, you with your strong muscles can hold it about half an hour. And that is the very most time that I will be in returning with some of my friends bringing log props and food and pulque."

"All right," said the Coyote. "I suppose I could hold this thing for half an hour. I guess I do not know my own strength. But only hurry. And remember, half an hour, Brother Fox."

"Yes, yes," said Mr. Fox, easing away from the cliff, "only push harder, now that I am not helping you. Harder! Harder!" And Mr. Coyote strained and put his shoulder to the cliff, digging his feet deeper into the ground.

"Until half an hour, no more, Brother Coyote," called the Fox over his shoulder. And he was off galloping with light jumps across the level desert, away from Mr. Coyote sweating and panting against the cliff.

A half hour passed. And no Señor Fox. Señor Coyote was still at his post pushing with all his might. An hour passed, and still Brother Fox did not appear. Mr. Coyote became terribly tired and impatient. From time to time now he began to glance up to the top of the cliff and relax his hold for just an instant. But every time he relaxed, it seemed that the cliff would begin falling. So he would almost fall himself in his haste to push harder.

Coyote Wisdom

The sun went down behind the distant hills and up came the moon over the mountains to the east. And Mr. Coyote turning his head painfully over one shoulder and then the other could not see Mr. Fox or anyone else anywhere on the landscape.

All night long while the moon traveled overhead to the other horizon, Señor Coyote was pushing against the cliff and howling and calling for the Fox. But he got no answer.

The moon went down and up came the sun where the moon had come before, and what did the sun see but Señor Coyote up past his knees in the hole his feet had dug. There he stood whimpering and gasping for breath and cursing, and yelling for Mr. Fox.

"I have no strength left in my arms to hold this cliff," he half sobbed aloud. "Maybe with good luck I can run faster than this cliff can fall. It is my only chance."

So Señor Coyote took a deep breath, shut his eyes, and sprang out of his hole and dashed from the cliff, running so fast he seemed to be flying with only his ears and tail for wings. When he was about a quarter of a mile away, he looked back expecting to see the great stone cliff lying on its side in an immense cloud of dust. But there it was, upright, as always before. Mr. Coyote could not believe his eyes. "It cannot be," he said, when he was able to get enough air to spare some on words. "How can it be?" He sat down on the ground, and when his strength returned came also his reason; and the idea came to him all at once that the Fox had fooled him another time. Up into the air he jumped cursing and yelling and shouting what he would do to Mr. Fox the next time he saw him.

And Señor Fox, where was he? *Quien sabe?*

Paisano Saves Rabbit from Rattlesnake

Many are the tricks of the Paisano, called by the gringoes the chaparral bird or roadrunner. He has many ways

The Little Animals of Mexico

of fighting his enemy the rattlesnake, such as building a corral of thorns around him, and throwing prickly pear in his pathways. But the strangest thing of all that he ever did to the rattlesnake was the time he saved the rabbit's life.

The snake was *enborrachando*[1] the rabbit, swaying his head from side to side and crawling closer and closer to the little helpless animal who could not move at all but stood there trembling unable to escape from the rattlesnake's spell.

Just when the big jaws of the rattlesnake were about to close down on the rabbit, out of the brush came this little *animalito*, the Paisano, running on his long legs. Up to the snake he ran, holding a long thorn in his beak; and while the snake's jaws were yawning wide, the Paisano, darting from the side, put the long thorn into the snake's mouth, straight up and down, propping his mouth open. Now the snake was helpless, and the little rabbit was free, and the Paisano was very happy.

[1]Literally, making the rabbit become drunk; charming.

"He put the thorn in the snake's mouth"

The Coyote:
Animal and Folk-Character

By LILLIAN ELIZABETH BARCLAY

THE tales about Old Man Coyote, the most popular and colorful character in the legendary lore west of the Mississippi, seem to be inexhaustible, for in every language and dialect (and there are many Amerind languages and dialects), a different cycle is found. Yet, in all these cycles runs a thread of strange similarity. If all the coyote tales told by the Amerinds were collected, there would be enough to fill several volumes. To make such a collection, carefully edited, with all variants of each tale properly placed, would be a worthwhile but stupendous undertaking.

As a trickster, Coyote is to the western Indian what Br'er Rabbit is to the southern Negro, what Reynard is to the European. He is more vivid than either of the other animals.

The fables about him are unlike the fables of European literature; there is no bitter meaning underlying the laugh, no casting of ridicule on institutions of society. They are beast comedies, not beast satires. They come from the folk, not from the literary artist. They may point a moral; they endlessly iterate fancies of aboriginal races about the origins of man, earth and a thousand physical factors of the observable universe, thus revealing a whole system of religion and philosophy. But many of them are stories for entertainment, fairy tales, the animal comedy, as people who looked upon all other animals as brothers saw that comedy.

The literature of Reynard the Fox may have more finish and polish, due to centuries of telling and retelling, writing and rewriting before Don Coyote, along with America, was discovered by Columbus; but the literature of coyote is broader in scope, ranging from tale to pure myth. It is as vivid and as arresting as the land in which he lives.

The first American folk tales heard and recorded by Europeans are found in the reports of the Jesuit Fathers, who, beginning in 1633, chronicled tales current among the tribes with whom they came into contact. Among those tales were several unusual ones about coyote. Since that time, priests, adventurers, explorers, ethnologists, and naturalists have recorded much fact and fiction concerning this animal character. Thanks are due these faithful collectors for gathering such a wealth of material for posterity's profit and enjoyment. Much of it, however, is not well written. Not until recently, comparatively speaking, has appreciation of the literary value of the vast body of native American folk tales come to the fore. At present the literature of the subject, already great, is being rapidly augmented in all fields of writing. There are books that deal with usual, unusual, and sometimes amazing episodes of animal life in a charmingly interesting and scrupulously honest and accurate way not found in similar books of an earlier date. There are many collections of Indian folk tales, some of which lack the brightness and vivacity that such retellings should have. It takes an understanding heart and a flare of genius to develop from the literal translations of the ethnologists and folklorist tales that are vivid, authentic, and readable, that lose none of the flavor given by the originators. Some few writers have achieved this

distinction, among them Frank Hamilton Cushing and
Mourning Dove (Humishuma).

I

The Coyote as Representative Animal
of the Southwest

The coyote, along with the cowboy and the rattlesnake,
is an integral part of Western and Southwestern North
America. Oren Arnold says he "probably is the one wild
creature that is most associated with the West and the
Southwest. He is part of our daily living here, an old timer
likely to be seen or heard any day."[1] Ernest Ingersoll calls
him "a true westerner," typifying the "independence, un-
restrained gaiety, and brisk zeal which enter into the heart
of him who sights the Rocky Mountains."[2] Charles F.
Lummis identifies him with the very landscape,[3] and to
John C. Van Dyke, he belongs to the desert country as
essentially as do the dry arroyos and washes along which
he skulks.[4] James W. Steele thinks that the representative
animal of the West should not be the buffalo but the
coyote, because he comes closer than the buffalo to being
the figurehead of the great West. He should, therefore,
adorn its escutcheons.[5]

The word *coyote* is an *aztequismo,* having no counter-
part in Castilian.[6] It comes from the Nahuatl word *coyotl,*[7]
the radical meaning of which, according to scholars, is
variable. Robelo, after explaining that the word *cocoyotla*
is plural, so made by the duplication of the first syllable,
writes: "The name coyote can be a corruption of *cocoyoc-*

[1]*Wild Life in the Southwest,* p. 51.
[2]"The Hound of the Plains," *Popular Science Monthly,* 30:350.
[3]"The Coyote," *The Land of Sunshine,* 3:215.
[4]*The Desert,* p. 159.
[5]"Figurehead of the Frontier," *Outing,* 50:407.
[6]Robelo, *Diccionario de Aztequismos,* 1904, p. 131.
[7]Simeon, *Dictionnaire de la Langue Nahuatl ou Mexicaine,* p. 109.

The Coyote: Animal and Folk*Character

tla, which is composed of *cocoyoctic,* hole or hollow thing, and of *tla,* a particle indicating abundance, and meaning, 'Where there are many holes'."[8] This explanation gives rise, perhaps, to Brinton's view that the root of the word *coyote* meant hole, the animal being so named because of his habit of burrowing his den. Fifteen years after making the explanation just given, Robelo issued this one: "The name properly is *coyohuacca,* which is composed of *coyotl,* from which has been formed the *aztequismo* coyote, and *huaqui,* meaning lean. This interpretation is authorized by the hieroglyphic, which consists of a coyote with bristling hair and tongue hanging out, indicating a lean and hungry animal. The name properly must be *coyohuacca,* because the names terminating in *qui* converted the *qui* to *ca,* and now they do not take another ending."[9]

A study of the hieroglyphic and its variants and the explanation and the derivation of the word itself in Pena-fiel's *Nomenclatura Geografica de Mexico*[10] would indicate that the latter theory is the better supported by fact, though the hole in the body of each variant of the hiero-glyphic is somehow significant. But whatever the root or its original meaning or the reason for giving the name to this particular animal may be, it is certain that both animal and name are indigenous to America.

Pronounciation of the word *coyote* varies with the local-ity. The correct Spanish pronunciation is given as ko-yo-ta, almost koi-o-ta, but in western United States usage almost universally makes the first syllable ki, with the pronuncia-tion either ki-o-te or ki-ot.[11] A provincial pronunciation is ky-ute.

Not always has the word been spelled coyote. F. W. Beechey in *Narrative,* printed in 1831, wrote it cuiota,

[8]*Nombres Geograficos Indigenas del Estado de Morelos,* p. 20.
[9]*Diccionario de Aztequismos,* Nueva Edicion, 1912, p. 108.
[10]Penafiel, *Nomenclatura Geografica de Mexico,* Secunda Parte, p. 68; Atlas, p. 23.
[11]Webster, *New International Dictionary.*

which is, according to Seton, the earliest form of the word found in English print.[12] Seton is also responsible for the information that "Cased Wolf" is an old trade name for coyote, because its skin was cased like that of the muskrat.[13]

Besides having an untold number of nicknames, El Señor Coyote has more given names than a crown prince. The sur- or scientific name for the most generally known type (according to Lantz there are a dozen species, eight of which roam the United States[14]) is *Canis latrans Say.* Indians, however, use no such generic term. Coyote was one of the Animal People, and as such had a very special and meaningful name. Among the tribes he is variously called Skinkoots, Mes-cha-cha-gan-is, Huk-sa-ra, Hatelwe, Cin-au-av, Song-toke-cha, Mee-yah-slay-cha-lah, and Sin-ke-lip, just to mention a few of the designations. What the farmers and the ranchers whose sheep he kills and whose chicken houses he raids call him is more pronounceable but scarcely as printable.

The Okanogan Indians tell a tale about how coyote got his name. The Spirit Chief, according to Mourning Dove, announced that on a certain day he would give names to all the Animal People. He who came first should have the choice name, and so on down to the last comer, who should get the least desirable name. Coyote, who did not like his name, Sin-ke-lip, or Imitator, was gleeful. He planned to stay awake all night and thus be the first to appear next morning. He decided on Grizzly Bear, the name of the ruler of all four-footed people, as his first choice, on Eagle, ruler of birds, for second choice, and on Salmon, the good swimmer, for third. Half the night passed and he became sleepy. So he braced his eyes apart with two little sticks. "Now I can stay awake," he said. But before long he was fast asleep,

<hr>

[12]*Lives of Game Animals,* Vol. I, Part II, p. 355.
[13]*Ibid.*
[14]*Coyotes in Their Economic Relations,* p. 7.

The Coyote: Animal and Folk-Character

although his eyes were wide open. The sun was high when his wife called him. Only half awake and thinking it was just dawn, he ran fast to the lodge of the Spirit Chief. Seeing none of the Animal People there and smiling broadly at his cunning in being first, he asked for the name Grizzly Bear. The Spirit Chief said, "That name was taken very early today." Coyote could hardly believe anyone could have come earlier than he. Then he asked for the name Eagle, then for the name Salmon. At last it dawned on him that something was amiss. His gay spirit drooped and drooped when he found that all the names but Coyote had been taken. No one had wanted that name. The Spirit Chief at last said, "That is the only name left. You must take it. It is good for you. But to compensate you for the unpopular name, I shall give you special magic power, which will make you wiser than any other animal. I have important work for you to do: to conquer the People-Devouring Monsters. For doing that, for all the good things you do, you will be honored and praised; but for the foolish and mean things you do, you will be laughed at and despised. That you cannot help; it is your way." So coyote he is and wise he is today, being sometimes praised and often blamed and despised. And ever after that night his eyes were different. They grew slant from being propped open while he sat by the fire waiting for daylight.[15]

Like the Indians, authors of short stories with coyote as the central figure choose for him such special names as suit their interpretation of his character, some of the more interesting being Kiyi, Kiote, Gray Dusk, Bareribs, Skeezix, Tito, Kip, Señor Yip-yap, Romulus. Of the appellations bestowed upon him in the past half century by American writers, Ishmaelite seems to be most popular. Others are Desert Serenader, Scavenger of Sagebrush Land, Father

---

[15]Mourning Dove, *Coyote Stories*, pp. 15-28.

Coyote Wisdom

Coyote, Hobo of the Hills, God's Dog or The Medicine Dog, Desert Bohemian, Vagabond of the Desert, Mugwump of the Plains, Voice of the Night, Wingless Vulture of the Plains, Prowler of the Night, Pariah of the Skyline, Wild Dog of the Desert, the Charlie Chaplin of the Desert, Shaggy Fellow, Furry Gangster of the Desert, Desert Troubador, Esau among the Tribes of the Desert, A Wanderer O' Nights and a Lier-by-Day, the Patti of the Plains, and Don Coyote.

It is odd how man reacts when animal names are applied to him. If he be called a fox, he is a little flattered; if he be called a coyote, he is ready to fight. For years the appellation coyote, like that of rat or skunk, has gathered to itself an opprobrium, due, perhaps, to the animal's legendary traits of being a cowardly braggart, and his factual traits of liking carrion. But since each animal has at least a few bad traits and since coyote has no more than the average, it should follow that the name coyote should be no more resented as an epithet than the name of any other animal usually accepted with equanimity. Charles F. Lummis, indulging in a bit of cynicism at man's expense, remarks: "So far as concerns man and his one flatterer, the dog, the coyote shines brilliant by comparison. . . . Seeing the wild dog with so much wit, and the tame one so perennially witless (for the hounds never learn the joke), one might wonder at it—if one did not remember that the domestic *canis* is handicapped by long looking up to the least observant animal that goes on legs."[16] Man does not like being called dog either. Yet, South Dakota accepts the nickname of Coyote proudly, and the Wichita Falls high school football team are the Coyotes.

It is interesting to study word pictures of the coyote. Horace Greeley describes him as a "sneaking, cowardly little wretch of dull or dirty-white color, much resem-

---

[16]"The Coyote," *Land of Sunshine*, 3:215-216.

bling a small, short-bodied dog set up on pretty long legs."[17] "He is similar to the gray wolf," says Oren Arnold, "Although one-third smaller. He looks much like a police dog, with a thinner nose and a furtive, wild look in his eyes. When fat or otherwise in fine condition, he is a handsome animal,"[18] implying that oftentimes he has a lean and hungry look. "Far from being the starved-looking creature described by many writers, the coyote," explains Jack O'Conner, "is usually sleek and fat; and in the long cold winters of the higher elevations, his coat becomes a glossy thing of beauty. A thin coyote means either that he is very old or that there is nothing left to eat in the country."[19] Theodore Roosevelt judges that coyotes have an average weight of thirty pounds and that they are about "one-third the size of the big gray timber wolves of the Northern Rockies."[20] Another asserts that the carcass of a skinned coyote is often no bigger than that of a large Western jackrabbit. There is a "whimsical cock to his head," writes Lorene Squire of an eleven-year-old coyote, "with eyes happy and bright, like a happy and carefree dog intent upon some absurd adventure," when unmolested. But when he is cornered, the happy yellow eyes suddenly glare green, "in them a gleam of demon's laughter."[21] He looks candid enough at play, remarks L. W. Rakes, but wild and vicious when scared, his face giving him the expression of a man who has beard and mustache.[22] Irene Finley, who with William Finley not only writes of coyotes but also photographs them beautifully, describes one thus: "He is golden tawny, medium-sized, pointed-

---

[17] *An Overland Journey*, p. 92.
[18] *Wild Life in the Southwest*, p. 46.
[19] "Furry Gangster of the Desert," *Readers Digest*, 28:47.
[20] "Wolf Hunt in Oklahoma," *Scribner's*, 38:513-532.
[21] "The Hunt of the Coyote," *Nature Magazine*, 22:151-154.
[22] "Shaggy Fellow," *Catholic World*, 125:217-221.

eared and -nosed, with clear, deep yellow eyes, a trim, slinking shadow."[23]

Indians have a why-story for most of the phenomena of nature. One such story comes from the Solians, who tell "Why Coyote Has Yellow Patches Behind His Ears."

"Coyote, wanting to be as beautiful as Rabbit, asked him, 'What did you do to have such beautiful yellow shoulders?'

"Rabbit, who was afraid of Coyote, replied, 'Why, my neck is yellow because I am always going into holes in the ground.'

" 'Good!' said Coyote. 'Then I'll go into holes, too!'

"He found a hole and went in. Then Rabbit got some hay, threw it into the hole behind Coyote, and set it on fire. Coyote was badly burned in trying to get out of the hole, and on this account he has a yellow patch behind his ears!"[24]

Another Indian story, Pima, relates "Why Coyote Is the Color of Dirt"—even if he isn't.

Once upon a time the coyote was a beautiful, bright green. He did not like being green, because he looked just like the grass and the leaves on bushes and trees. "I wish I were some other color," he said to himself, as he walked along the path. Soon he came to a lovely little lake. Coyote did not know that it was a Magic Lake. Just as he began to lap a drink of water, he saw a very ugly, black and brown bird standing on the shores. It sang a song, then dived into the water, bathed for an hour, and then came out in its bare skin. It stood on the shore, sang the song again, dived again into the water, bathed, came out, and repeated the performance twice more. The last time it came out fully dressed in beautiful blue feathers. Coyote

[23]"The Wild Dog of the Desert," *Mentor*, 12:28-29.

[24]Mason, "The Language of the Solian Indians," *American Archaeology and Ethnology*, XIV:88, Cal. U. Pub.

» 44 «

had never before seen anything so gay and lovely. He asked, "How is it that all your ugly color has come out of you and that now you are all blue and gay and beautiful? You are more beautiful than any other thing that flies in the air. I want to be blue, too."

"Oh, this is a Magic Lake," replied Bluebird. "If you will bathe here for an hour four times each morning for four mornings and sing a Magic Song each time, you will be blue, too."

"I'll do it," said Coyote. "Will you teach me the Magic Song?"

And Bluebird taught him this song:

> The blue sky is
> In the blue water;
> I went in —
> I am all blue.

Then Bluebird flew away. Coyote stayed by the lake for four days and nights. He was afraid that if he went away he would not find the lake again. For four mornings he bathed four times in the Magic Lake and sang the Magic Song. And it happened just as Bluebird said. On the last morning he shed his coat with the first bath and with the last came out a beautiful blue. He was happy as he walked along. He looked this way and that, to see if anyone were watching him. "I want everyone to see how beautiful I am," said Coyote. Then he watched his shadow to see if it were blue. All at once he fell over a stone and rolled in the dirt. Up he jumped and tried to brush off the dust. But he could not, and the beautiful blue color was gone.

Coyote could never find the Magic Lake again. So to this day all coyotes are the color of dirt.[25]

As for his character, writers about the coyote, considered in the aggregate, have made him a super Dr. Jekyll

---

[25]Russell, Bureau of American Ethnology, Vol. 26, p. 245 (paraphrased).

Coyote Wisdom

and Mr. Hyde. T. Shoemaker[26] catalogues him as crafty, alert, knowing, cunning, sly, watchful, wise, a marauder, a killer, hated by man and other animals. Pertinacity, zeal, sagacity, endurance, trickery, impudence, piracy, thievery, unmannerly deportment, strategy are some terms applied by other writers. "Every man's hand is against him, and with reason," states one. "He displays a cunning, exceeded only by his cowardice," declares another. "He has a lot of patience, and a sense of humor," defends J. Frank Dobie. Lorene Squire argues that he is just a plain contradiction, a part of him the drift of the wind, part like a little dog Trixie, part a lone Gypsy always wandering, another part like a great, gray wolf, and the rest of him just plain devil—a mean, sneaking, cowardly, low-down chicken stealer, but never a cringer or beggar, sometimes mocking, other times impudent, always independent and airy, but ever loyal to his own.[28] "A beautiful coyote hide wraps up more deviltry than any other hide of equal dimension stretched over an animated form," observes Enos A. Mills. "His successful cunning and his relentless ways of getting a living cause him to be cursed by those whom he plunders. But he is always interesting and appears to enjoy life even in midst of lean times. He is the Clown of the Prairie. He is cynical, wise, and a good actor. He has a liking for action and adventure. He really is a happy fellow, something of a philosopher and full of wit."[29]

Ingersoll sums him up thus: "He is the Ishmaelite of the desert; a consort of rattlesnakes and vultures; the tyrant of his inferiors; jackal to the puma; a bushwacker upon the flanks of the buffalo ranges; the pariah of his own race, and despised of mankind. Withal, he maintains himself and his tribe increases; he outstrips animals fleeter

---

26"Kiote," *Outlook*, 101:679.
28"The Coyote of the Plains," *Nature Magazine*, 17:162-167.
29*Watched by Wild Animals*, p. 86.

than himself and foils those of far greater strength; and he excels all his rivals in cunning and intelligence."[30]

Of all the indictments against coyote, cowardice seems least justified by facts. It is not cowardice but judgment that causes the coyote to avoid making a target of himself, and his resourcefulness in this respect has caused disgruntled hunters, trappers, and property owners whose premises he has raided to proclaim him a coward. He has courage enough to go his way and make his raids in spite of the best efforts of all who would prevent him. No cowardly creature would persistently take chances in raiding melon patches closely guarded or in killing sheep inclosed near a house.

Oren Arnold writes: "It is rare that you find a true coward among Nature's children, and certainly coyote is not one. That unfair blot on his character is due to the fact that he runs away from man and packs of dogs, and uses his cunning when hunting food. But the truth is, he would be stupid not to. Why is it cowardice to run from a creature of far greater intelligence and size, who in his bravery also carries a deadly gun? Why is it cowardice for coyote to run away from two or more trained fighting dogs, all bigger than he and all backed by armed men? Why is it cowardice for a coyote to run when an angry bull charges, or an enraged stag? The horns or paws of each are deadly. Wouldn't you run, too? Why is it cowardice if a coyote stalks and kills smaller creatures than he, or sometimes slays a calf or a lamb? Doesn't your cat catch anything he can? This is Nature's way, for the big animals to prey on the smaller."[31]

"He is a wag—and, like most wags, timid; though I deem it no honor to their intelligence that many call him a

---

[30]*Wild Neighbors*, p. 100, and "The Hound of the Plains," *Popular Science Monthly*, 30:360. (Quotations in two sources differ slightly.)

[31]Arnold, *Wild Life in the Southwest*, pp. 47-48.

coward. Do they expect a thirty-pound dog to attack man?" questions Lummis.[32] "He displays both courage and fighting blood whenever there is anything to be gained by such display," Enos Mills concedes. "Recklessness and rashness do not constitute bravery."[33]

There have been instances of coyote's crippling or killing as many as two attacking dogs, and hunters can tell more than one story of a coyote's fierce bravery against unfair or overwhelming odds. One such story is told by a hunter of the Biological Survey in Colorado who witnessed a battle royal between a coyote and a bobcat, with the coyote pushing the fight. There certainly was no sign of cowardice on coyote's part in that duel of skill and strength.

Hunters on horseback with a pack of six hounds were once on the trail of a coyote that ran 'til exhausted, relates Lorene Squire. Knowing that at last he was done for, coyote suddenly turned, his eyes gleaming, and waited. "Then the pack was upon him. The men on horseback saw a scramble of yellow, bleeding hounds and now and then one bloody, shaggy demon, green-eyed, slashing here and there. Then they could no longer see him. They parted the dogs; there lay a mangled piece of yellow fur—and two dead fox hounds. The remainder of the pack was sadly slashed and torn.

" 'I'm glad to see that sneakin', dirty, worthless four-flushin' coyote killed,' said a huntsman on a heavy Western saddle. 'I didn't think them hounds could do it.'

"The owner of the hounds looked quizzically at these native huntsmen. Then he surveyed his torn and depleted pack. He picked up the thirty-pound carcass of coyote. 'So this is what you call the cowardly coyote?' he said."[34]

---

[32]"The Coyote," in *The Land of Sunshine*, 3:218.
[33]*Watched by Wild Animals*, 94.
[34]"The Hunt of the Coyote," *Nature Magazine*, 22:151-154.

The Coyote: Animal and Folk-Character

Indians say that coyote, unlike man, never kills wantonly, but only for food. As a matter of fact, given a chance, he may in an hour kill more kids out of a flock of goats than he can eat in a week—but then he is not particular about having his meat fresh. His business in life is not essentially different from that of man; namely, to find and get his daily meat. He looks for this with diligence and singleness of purpose, with skill and cunning and an animal patience which far excels the virtue known by that name in men and women. The qualities of skill and patience are particularly well shown in his killing, without coming to grief, a porcupine.

Often are yarns told of ferocious coyotes, as well as of wolves, attacking some human being. Vilhjalmur Stefansson, the explorer, has disposed of such reports in a book called *Adventures in Error*. Various instances of rabid coyotes biting human beings have been recorded, but a coyote with the rabies is not himself, and rabies among these animals are rare. Lummis affirms that: "Nothing can be more ridiculous than fear of coyote. A hunter would sit down as unconcerned amid a thousand coyotes as if they were rabbits—unless he had something stealable. As a sneak-thief the coyote is as enterprising as his big grey cousin is a highway robber and assassin. I have several times had a coyote step across me while I slept; and among the diversions of our wedding journey in the wilderness was the waking one night to find two coyotes fairly over us, trying to get saddle-bags from between our heads and the big pine tree which was our hotel. It needed no more than the creak of any eyelid to send the interlopers flying."[35]

Coyote is neither a pariah nor a hermit. Instead he is noted for being sociable and coöperative with his own kind. Mills reports seeing one or more coyotes staying near a crippled coyote as though taking care of him, and en-

[35]"The Coyote," *The Land of Sunshine*, 3:218.

deavoring to lure away any hunter who approached. Coyotes will assist each other by hunting in relays. They have a system of intercommunication, including signal stations, which may be a stone, a tree, a post, or an old buffalo skull, at which a coyote may leave a message, or learn by odor of the last comer. The whole country is marked by these intelligence depots. Coyote uses his voice to ask for information, to call for help, and to give warning. A leader may search out food, scout the lay of the land, and look out for traps or poison. When assured that all is quiet and clear, he will signal the pack to come. He may mount an eminence and broadcast his message, which will be picked up and relayed, so that within a few minutes the latest news or order or an urgent warning reaches all coyotes within a radius of many miles.[36]

Many are the tales illustrating coyote's love of play, his penchant for teasing or joking, and his sense of humor. A hunter rode up on three coyotes yelping and howling around a tortured panther perched on a stump. The coyotes were teasing the panther and nothing more, and they were having the time of their lives.[37] A coyote often makes a monkey of a dog. Ernest Thompson Seton tells a story that well illustrates the point.

Chink, a conceited and lively puppy, had attached itself to the naturalist's camp on the Yellowstone. A coyote had also attached himself to the campers, pilfering the garbage pile and often sitting on a ridge about two hundred yards away and there making observations on human ways. One day a camper sicked Chink after his impudent cousin.

"Burning to distinguish himself, that pup set off at full speed, and every time he struck the ground he let off a war-whoop. Away went the Coyote and it looked like a good race to us, and to the Picketpin ground-squirrels

---

[36]Mills, *Watched by Wild Animals*, pp. 86, 96; Seton, *Lives of the Hunted*, p. 309.
[37]Dobie, *On the Open Range*, p. 28.

that sat up high on their mounds to rejoice in the spectacle of these, their enemies, warring against each other.

"The coyote has a way of slouching along, his tail tangling with his legs, and his legs loose-jointed, mixing with his tail. He doesn't seem to work hard but oh! how he does cover the prairie! And very soon it was clear that in spite of his magnificient bounds and whoops of glory, Chink was losing ground. A little later the coyote obviously had to slack up to keep from running away altogether. It had seemed a good race for quarter of a mile, but it was nothing to the race that began when the coyote turned on Chink. . . . His war-whoops gave place to yelps of dire distress, as he wheeled and made for home." The coyote not only outraced him but during the chase ran circles around him, nipping him here and there to emphasize the joke and not stopping till the ambitious pup was hidden under his master's bed. Thenceforth, as his actions showed, whether anybody sicked him on or not, he was determined to leave coyotes alone.

"The Coyote, however, had discovered a new amusement. From that day he simply 'laid' for that little dog, and if he found him a hundred yards or so from camp, would chase and race him back in terror to some shelter. At last things got so bad that if we went for a ride even, and Chink followed us, the Coyote would come along, too, and continue his usual amusement."[38]

Whether the following incident was just plain teasing or a game of tag entered into mutually, George Bird Grinnel was not quite sure. Riding out to look at a bunch of cattle, he saw a badger and a coyote going over a hill. "I had no gun," he says, " and the coyote seemed to know it, for he paid no attention to me, but appeared to be playing with the badger. He would prance around it, make a feint of biting it, and then run off a little way, the

---

[38]Seton, *Wild Animals at Home*, pp. 8-10.

badger immediately running after him. This he did until the badger had gone sixty or seventy yards, then I got so near the two that the badger saw me and ran into a hole, and the coyote trotted off forty or fifty yards and lay down. . . . Either the two animals were playing together, or else the coyote was teasing the badger."[39] As a matter of fact, it is known that coyotes "dog" badgers in order to catch and eat wood rats that the badgers dig out of nests in prickly pear; also that badgers sometimes dig out and eat rabbits that coyotes run into holes. It would be natural for the mutual interdependence of the two animals to result at times in playfulness.

Shoemaker describes Kiote as sitting patiently on his haunches and watching a badger, an animal too tough for him to tackle, dig out a ground squirrel. "The badger dug and dug, and presently emerged with his prey. Immediately Kiote began to harrass him, yelping and snapping in the badger's face. After a particularly well-feigned attack, the badger would drop his dinner and throw himself on his back in an attitude of defense." Kiote trotted off with the unearned morsel, leaving the badger to dig another hole.[40]

The coyote's sense of humor is often more ironic than playful: "I have," says Enos Mills, "seen a coyote look at a deserted and tumble-down building and strike an attitude of mocking at the failure of man. Sometimes he catches a chicken while the family is away, and carrying this to the back porch to feast, leaves the unconsumed feathers there."[41] He has been known to leave a sign, universally understood as connoting contempt, on an unsprung steel trap.

The saying, "smarter than a steel trap," may be derived from this gesture. "Next to God," says the *pastor*, a goat

[39]Grinnell, "About Wolves and Coyotes," *Forest and Stream*, 7:512.
[40]"Kiote," *Outlook*, 101:679.
[41]Mills, *Watched by Wild Animals*, p. 86.

The Coyote: Animal and Folk-Character

herder, in J. Frank Dobie's *Tongues of the Monte,* "the coyote is the wisest creature in the world." His judgment in keeping beyond gun-shot and in determining when a man is armed or not armed has been the subject of extensive comment. "If he is not a mind reader," says Dr. W. T. Hornaday, who cannot be classed with Mills and Seton as "romantic naturalists," "his actions belie him. Twice in Montana, each time for two weeks, have I tried my utmost to shoot a coyote, but during those periods not one would offer more than a running shot at three hundred yards or more. Twice, however, when I was riding quite unarmed, coyotes sat down beside the trail, waited for me to approach within forty yards, then yawned in a bored manner, and slowly trotted off."[42]

Such close observers as Mary Austin and Enos Mills say that coyote recognizes landmarks and steers his course by them, showing that he is himself a pretty close observer. But he is not only an observer; he seems also to reason. Imogene Humphreys relates how Kiyi, daughter of a coyote mother and a collie father, procured a chicken dinner.

"We had two hens in a small pen. One was old and scrawny, the other a pullet. One day I noticed Kiyi did not eat her dinner. She lay beside the dish. There was a peculiar look in her eyes. I watched her. She watched me. For a long time she did not make a move. Then, when my back was turned, she took a small bit of food and went toward the chicken pen. Then she put another bit of food a short distance from the first. Finally she laid a trail of food up to her box where the chain was fastened. Then she lay down to wait. Over the fence came the pullet. She clucked along from one bit of food to the next bit. When she was within leaping distance, Kiyi leaped. Later she tricked the old hen."[43]

---

[42]*American Natural History,* 1904, p. 24.
[43]"Kiyi," *Nature Magazine,* 22:283-284, Dec., 1933.

Coyote Wisdom

A coyote, it is claimed, always comes up to a chicken coop on the leeward side, so as "to hear you approach, and for the wind to take his noise and odor away from you."[44] The yarns that trappers spin about the coyote's cleverness in detecting poison and avoiding traps are matched by instances of coyote strategy recorded by naturalists. Pronouncing the trick a stock joke — with the coyote — better known than appreciated by ranch folk, Lummis tells how one coyote will excite dogs that feel responsible for a chicken yard or sheep corral, toll them off on a will-o-the-wisp chase, and then how, when they return with lolling tongues and depressed tails, they will find that the accomplices of their mocker have stolen a sheep or a chicken.[45] Grinnell details the manner in which a single coyote tolled a dog, which had with joy been practicing the art of chasing coyotes away from a ranch house at night, into an ambuscade of a half-dozen other coyotes. They would have killed Shep if a man with a gun had not gone to the rescue.[46]

According to stories "as many as an ox has hairs," the coyote can out-possum a possum himself. As Inocencio, in J. Frank Dobie's *Tongues of the Monte*, tells one *cuento*, there was "a householder whose chickens slept in some mesquites inside a corral of solid adobe walls. The gate opening into it was solid and it was always kept shut. There was a hole, a very small hole, in the wall even with the ground, and through it the chickens went in and out.

"Well, one night a coyote got through the hole. . . . The morning following, the householder went out as usual to inspect all his little animals. There in the corral the ground was covered with feathers, with chickens without any heads and heads without any chickens. It was a barbarity.

44"Shaggy Fellow," *Catholic World*, 125:217.
45"The Coyote," *The Land of Sunshine*, 3:215.
46"About Wolves and Coyotes," *Forest and Stream*, 47:511.

The Coyote: Animal and Folk-Character

And there over in a corner was the assassin swelled up like a heated bladder of a hog. His legs were sticking out, his mouth open, and all else was in the manner of an animal that is well dead from having been herbed. It was in the time of summer and the hide was of no value. The man thought, 'This coyote filled his stomach so full he could not pass through the little hole in the wall and then he died from something wrong in his system.'

"He called the boy to drag the creature away. The boy came and gave the body some kicks and tied a rope on its hind legs and went dragging it over rocks and gullies and through little thorn bushes. He dragged it something like a hundred *pasos*. The man was standing watching him all the while. Then the boy stopped. 'Take it farther still,' the man yelled at him, 'so that it will not stink to us.' Then the boy went on a distance farther. He took the rope off the legs and gave the body some more kicks and started back to the house.

"The man was still watching. When the boy was half-way back, the man saw the coyote raise up his ears and then his head. All was safe. He leaped to his feet and galloped off into the brush. The coyote can play dead better than a possum. He is *muy astuto, muy diablo*."[47]

One of coyote's characteristics, not a very favorable one, is his liking for carrion and his enjoyment of rolling in offal. Mary Austin insists that he is not a scavenger by choice, preferring his own kill, but being, on the whole, a lazy dog, is apt to fall into carrion-eating because it is easier. She relates that "once at Red Rock in a season of green pasture, which is a bad time for scavengers, we saw two buzzards, five ravens, and a coyote feeding on the same carrion, and only the coyote seemed ashamed of the company."[48]

---

[47]*Tongues of the Monte*, p. 274.
[48]*The Land of Little Rain*, p. 54.

Coyote Wisdom

Mills reports an incident so similar as to appear to be the same one: "He has a liking for carcasses, no matter how smelly or ancient. I once saw a coyote feeding on a dead mule along with ravens and buzzards. He did appear to be a trifle ashamed of his companions; for though he seeks adventures and is almost a soldier of fortune, he has a pride that does not sanction indiscriminate associates."[49]

There have been many attempts to describe the "music" of the coyote. "A coyote's song is more conducive to sleep, more musical, more pleasing than the music from a neighbor's radio," remarked J. Frank Dobie in a lecture. In *On the Open Range* he writes, "I like to hear his lonely and eerie howl in the night. I like to ride along and know he is watching me from behind some prickly pear bush. Coyotes are good company."[50] "A coyote," observes Oren Arnold, "has the most famous voice in the wilderness—a dog-like yelping, half bark and half growl. Two coyotes on opposite hills, calling each other, will sound like a dozen or more."[51]

This multiplicity of sound is remarked by Jack O'Connor: "The coyote is among the noisiest of animals, giving at dusk a short, yipping bark that re-echoes through the cañons so that half a dozen coyotes seem like a hundred to the uninitiated. But in the serious business of running game he is silent except for little half-suppressed yelps of excitement."[52]

C. F. Holder corroborates the impression of the one sounding as many: "Don Coyote yelped, becoming so enthusiastic over the melody of his song that notes fairly piled on one another, gathering volume until they became ventriloquistic and went echoing far and wide, conveying the impression to the one startled listener that a pack of

---

[49]*Watched by Wild Animals*, 93-94.
[50]*On the Open Range*, 27.
[51]*Wild Life in the Southwest*, p. 43.
[52]"Furry Gangster of the Desert," *Reader's Digest*, 28:48.

The Coyote: Animal and Folk*Character

particularly ferocious coyotes was surrounding the camp."[53]

Enos Mills also describes coyote as a ventriloquist, saying: "He has a remarkable voice. It gives him a picturesque part. Usually his spoken effects are in the early evening; more rarely in the morning. Often a number, in a pack or widely separated, will engage in a concert. It is a concert of clowns; in it are varying and changing voices; all the breaks in the evening song are filled with startling ventriloquistic effects. The voice may be thrown in many directions, and the efforts of two or three coyotes seem like those of a numerous and scattered pack."[54]

"One man in a million," says Charles F. Lummis, "can become a ventriloquist; every coyote is one at birth. He is the only breathing thing that has this unvarying birthright. ... He can so 'place' his voice that you shall not know if it came from north, east, south, or west. As a multiplier— well, hearing one coyote, no newcomer but will swear it is a dozen. ... That wail is the strangest, weirdest, most baffling sound known to any wilderness—a wild medley of bark, howl, shriek, and whine utterly confounding; and as to its articulation, glib as nothing else I know except the sound of irregular musketry. The swift patter of vocables is something almost indescribable. It is this voice which has earned him his scientific name—which is unscientifically applied. He is not a barker (*latrans*), but a bewailer, and should be ticketed *ululans*."[55]

"His voice," asserts J. W. Steele, speaking of one certain coyote, "was the principal part of him. He threw back his head in an ecstasy of discord and gave it to the wind and the silence in a quick succession of staccato yelps that made two of him seem like two hundred. Nobody ever knew why he did it, the common opinion being that it was for amuse-

[53]"Don Coyote," *Outing*, 45:692.
[54]*Watched by Wild Animals*, p. 96.
[55]"The Coyote," *The Land of Sunshine*, 3:216.

ment; not for others, but for himself, like a man practicing upon a brass horn."[56]

One must have spent an hour or two vainly trying to sleep before he is in a condition to appreciate fully those short, sharp barks, given in quick succession, growing faster and the pitch getting higher until they run into a long-drawn, lugubrious howl in the highest possible key. Rakes explains how this lugubrious "music" is made: "He opens his mouth rather widely, the more widely, the higher the pitch. Then the lower jaw is vibrated slightly up and down."[57]

The poets have found in the coyote's song inspiration for a song of their own. To John Curtis Underwood, well-known writer of free verse who hails from Santa Fé, coyote's song is not melody, but a discordant howl.

He howls as a leper howls
When health and wholesomeness and human touch are taken
 from him.
He howls as evil men must howl in evil dreams,
Seeing lost happiness they maimed and murdered.
He howls as a blind man howls when his eyes are put out.
He howls as madmen howl at shifting shapes that trick and
 betray them.
He howls as devils howl when Hell damns the innocent.[58]

E. A. Brinninstool attempts to translate coyote's song into words in the refrain to his poem, *The Desert Serenader*.

Bow-wow-wow, ki-yi-i-i-yee-ip-ip-eow-ow-ow!
Bow-wow-ki-yi-i-i-ee-eouw-eow-ow-ow-eow-ow-ow!
Yee-ee-ee-yeow-wow-ow-ow-ki-yip-ee-i-ow-ow![59]

In "The Coyote's Song,"[60] Ernest Thompson Seton ex-

[56]"The Figurehead of the Frontier," *Outing*, 50:407.
[57]"Shaggy Fellow," *Catholic World*, 125:217.
[58]"Coyote," in *The Trail's End*, p. 59.
[59]*Trail Dust*, p. 000.
[60]*Wild Animals at Home*, pp. 13-14.

The Coyote: Animal and Folk-Character

presses the joyful thrill he gets when he hears "the Patti of the Plains" sing his song in the dusk or at dawn:

I am the Coyote that sings each night at dark;
It was by gobbling prairie-dogs that I got such a bark.
At least a thousand prairie-dogs I fattened on, you see,
And every bark they had in them is reproduced in me.

REFRAIN:

I can sing to thrill your soul or pierce it like a lance,
And all I ask of you to do is give me half a chance.
With a yap-yap-yap for the morning
And a yoop-yoop-yoop for the night
And a yoww-ow-wow for the rising moon
And a yah-h-h-h- for the campfire light.
Yap-yoop-yow-yahhh!

I gathered from the howling winds, the frogs and crickets, too,
And so from each availing fount, my inspiration drew.
I warbled till the little birds would quit their native bush,
And squat around me on the ground in reverential hush.

I'm a baritone soprano, and a bass and tenor, too.
I can thrill and slur and frill and whirr and shake you through
    and through.
I'm a Jews' harp—I'm an organ—I'm a fiddle and a flute.
Every kind of touching sound is found in the coyoot.

I'm a whooping, howling wilderness, a sort of Malibran,
With Lind, Labache, and Melba mixed and all combined in one.
I'm a grand cathedral organ and a calliope sharp,
I'm a gushing, trembling nightingale, a vast Aeolian harp.

I can raise the dead or paint the town, or pierce you like a lance
And all I ask of you to do is to give me half a chance.
Etc., etc., etc.

Although I am a miracle, I'm not yet recognized.
Oh, when the world does waken up how highly I'll be prized.
When managers and vocal stars—and emperors effete
Shall fling their crowns, their money bags, their persons at my
    feet.

I'm the voice of all the Wildest West, the Patti of the Plains;
I'm a wild Wagnerian opera of diabolic strains;
I'm a roaring, ranting orchestra with lunatics becrammed;
I'm a vocalized tornado—I'm the shrieking of the damned.

Coyote Wisdom

Though the original habitat of coyote was Western North America, reaching from Central America on the south to Manitoba on the north and from the Pacific on the west to the Mississippi River on the east, the coyote is now found in Alaska and clear to the Atlantic. Facing new conditions as they arose with advancing civilization, coyote has adapted himself to every kind of environment, from open valley and plains to brushy and mesquite-covered slopes, into the rough foot-hill country, upon plateaus, and even above the timber line. So, unlike most of the important wild creatures of the West, which have been reduced in numbers and in range if not exterminated, he has thrived on civilization, and has enormously extended his realm.

Two articles of interest and significance, "Coyotes Move East by Modern Methods" from *Scientific American*, June, 1936, and "Go East, Young Coyote, Go East" from *Literary Digest*, September 3, 1932, give two reasons for the spread of coyotes in Eastern United States. These are: (1) Easterners touring the West buy coyote pups for pets, ship or take them back home, find half-grown coyotes undesirable as household companions, and free them; (2) sportsmen import them for hunting (some believing they are importing foxes and others knowing the truth), turn them loose for the chase, and let many of them escape. Freed, all these coyotes grow up and breed. The East is now howling as loudly as ever a coyote can howl for Federal aid in exterminating the pests.

Coyotes can give human beings pointers on marriage, homelife, and the upbringing of children. They are monogamous and mate for life, hunting, playing, working together or in close coöperation. The "wife" selects the home and is its owner and general manager. The dens are often among rocks or in washed-out places along banks of streams. They may be made entirely by coyotes, though they are usually the dens of badgers or some smaller animals, enlarged and rearranged. The nest may be lined with grass and fur or it may be bare. Often there is more than one entrance, each excellently concealed, just as there are different "rooms." "The den has other uses besides its nursery or main purpose," writes Seton. "The father needs a den of his own—a bachelor apartment—when he is not an acceptable member of the home group. The mother may need another den. She does not wish to be pestered with the pups the whole time, and other nursery dens are needed for a change-off, probably to help in getting rid of insect parasites."[61] Both E. A. Mills and A. S. Barton say that the young coyotes scratch out for themselves little pockets leading from the main den. The family may have several dens: some for mere sleeping or resting places for the heat of the day; others for emergency quarters in case the home place has been discovered by an enemy.

The mating season is during the latter half of February, and the young are born sometime in April. The average coyote family numbers six or seven cubs, though it may number from three to ten. The father helps the mother take care of the children, brings his share of food to them, and helps in protection against hunters and other enemies. Together the parents teach the children tricks of living, and evidently they issue orders about ranging from home-base until their young are old enough to fend for themselves. The mother and the father have a special warning cry to give notice of danger, and, like other wild creatures, they try to lure the enemy from the den by pretending an injury or trying some other trick. If the den is discovered, the family at first opportunity vacates it. There is evidence that the mother continues at times to look after the welfare of her children, even after they are old enough to shift for

---

[61]*Lives of Game Animals*, Vol. I, Part II, pp. 370-371.

Coyote Wisdom

themselves, giving warning of danger, decoying the enemy, or attacking him, if need be.

Although the average span of coyote life is ten years, individuals are known to have lived twenty years or more. Coyotes have an individual range approximating less than a radius of five miles, and these individual ranges overlap so that six or eight couples may appear to have the same range. The coyote is generally silent by day, doing most of his howling, as well as his prowling, by night. Like the elephant, he never forgets. His inquisitiveness, boldness, and curiosity are often responsible for his undoing, but his natural sagacity offsets this and helps maintain a balance of accounts. He often stores food against the proverbial rainy day.

W. P. Webb[62] thinks that coyotes "eke out a rather miserable living on insects, rodents, prairie-dogs, and the helpless young of small animals." But when one reads the long list of his prey, culled from various sources, one wonders about that "rather miserable living": mice, rats, prairie dogs, squirrels, jackrabbits, cottontails, quail, grouse, pigs, sheep, calves, goats, and occasionally antelope and deer. Coyotes do not molest calves to any great extent, because the mother cow is a good protector. "If ranges are poor and the cattle are weak," writes W. H. Robinson in *Under Turquoise Skies*, "two or three coyotes may catch an enfeebled mother away from the rest of the herd and rob her of her calf, or snapping at her from under her body, kill her as well. However, if her bellowings reach the ears of nearby cows, they run wildly to her resuce, and with lowered heads and threatening mien, present a front that usually sends the coyotes off discomfited."

But to continue the inventory of food eaten by coyotes: They are known to eat plums, mesquite beans, watermelons, peaches, apricots, prunes, grapes, juniper berries,

---

[62]*The Great Plains*, p. 50.

hackberries, Mexican persimmons, berries of the coma, brazil, and other growth of the Brush Country of Texas and of Mexico, and the fruit of prickly pears. They even eat crickets, grasshoppers, beetles, and horned frogs. Without much undue exaggeration one might say that coyote is as omnivorous as man.

In *Under Turquoise Skies* Robinson writes: "The ranchers think him shrewd, but do not love him for this quality. He robs their chicken yards and picks up straying turkeys; he makes nocturnal visits to their melon patches, and not satisfied with eating one or two to satisfy a frugivorous hankering, will bite into half a dozen or more cantaloupes or watermelons to an agriculturist's natural disgust. The coyote is particularly pestiferous to a sheep herder. One will camp on the trail of a band of sheep indefinitely and woe to the sheep or the lamb that strays from the rest of the herd and the protection of the herder and his dogs. A lamb may be killed and wholly devoured in a time no longer than it takes a man to consume a couple of doughnuts in a quick lunch stand. . . . Still, to the agriculturist he is really more of a blessing than a pest. All rodents lay toll upon crops, and the coyote is a perpetual enemy of these hungry little pilferers."[63]

Among the beneficial habits credited to the coyote are these: He destroys rabbits, prairie-dogs, rats, and other rodents and he is useful as a scavenger. His injurious habits include the killing of game and farm animals and fowls. Aside from advocating extermination as a cure for the coyote evil, the Biological Survey suggests that just as owners protect their property from other dangers, they should protect their fowls and live stock from coyotes and other prowling beasts (including dogs, for coyotes are often blamed for damage done by dogs) by proper housing and fencing.

[63]*Under Turquoise Skies*, pp. 316-317.

Coyote Wisdom

To exterminate or not to exterminate has been and continues to be a moot question. Because the coyote's depredations on stock cost ranchmen and farmers some $500,000 a year, they asked state and federal aid in exterminating him. So in many states a bounty has been placed on Don Coyote, and the work of extermination goes merrily on. No fair play is accorded coyote. He is hounded for the bounty, for his pelt. Trappers have redoubled their efforts; forest rangers do their bit; poison is used; and dogs have been trained to go into dens to bring out the young, which are scalped for the bounty. In some vicinities farmers and ranchers have paid their taxes by means of bounty money; trappers and hunters have made a rather good living out of it.

For some years bounty-paying rode a crest of public opinion biased against coyotes. Then along in 1926-1927 a reaction set in. "Save the coyote," became the cry of stockmen and farmers in Nevada, the Dakotas, California, Canada, who embarked on a campaign to protect the coyote against the warfare waged by federal and state agents. The stockmen had much the same feeling expressed in an article printed in the *Literary Digest* for March 26, 1927: "Kansas, which once ranked the coyote in the category of evils alongside beer, cigarettes, Wall Street, and the octopus, has recently decided that if the state had not been so industrious in killing off the coyote, it would not have so many plagues of long-legged rabbits." On the other hand, New Mexico is this year planning to place a bounty on the coyote, while Alaska recently appropriated a large sum for the purpose of extermination.

The Coyote Hunt is gaining favor, supplanting the more formal and ceremonious Fox Hunt of the East because it is more exciting. Such hunts have always been popular in the West and the Southwest. In *Scribner's*, November, 1905, Theodore Roosevelt describes vividly a large and prolonged wolf and coyote hunt. A March, 1925, issue of the *San Antonio Express* carried a news story of a three-day meet of the Southwest Texas Wolf Hunters Association in Atascosa County in which one hundred and fifty men and sixty dogs took part. They killed twelve coyotes. This association holds a hunt each March near San Antonio. Bull-dogging and hunting by automobiles and airplanes are gaining favor for the sake of the thrills furnished by such sport, if sport it can be called. The *New York Times* for March 29, 1931, bannered a story about Kansans at Dodge City having a new sport, chasing coyotes in planes. In New Mexico on November 11, 1936, a large crowd gathered to see men take off from a fast-moving automobile to try to win the world's first "coyote-doggin'" championship.

With the evidence all in, it seems safe to say that coyote is not necessarily a bad citizen, but is, on the other hand, quite a good citizen, as citizens go; that he is more sinned against than sinning; that he has an economic value, a sports value, and a sentimental value; that he is a fitting symbol of the West and the Southwest. No ending seems more suitable to a chapter on "The Coyote as a Representative Animal of the West and the Southwest" than the conclusion of Ernest Thompson Seton's eulogy, called "The Spirit of the West."

"Sheep-men may rage and governments set a blood-price on your head—but wise are you as you are swift and brave.

"From all parts of the West comes the same rejoiceful news—the Coyote holds his own and is even winning wider lands, and defies the cleverest machinations of the all-destroying Whiteman. How complete was the Redman's understanding when he called you the "Wonder Dog," and made you the incarnation of the Deity, the one who brought the divine fire to earth in the beginning, the one who will live to see it die when all the world is dead.

"If ever the day should come when one may camp in the

West, and hear not a note of the Coyote's joyous stirring evening song, I hope that I shall long before have passed away, gone over the Great Divide, where there are neither barbwire fences, nor tin cans, nor hooch-houses, nor improvement companies, nor sheep-herds, nor flies, but where there is peace, and the Coyote sings and is unafraid."[64]

II

The Coyote in Amerind and Mexican Folk Tales

THE coyote of today may be a howling pest, but, according to many an Amerind tale, his ancestor—the first of his kind—was divine. In some creation myths he figures as the Great Spirit or World Creator; in others, he is the Great Spirit's first lieutenant. Mourning Dove (Humishuma), an Okanogan Indian, places Coyote in the latter category. In the Preface to her book, *Coyote Stories*, she says:

"The Animal People were here first—before there were any real people.

"Coyote was the most important because, after he was put to work by the Spirit Chief, he did more than any of the others to make the world a good place in which to live. There were times, however, when Coyote was not busy for the Spirit Chief. Then he amused himself by getting into mischief and stirring up trouble. Frequently he got into trouble himself, and then everybody had a good laugh—everybody but Mole. She was Coyote's wife.

"My people call Coyote Sin-ke-lip, which means Imitator. He delighted in mocking and imitating others, or in trying to, and, as he was a great one to play tricks, sometimes he is spoken of as Trick Person.

---

[64]Seton, *Lives of Game Animals*, Vol. I, Part II, pp. 416-417.

The Coyote: Animal and Folk-Character

"Our names for the Animal People is Chip-chap-tiqulk, and we use the same word for the stories that are told about the Animal People and legendary times. To the younger generation, chip-chap-tiqulk are improbable stories; that is a result of the white man's schools. But to the old Indians, chip-chap-tiqulk are not at all improbable; they are accounts of what really happened when the world was very young."[1]

Coyote was in such high honor with the Nahuas that they gave him a temple of his own, with a congregation of priests devoted to his service, his statue carved in stone, and an elaborate tomb at his death.[2]

In the Creation-of-Man myths, told by the Miwok Indians, Coyote himself is the great High Mogul, who, after he had finished fashioning the earth and all the inferior creatures, called a council of animals together for the purpose of devising man. Each speaker wanted man made just like himself. Coyote said it was nonsense; he did not think himself the most perfect animal that could be made, and he announced it as his theory that man should be formed by taking the best points of all the others—strong voice like a lion; lack of tail like the bear (since, in his opinion, a tail was only a harbor for fleas); the sharp eye of the elk, and so on. "But," said the autocrat, "there is surely no animal from whom man can borrow wit besides myself, and therefore he shall resemble Coyote in being cunning and crafty."

The council broke up in a row, and there was a general battle, after which every animal set to work to make an earthen image after his own idea. Night came before any models were finished, and all sculptors went to sleep, except Coyote, who, when camp became still, destroyed the other

---

[1]*Coyote Stories*, p. 7.
[2]Brinton, *Myths of the New World*, p. 145.

models, and made the composite he had suggested, and gave it life at dawn.[3]

Stories of the origin of death are prevalent from Greenland to Mexico. In the West the beneficent intentions of the Creator are thwarted by Coyote, whose interference brought into the world toil, pain, and death. "I was the oldest in olden times, and if a person dies, he must be dead," says Coyote to Earth-Maker in a Maidu myth. His son is the first to die. When Coyote tries to revive him, Earth-Maker reminds him of his own decree, which must stand. Then Coyote weeps. His are the first tears in the world.[4]

A Shoshonean myth tells how Coyote and his younger brother debated the lot of mortals. Coyote decreed that man must die and that he must work for all he receives, for if he has no labor to perform, he will be worthless; he will engage in quarreling and fighting and thus destroy himself and the world.[5]

Many of the incidents of the deluge of Biblical and Noahian fame are duplicated in Amerind deluge-myths. There is generally a raft or an *olla* on which the hero is saved, the landing on an eminence, the subsequent re-peopling of the world, the confusion of tongues, and the dispersal of mankind. Bartley Burr Alexander thinks there is no question but that these myths are aboriginal and pre-Columbian.[6]

The Wappo Shochamai make Coyote a rebuilder of the world after the great flood. All living creatures were drowned except Coyote. Seeking all over the world the sites of antediluvian villages, he gathered the floating tail

[3]*Myths of the Miwoks*, University of California Publications in American Archaeology and Ethnology, Vol. 12, pp. 283-328.
[4]First Annual Report, Bureau of American Ethnology, pp. 44-45. (These Myths are also to be found in Alexander's *Myths of All Races*, Vol. 10, pp. 116, 217-218, 234-235; Thompson, *Tales of North American Indians*, p. 29.)
[5]*Ibid.*
[6]Alexander, *Myths of All Race*, Vol. 10, pp. 299-300.

The Coyote: Animal and Folk-Character

feathers of hawks, owls, buzzards, and eagles and planted one wherever a wigwam had stood. In due time these feathers sprouted, branched, and finally turned into men and women.[7]

Pima-Papagos do not give Coyote credit for making man. Their story, as related by Robinson, is that after the waters of the flood had subsided, the trinity of high gods, Jewerta Maki or Earth Magician, See-a-boo or Elder Brother, and Coyote, cunning child of the Sun and the Moon, "met to create for the second time men, beasts, and birds to inhabit the earth. Each in his mind had determined upon certain changes, as the first batch had not turned out very well. When they had reached their rendezvous, the three sat down, their backs to each other, and each with a lump of moist clay in front of him, started his modeling. The Earth Magician, being himself a sort of super-Pima, decided he could do no better than to make his men a good deal like himself. Elder Brother, in his haste to make some people that would be superior to those of Jewerta Makai, scratched one of his fingers, causing it to bleed copiously. The blood stained the clay, and, as a result, his creatures came to be the cruel Apaches. El Coyote was considered to be a bit lower in the social scale than the other two; so to him was left the job of making the beasts and the birds, with the left-overs to be turned loose as reptiles. Somewhat of the same mind as Earth Magician, Coyote started in by making one beast in his own image, and, naturally having a special affection for him, endowed him with his personal cunning, which attribute the mortal coyote has to this day."[8]

Coyote, says the Mandan, was not satisfied with the animals he had created, for many had grievous faults. For

---

[7]University of California Publications in Archaeology and Ethnology, Vol. 19, pp. 67-69.

[8]Robinson, *Under Turquoise Skies*, p. 314.

instance, Dog, who could talk, tattled on the Master's wife. So Coyote had to take away his power of speech. That is why all dogs just bark today. Coyote also had to alter the nature of Elk so that he would not eat man, and to dull the eyesight of Buffalo for the good of the hunter.[9]

In numerous tales Coyote is shown as a serious benefactor of man. Rememberers of tribal history in the Northwest told Mourning Dove how Coyote conquered and domesticated four people-devouring monsters. The fact that the first monster in the tale is the horse dates it as post-Columbian, since horses were unknown in America before the Conquest; yet horse could have been substituted for some earlier monster in the same tale.

"For many suns Coyote had been traveling towards the sunrise. He had crossed the Rocky Mountains and was in the Great Plains country. Sin-kit-zas-cow-ha (Horse) lived there. He was a dangerous monster and he was much bigger than is any horse today. As soon as he saw Coyote, Horse took after him."

Coyote had to call on his magic. "His power heard" and caused three trees to grow out of the ground straight ahead of him. Coyote got in one, but Horse pawed it down. He was in the third tree and it was about to fall when Coyote jumped on Horse's back. His "power" had provided a whip, and now Coyote used it. Horse "bawled and bucked; he whirled around and around; he stood on his hind feet and on his front feet; he threw himself; he rolled—tried all his tricks," Coyote meanwhile never ceasing to ply the medicine whip. In the end Horse begged for mercy, and when Coyote dismounted to survey the conquered monster, he saw that he had beaten him down until he was as small as horses are now.

" 'From this sun you are for people to ride,' Coyote said.

---

[9]Beckworth, *Mandan and Hidatsa Tales*, pp. 300-302. (Also found in Zuni Lore, "Why Dogs Cannot Talk," Vol. 31 of *Journal of American Folklore*, pp. 464-467.)

The Coyote: Animal and Folk·Character

'Only when first ridden will you buck and be mean. Even
old men will be able to sit on you. And old women will use
you for carrying their camp things. On you they will put
their heavy packs of roots and berries and meats.' "

Thus was Horse domesticated, and the subjection of the
other monsters followed.[10]

There are many stories about Coyote and Sun, Coyote
and Moon, and Coyote and Stars. Coyote even had dealings
with meteors. The Shastika Indians say that originally the
Sun had nine brothers, flaming hot with fire, so that all the
world was likely to perish; but Coyote slew them and saved
mankind from burning up. There were ten moons, also, all
made of ice, so that in the night people nearly froze to
death. Nine of these Coyote slew with his flint knife, carrying heated stones to keep his hands warm.[11]

The Ho-sem-i-tahs of River Merced Valley say that
when the world was very young, the Indians had no fire,
no sunshine. Their homes were cold and the valley was in
dim, cold twilight. Coyote, who had been on a long journey, told the chieftain of a wonderful land beyond the
granite walls of their valley. The country had light and
warmth. The chieftain and the tribe hooted Coyote as a
mere teller of tall tales. To prove his story, Coyote went
away again to that country. The blazing light was hanging
on a pole. While he watched, the chief took it to his wigwam. Then it became dark. The women began to hunt
sticks to keep the fires lighted. Coyote turned himself into
a stick and was picked up by a woman, taken into the
chief's wigwam, and thrown into the fire. Turning himself back into himself, he seized the ball of fire in the
blanket and raced back to his own tribe in Yosemite, hotly
pursued by the enemy. There was threat of war. His chief
commanded Coyote to talk with the Spirit Chief to find

---

[10]Mourning Dove, *Coyote Stories*, pp. 41-48.

[11]Ingersoll, "Coyote, The Hound of the Plains," *Popular Science Monthly*, 30:360.

out how they might keep the ball. The Spirit Chief said, "Hang the shining ball in the sky to give light and warmth equally to all tribes of men. When it shines from the sky, it will be day; then when I take the bright ball under the shadow of my robe, it will be night and time for sleep and rest.[12]

According to the Navajos the stars in the heavens are so arranged because of Coyote's mischief-making proclivities. After the sun and the moon had been made in the heavenly workshop, the old men set about embroidering the sky with stars in beautiful patterns. But just as they made a beginning, Coyote rushed in and contemptuously scattered the pile of stars over the floor of heaven, just as they are now.[13] The Chochiti's version for the hodge-podge arrangement of the stars is only slightly different. The jar in which the stars were kept was entrusted to Coyote to hold while they were being hung in the sky. Just after the old man had hung the Shield Stars (Dipper), The Pot-Rest Stars (Three Stars), and Siwasila (Morning Star), Coyote dropped the jar. All the other stars jumped out and spread themselves everywhere over the sky.[14] Credit for making the moon and the stars is given to Coyote by the Pima Indians, who know because Coyote has so told them in this song:

> I have made the moon!
> I have made the moon!
> Hurling it high
> In the four directions.
> To the east I threw it
> To run its appointed course.

[12]Squier, Emily Lindsey, "The Coyote Who Talked With God," *Good Housekeeping*, 77:30-31.

[13]*Myths, Prayers, and Songs of Navajos*, University of California Publication in Archaeology and Ethnology, Vol. 5, pp. 21-63.

[14]Benedict, Ruth, Bureau of Ethnology, Bulletin 98, p. 5.

The Coyote: Animal and Folk-Character

I have made the stars!
I have made the stars!
Above the earth I threw them.
All things above I've made
And placed them to illumine.[15]

How Coyote got fire for man has many versions. It seems that the Great Spirit had made the fishes, the mammals, and finally man. But man had no fire to cook his food or to keep himself warm. In the beginning the Great Spirit had put fire into a cask, which was guarded by two sleepless hags, either far toward the rising sun or on the bed of the ocean. Again the story is that one small and much favored tribe has fire which it jealously guards. But wherever fire is or however kept, Coyote discovers it, steals it, and with the help of such as Squirrel, Frog, Robin Redbreast, Eagle, Hawk, Hummingbird, or other Animal People, takes it to man in relay fashion.

The origin of the seasons is a tale the Kutenai tell. It had been winter a long time, and food was getting scarce. Squirrel, who shared her small store with Coyote, said, "Soon there will be no more food, and Spring is far away. What shall we do?" Now the seasons were kept tied up in a bag and safely guarded in a distant town. Coyote thought and thought, then made a plan. He would station the swiftest runner just outside the town and the strongest person on the prairie. Then one who could walk secretly would go into the town and enter the tepee of the Old Woman who kept the seasons. All worked out well. The boy secretly entered the tepee, clapped warm gum over Old Woman's mouth so she could not give the alarm, grabbed the bag containing the seasons, and ran forth. The Swiftest Runner carried it to the Strongest Person, who tore the package open and let Springtime out. Wind came,

---

[15]Twenty-sixth Annual Report, Bureau of American Ethnology, p. 273.

snow melted. Ever since there have been seasons and food.[16]

Of interest equal to the myths are the fables and the tales wherein Coyote is the sly, tricky fellow that no one loves or trusts, the "joker and the butt of jokes" that usually comes out second best, the braggart, the envier, the imitator. Peshlikai, a Navajo, tells a story of how Coyote wanted to make his children beautiful like the fawns.

"Long ago when the animals were people, Coyote left her pups in her lair and started out after adventure. As she went along, she met Deer with her two little fawns trotting behind her. They were beautifully spotted and at once attracted Coyote. She put herself out to be nice and particularly friendly, and according to the fashion of animals of that time, she shook Deer's hand in warm greeting. 'Where do you come from, and where are you going, cousin?' she asked.

"She was not Deer's cousin at all, but it suited her purpose to feign relationship.

" 'We are looking for a good place to eat, where the grass is fresh and water clear,' answered Deer.

"Coyote, unable to restrain her inquisitivieness and envy any longer, said, 'Cousin, what pretty children you have.' She pawed the fawns over. 'How did you give them their beautiful spots, my cousin?'

" 'I have done nothing to them,' Deer replied. 'They were always like that. They were born that way.'

" 'Cousin, do not conceal anything from me. You must have done something. You are not spotted. I know you must have done something to them. How came your two children to have such pretty spots if you have not done it for them? Please tell me. My children are plain, and I want to make them as pretty as yours.'

" 'There is nothing. It is just their nature.'

[16]Bureau of American Enthology, Bulletin 59, pp. 179-181.

The Coyote: Animal and Folk-Character

" 'No, you are hiding it from me. You must tell me. You are not my true friend.'

"Deer began to be puzzled and alarmed. Coyote was smart, she had always heard, and ever ready to trick another animal. She feared to deny longer, lest Coyote wreak vengeance on her for a fancied wrong. 'I must get away from her,' she thought. 'I shall tell her anything to escape.'

" 'Well, cousin,' she said, 'let it be so; I shall tell you everything. It is my secret, but since you must know, I shall share it with you. Well may you wonder, but I burn spots on my children. I put them into a hole in the ground, so there is only a small opening at one end. In front of that I build a fire of cedar. You know how that sparkles and snaps. Then the wood pops and sparks fly on my children and make the spots. When the fire dies down, I take them out and they are pretty. Now can you do this with your own children, too. Only you must watch closely and let them stay in long enough to become spotted all over. Don't let them out too soon. When you look in and see their teeth, then you will know they are laughing and that they are properly spotted. That is the time to take them out. You will see how pretty they are.'

"Coyote was delighted at having at last learned the cherished secret. 'Thanks, cousin, many thanks,' she said. 'I see you are really my friend, and will never deny me the truth. Thanks again. Now I must go home at once.'

"She started, much to the relief of Deer, who no longer had to fear her mischief. All the way home Coyote ran at full speed, never stopping, so eager was she to make her children beautiful. 'Children, children!' she cried to the brood of pups that came running out and frisked about her. 'Now you are going to be pretty! Wait till you see how beautiful I shall make you with fine spots all over.' . . .

"Coyote, followed by her young, looked among the rocks until she found a suitable hole with a small opening.

Coyote Wisdom

'Come, children, go in! This is just the place. Now you will surely soon be beautiful.'

"The cubs crawled in and she gathered a pile of cedar and split it fine. She piled the wood up at the opening and lit it. Inside the pups were laughing and happy. 'Now we shall be made beautiful,' they all said.

"Soon the fire blazed up, roaring. Everytime it snapped and crackled, Coyote's heart was glad. Everytime a spark popped she said to herself, 'Another pretty spot on them.'

"The pups began to yelp. 'Stop crying!' Coyote ordered. 'Think how pretty you are being made!'

"Still they yelped and howled, until Coyote grew weary of commanding them to cease. The fire grew hotter and bigger and finally it grew quiet in the hole. Coyote let the fire die down. When she looked inside the cave, she saw the gleaming teeth of the cub that was nearest. . . .

"She raked the embers and ashes aside, and one after another took the cubs out. . . . They were cooked dead. Coyote, the trickster, had herself been tricked."[17]

Nearly every race of people has its own story of the Tortoise-and-Hare race, and among the Indians there are many versions, with the hero in each far cleverer than Aesop's hero. This tale was told by a Navajo to Clara Kern Bayliss:

"One afternoon Coyote met Turtle, hitching along in the unsteady walk that turtles have, and he said to it, 'You are the slowest and clumsiest traveler I ever saw. You move about as fast and as gracefully as a piece of bark with beetles under it.'

"Now Turtle knew that he was a slow coach, and just because he was so well aware of it, he was sensitive on that subject. It always vexed him to be taunted with this defect;

---

[17]Kroeber, H. R., "Navajo's Fairy Tale," *Overland Monthly*, 54:456-458. (This story, identical in detail, is in the Eleventh Annual Report of the Bureau of American Ethnology, pp. 153-154.)

so he spoke up very loudly and scornfully and said, 'You don't know what you are talking about, Coyote. Why, I can beat *you* running!' ... Turtle knew he couldn't do any such thing. But he didn't like to hear Coyote laugh at him. ...

" 'Tomorrow,' said Coyote, 'we'll start from this ant-hill and go to that dead stump of a tree at the edge of the wood. But by the time you've crawled a yard, if you'll stand upon your hind legs and turn your ugly woggle-eyes in that direction, you'll see me waiting for you at the stump.' ...

"Turtle lay awake all night studying out what he should do, and it was growing light in the east before he had made up his mind. Early in the morning he went to some other Turtles and asked them to assist him.

" 'Brothers,' said he, 'Coyote and I are to run a race today, and if you will help me, I know how we can fool him and take some of the brag out of him. I want each of you to dig a hole along the course we are to run, and take your station several yards back of the hole. When you see Coyote coming, run as hard as you ever can till he has passed you. Then hide in your hole.' ...

"Four Turtles volunteered to do as they had been told. The Turtle himself went to the anthill where he was to meet Coyote, while one of the others went to the goal and waited. Pretty soon Coyote came up prancing and capering. In his frisking he disturbed the ants which lived in the hill, and they swarmed out and began to bite and sting him so he had to go off a little way and roll in the sand until he brushed them away.

"Then they got ready to start. Turtle gave the command, 'one-two-three, go-o!' Coyote dashed off—and Turtle crawled into his hole.

"When Coyote got over the first ridge, what was his amazement to see Turtle ambling along ahead of him. He didn't know what to make of it; but putting on all the

Coyote Wisdom

speed that was in his nimble legs, he soon passed the plodder. No sooner was Coyote safely by than the other popped into his hole.

"Away went Coyote sniffing like the wind, fairly flying, but when he got to another ridge there was Turtle ahead of him again!

" 'Why, what can this mean?' thought he. 'I never saw Turtle run like that! This fellow must have magic in him.'

"He dashed down the slope, running like mad and soon got ahead of this Turtle also—and it at once crawled into the ground.

" 'Now,' thought Coyote, 'I've seen the last of Turtle.' He ran his utmost, but when he got to the end of the course, behold! there was Turtle sitting quietly on the stump, waiting for him and pulling his blanket closer around himself."[18]

There is a similar story told in the Tee-wahn tribe of the Pueblo Indians. In this tale the race is between Cotton-tail and Coyote. They arrange to race around the world, Cotton-tail to run underground and Coyote above ground. Whichever comes in first is to kill and eat the other. Cotton-tail asks for four days' grace. In that time he arranges with members of his tribe. At the four corners of the earth are to be rabbits in holes. As Coyote comes to each corner, Cotton-tail is to pop out and taunt him, then jump back into the hole as if he were rapidly running underground. So Cotton-tail wins the race, but Coyote runs away without paying forfeit.[19]

"And the Best Man Won" might caption a story of how Cricket out-generaled Coyote. The following is a "dressed-up" version of a literal translation from children's tales of the Picuris Indians.[20]

---

[18]Bayliss, *Old Man Coyote*, pp. 31-36.
[19]Lummis, *Pueblo Indian Tales*, pp. 99-100.
[20]Forty-third Annual Report, Bureau of American Ethnology, pp. 383-387. (This is my own version, based upon the text given in the Annual Report.—L.E.B.)

The Coyote: Animal and Folk Character

Once upon a time Coyote, taking his early morning stroll, came upon Cricket basking in the sun. As he passed, he stepped on Cricket, who said, "Dust and devils! Why don't you look where you are going and why don't you speak?"

"Why," sniffed Coyote, "I never speak to such looking persons as you!"

"Be it so," replied Cricket. "But look you! I'll prove that I am the better man. Tomorrow we fight a duel."

"By the moon, that's an excellent idea!' yipped Coyote. "It will be fun and the spoils of victory will be mine."

So each went his way, after agreeing on the time, the place, and the terms.

That night Cricket called his people together. There were the Bumblebees, White-striped Bees, Honey Bees, Wasps, Yellow-Jackets, Mosquitoes—all insects that sting and bite. And Coyote called together his forces, the Wild Cat, the Bear, the Mountain Lion, and all other beasts of prey.

So the next day to the banks of the Picuris River they came, Cricket to the west and Coyote to the east. Then Coyote said to his men, "Wait here."

He went to Cricket and asked, "Are you ready?"

Cricket replied, "Even so. But send your best man first to meet mine."

Coyote ordered forward Mountain Lion. Cricket called out the Bees, who stung Mountain Lion in the eyes, the ears, all over his body. So he gave up and rolled in the dust. Cricket laughed.

Coyote now sent Wild Cat forward. Cricket gave orders for Yellow-Jackets to advance. They stung Wild Cat here and there and everywhere. "Terror and blood!" yelled he, and away he went like greased lightning.

Again Cricket laughed and taunted Coyote. "Why don't you send someone worthy of our mettle?"

Coyote Wisdom

Coyote, infuriated, exclaimed, "I'll come myself!" And he rushed madly forward, to be met by Hornets. How they stung him! They got into his eyes, his ears, his mouth; they bit him above and below. "Demons and Corpses!" he screamed, as he plunged into the river. Cricket was the better man.

The story about how Coon fooled Coyote into thinking the reflection of the moon in water was cheese and how Coyote in diving for it drowned himself is widespread both in Mexico and among the Indians of the West.[21] There was no cheese in America until the Spaniards introduced it. There were the corn cakes called *tortillas*, however, and one of the aboriginal tales is of how a woman carrying *tortillas* across a river fooled a coyote into jumping into the water and drowning.[22]

In an often-told tale Coyote was going along one day close to a wood when he heard Blackbirds calling excitedly, "Bring my bag! Bring my bag! It's going to hail!"

"Coyote, being very curious, came near and saw that they all had buckskin bags to which they were tying lassos, the other ends of which were thrown over the boughs of the trees. Very much surprised, the Coyote came to them and asked: 'Blackbird friends, what are you doing?'

" 'Oh, friend Coyote,' they replied, 'soon there will be a very hard hail-storm, and we do not wish to be pelted to death. We are going to get into these bags and pull ourselves up under the branches, where the hail cannot strike us.'

" 'That is very good,' said Coyote. 'Let me join you.'

" 'Oh, yes! Just run home and get a bag and a lasso. Then come back here and we shall help you.'

"So the Coyote got a large bag and a lasso, and came

[21]A good version of the story is told by Howard W. Wesley in *Puro Mexicano*, Pub. No. XII of the Texas Folk Lore Society (1935), pp. 214-215.
[22]Twenty-sixth Annual Report, Bureau of American Ethnology, p. 243.

The Coyote: Animal and Folk·Character

back to the Blackbirds, who were waiting. They fixed the noose around the neck of the bag so that it would be closed tight when the rope was pulled. Then they threw the end of the lasso over a strong branch and said, 'Now, friend Coyote, you get into your bag first, for you are so big and heavy that you cannot pull yourself up, and we will have to help you.'

"The Coyote crawled into the bag, and all the Blackbirds pulled with all their might till the bag was swung clear up under the branch. Then they tied the end of the lasso around around the tree, so the bag could not come down, and ran around picking up all the pebbles they could find.

" 'Mercy! How the hail comes!' they cried excitedly, and began throwing stones at the swinging bag as hard as ever they could."

After being pelted and ironically taunted for a long time, Coyote was released. When he saw the sun shining and noticed how dry the ground was, he realized how the Blackbirds had duped him. Until this day he tries to sneak up on them and eat them in order to get even.[23]

The didactic element is more prevalent in the Mexican than in the purely Indian tale. The Indian tales given, a few pages back, of Coyote's races against Turtle and against Rabbit—tales with interest depending entirely upon the turn of a trick—may be contrasted with the following Mexican account of another contest, which teaches that "the race is not always to the swift."

"One day Coyote said to Frog: 'Listen, let's run a race from here to the arbor over there.'

" 'Let's do,' said Frog.

"Then Coyote said, 'On the count of three, go!'

"He stepped forward, and she jumped to place. When Coyote said three, Frog, spying Coyote's bushy tail, think-

---

[23]Lummis, *Pueblo Indian Folk Stories*, pp. 27-29. In other versions of the story, Fox or Rabbit gets Coyote into the bag.

ing quick and acting quicker, jumped on it. Coyote ran a
desperate race, raising the dust all around, never knowing
about the burden he was bearing. After he had come to his
destination and turned round to see where Frog was jumping along, she hopped down without disturbing him,
jumped far over the line, and slyly said, 'You see how I
beat you!' "[24]

One of the most popular of Mexican folk tales resolves
itself into a discussion over the ethics of repaying good with
evil.[25] The conclusion is that even if such a reward is not
right, *es la costumbre.**

But that is not always the custom, as another tale will
show. Once upon a time as a traveler was going along his
way, he saw Coyote making a sign to him with his forefoot
to approach him. When he drew near, he saw a snake
wound around Coyote's neck. The snake, a cincoatl, had its
head beneath the armpit of the animal and was pressing
very tightly. The traveler, as he looked upon the scene,
asked himself, "Which one of these shall I help?" He decided to aid Coyote; so he took a stick and beat the snake,
which untwined itself, fell upon the ground, and escaped
in the grass.

Coyote also fled from the spot, but returned to meet the
traveler in a cornfield. He brought two hens in his mouth.
Placing them before the traveler, he made a sign that he
should take them. He followed the traveler home, and, to
show his gratitude, he daily supplied him with chickens.[26]

Coyote the Trickster having the tables turned upon him
by a Cock in Mexico leaves the same teaching that Russell

[24]*El Folklore Literario de Mejico*, pp. 54-57.

[25]A superior version of the story is by Riley Aiken in his "A Pack Load of Mexican Tales," *Puro Mexicano*, Pub. No. XII of the Texas Folk Lore Society (1935),
pp. 4-7.

*A version without ethical implications, of the same story, is told by Dan Storm,
under the title of "Señor Coyote Acts as Judge," in this volume.—*Editors.*

[26]Robello, *Nombres Geograficos*, p. 23.

the Fox left when he opened his mouth—and let Chaunti-cleer escape—in Chaucer's tale.

"One evening an old rooster, who felt himself neglected, left the barnyard and went to roost in a mesquite tree some distance from the house of his master. When he awoke the next morning, he saw a coyote sitting on the ground looking up at him.

" 'Good morning,' said the coyote.

" 'Good morning, sir.'

" 'I am glad to see you,' said the coyote, smiling his best smile. 'I have been wanting to get acquainted with you for a long time. How are you feeling?'

" 'I am feeling very well, I thank you,' replied the rooster. 'I hope you are well.'

" 'Yes, I never felt better,' the coyote answered. 'It delights me to be so near you and to have this opportunity to tell you of my friendship for you. Come down, won't you, so that we can have a real visit.'

"But the coyote cannot persuade the rooster to descend. 'The truth is,' the latter admits after much beating about the bush, 'I am afraid you will kill me and eat me up.'

" 'The very idea!' the coyote exclaimed. 'Don't you know we live in a civilized country that has a constitution and laws against killing people? Don't you know that civilized folks never eat each other? Sir, you mistake my motives.'

"About this time the rooster looked off towards the house where he lived. He seemed to be very much interested in something he saw.

" 'What are you looking at?' asked the coyote.

" 'Oh, I see a man,' the rooster explained, stretching himself and yawning.

" 'A man!'

" 'Yes, a man.' Then he added casually, 'The man is coming this way.' Also, 'The man has a gun, also a dog.' He began to shift around and remember that he must be getting home.

" 'Now, now,' taunted the rooster, 'you are making excuses. Come, tell me the truth. Why won't you stay and visit me?'

" 'The truth is,' the coyote yipped out in a sharp voice, 'that I am afraid the man will kill me with his gun or at least will make his dog try to chase me to death.'

" 'The very idea!' the rooster crowed. 'Don't you know we live in a country that has a constitution and laws against killing people?'

" 'Yes,' the coyote called back over his shoulder as he trotted off out of sight. 'Yes, I know all that, but there are some rascals who pay no attention to laws and the constitution. Adios!' "[27]

* * *

To include one example of each kind of coyote tale told among American Indians and Mexicans, to exemplify each motif, would make a very large volume. This collection may well end with two tales that exemplify in a rare way both fidelity to source and literary artistry. The first example is from Frank Hamilton Cushing's *Zuñi Folk Tales*. Cushing's "influence on the literary translation of aboriginal literature in the United States," wrote Mary Austin, in 1930, "has barely begun. It has raised up no successors of his proportions; perhaps the combination of literary skill and sound knowledge of the kind required does not often occur. Perhaps he was, in fact, a changeling, a throw-back to the mysterious little people, traces of whose life, so close to the earth, make a net-work of fairy lore over ancestral Europe. He remains uniquely the only man not of their blood who understood completely the soul of such lore among the Amerinds of the West."

---

[27]Dobie, *On the Open Range*, pp. 30-32.

The Coyote: Animal and Folk-Character

When the native folk tales of North America about Coyote are written down as they should be—if they ever are—there will be in them something of the quality here exemplified by Cushing.

"One day the Coyote went out hunting, leaving his large family of children and his old wife at home. It was a fine day and the sun was shining brightly, and the old Locust crawled out of his home in the loam of the arroyo and ascended to one of the bare branches of the piñon tree, where, hooking his feet firmly into the bark, he began to sing and play his flute. The Coyote in his wanderings came along just as he began to sing these words:

> Locust, locust, playing a flute!
> Locust, locust, playing a flute!
> Away up above on the pine-tree bough,
> Closely clinging,
> Playing a flute!
> Playing a flute!

" 'Delight of my senses!' called out the Coyote, squatting down on his haunches, and looking up, with his ears pricked and his mouth grinning: 'Delight of my senses, how finely you play your flute!'

" 'Do you think so?' said the Locust, continuing his song.

" 'Goodness, yes!' cried the Coyote, shifting nearer. 'What a song it is! Pray, teach it to me, so that I can take it home and dance my children to it. I have a large family at home.'

" 'All right,' said the Locust. 'Listen, then.' And he sang his song again:

> Locust, locust, playing a flute,
> Locust, locust, playing a flute,
> Away up above on the pine-tree bough,
> Closely clinging,
> Playing a flute!
> Playing a flute!

Coyote Wisdom

" 'Delightful!' cried the Coyote. 'Now shall I try?'

" 'Yes, try.'

"Then in a very hoarse voice the Coyote half growled and half sang (making a mistake here and there, to be sure) what the Locust had sung, though there was very little music in his repetition of the performance.

> Locust, locust, playing a flute!
> Locust, locust, playing a flute!
> Away up above on the pine-tree bought,
> Closely clinging,
> Playing a flute!
> Playing a flute!

" 'Ha!' laughed he, as he finished; 'I have got it, haven't I?'

" 'Well, yes,' said the Locust, 'fairly well.'

" 'Now, then, let us sing it over together.'

"And while the Locust piped shrilly, the Coyote sang gruffly, though much better than at first.

" 'There, now,' exclaimed he, with a whisk of his tail; 'didn't I tell you?' and without waiting to say another word he whisked away beyond the headland of rocks. As he was running along the plain he kept repeating the song to himself so that he would not forget it, casting his eyes into the air, after the manner of men in trying to remember or to say particularly fine things, so that he did not notice an old Gopher peering at him somewhat ahead on the trail; and the old Gopher laid a trap for him in his hole.

"The Coyote came trotting along, singing: 'Playing a flute, playing a flute,' when suddenly he tumbled heels over head in the Gopher's hole. He sneezed, began to cough and to rub the sand out of his eyes; and then jumping out, cursed the Gopher heartily, and tried to recall his song, but found that he had utterly forgotten it, so startled had he been.

The Coyote: Animal and Folk*Character

" 'The lubber-cheeked old Gopher! I wish the pests were all in the Land of Demons!' cried he. 'They dig their holes and nobody can go anywhere in safety. And now I have forgotten my song. Well, I will run back and get the old Locust to sing it again. If he can sit there singing to himself, why can't he sing it to me? No doubt in the world 'he is still out there on that piñon branch singing away.' Saying which, he ran back as fast as he could. When he arrived at the piñon tree, sure enough there was the old Locust still sitting and singing.

" 'Now, how lucky this is, my friend!' cried the Coyote long before he reached the place. 'The lubber-cheeked, fat-sided old Gopher dug a hole right in my path; and I went along singing your delightful song and was so busy with it that I fell headlong into the trap he set for me, and I was so startled that, on my word, I forgot all about the song, so I have come back to ask you to sing it for me again.'

" 'Very well,' said the Locust. 'Be more careful this time.' So he sang the song over.

" 'Good! Surely I'll not forget it this time,' cried the Coyote; so he whisked about, and away he sped toward his home beyond the headland of rocks. 'Goodness!' said he to himself, as he went along, 'what a fine thing this will be for my children! How they will be quieted by it when I dance them as I sing it! Let's see how it runs. Oh, yes!'

Locust, locust, playing a flute,
Locust, locust, playing —

" 'Thli-i-i-i-i-p, piu-piu- piu-piu!' fluttered a flock of Pigeons out of the bushes at his very feet, with such a whizzing and whistling that Coyote nearly tumbled over with fright, and, recovering himself, cursed the Doves heartily, calling them 'gray-backed, useless sage-vermin;'

and, between his fright and his anger, was so much shaken up that he again forgot his song.

"Now, Locust wisely concluded that this would be the case, and as he did not like Coyote very well, having been told that sometimes members of his tribe were by no means friendly to Locusts and other insects, he concluded to play him a trick and teach him a lesson in minding his own business. So, catching tight hold of the bark, he swelled himself out of his old skin, and, crawling down the tree, found a suitable quartz stone, which, being light-colored and clear, would not make his skin look unlike himself. He took the stone up the tree, and carefully placed it in the empty skin. Then he cemented the back together with a little pitch and left his exact counterfeit sticking to the bark, after which he flew away to a neighboring tree.

"No sooner had Coyote recovered his equanimity to some extent than, discovering the loss of his song, and again exclaiming, 'No doubt he is still there piping away; I'll go and get him to sing it over,' he ran back as fast as he could.

"'Ah wha!' he exclaimed, as he neared the tree. 'I am quite fatigued with all this extra running about. But, no matter; I see you are still there, my friend. A lot of miserable, gray-backed Ground-pigeons flew up right from under me as I was going along singing my song, and they startled me so that I forgot it; but I tell you, I cursed them heartily! Now, my friend, will you not be good enough to sing once more for me?'

"He paused for a reply. None came.

"'Why, what's the matter? Don't you hear me?' yelled Coyote, running nearer, looking closely and scrutinizing Locust. 'I say, I have lost my song and want you to sing for me again. Will you, or will you not?' Then he paused.

"'Look here, are you going to sing for me or not?' continued Coyote, getting angry.

"No reply.

The Coyote: Animal and Folk Character

"Coyote stretched out his nose, wrinkled up his lips, and snarled: 'Look here, do you see my teeth? Well, I'll ask you just four times more to sing for me, and if you don't sing, then I'll snap you up in a hurry, I tell you. Will—you—sing—for me? Once. Will you sing—for me? Twice. Two more times! Look out! Will you sing for me? Are you a fool? Do you see my teeth? Only once more! Will—you—sing—for me?'

"No reply.

" 'Well, you are a fool!' yelled Coyote, unable to restrain himself longer.

"Making a quick jump, he snapped Locust's skin off the bough, and bit it so hard that it crushed and broke the teeth in the middle of his jaw, driving some of them so far down in his gums that you could hardly see them, and crowding the others out so that they were regular tusks. Coyote dropped the stone, rolled in the sand, and howled and snarled and wriggled with pain. Then he got up and shook his head, and ran away with his tail between his legs. So excessive was his pain that at the first brook he came to he stooped to lap up water in order to alleviate it, and he there beheld what you and I see in the mouths of every Coyote we ever catch—that the teeth back of the canines are all driven down, so that you can see only the points of them, and look very much broken up. . . . And so also to this day, when locusts venture out on a sunny morning to sing a song, it is not infrequently their custom to protect themselves from the consequences of attracting too much attention by skinning themselves and leaving their counterparts on the trees."[28]

---

[28]Cushing, Zuñi Folk Tales, pp. 255-261. (There are several variants of this tale. W. D. Wallis has one version in "Folk Tales from Shumopovi," in Journal of American Folk Lore, Vol. 49, pp. 50-51. In "Myths of Owens Valley Paiutes," University of California Publication, Vol. 34, pp. 380-381, J. H. Steward tells "Coyote Learns Grasshopper's Song," "Coyote Learns Turtle's Song," and "Coyote Learns Dove's Song." In still another tale' "Coyote Learns Cottontail's Song." In the latter version, Coyote does not crush his teeth, but Cottontail outwits him). The quotation from Mary Austin used in introducing Cushing's tale is from Mary Austin's Introduction to the 1931 edition of Zuñi Folk Tales. See Bibliography.

Coyote Wisdom

Mary Austin in *One Smoke Stories* seems to adhere closely to the Indian way of telling a story. Certainly she achieves something universal and lovely. One of the best of that graphic and racy collection is "The Coyote Song."[29]

"Hear a telling of the song the Coyote gave to Cinoave and took away again, in the day when every man had his own song, and no one might sing a man's own song without his permission. Thus it was among our fathers' fathers. When his son was born, when he had killed his enemy or first made a woman to know him as a man, out of his great moment he made a song and sang it on his own occasions. Sometimes it was a song for the people, which he left as a legacy when he died. There were also songs to be sung while he was dying, by himself if he were able, or the friends who stood around him; or it might be the song was so secret that it passed only between the singer and his God.

"But Cinoave had no song. When the tribe came together for the dance of the Marriageable Maidens, or for the feast of the Piñon Harvest, Cinoave would busy himself gathering brushwood for the fire. Or he would sit apart from the others pretending to mend a pipe or sharpen an arrow, hoping not to hear the tribesmen whisper to one another, 'There is Cinoave, the man without a song.'

"This to Cinoave was sadness. For without a proper song, how can a man win favor of the gods or women? Thus say the fathers. Then, one day when he was digging tule roots by the river, the Coyote came by and said, 'What will you take for your sweet roots, Cinoave?'

"Said Cinoave, 'I will take a song.' For is not the Coyote the father of song-making?

" 'What kind of song?' asked Coyote, for though he meant to strike a bargain, he wished to hold out as long as possible.

---

[29] Austin, Mary, *One Smoke Stories*, pp. 34-38.

"Cinoave considered within. 'A song that will warm the hearts of the tribe and stir up their thoughts within them,' said Cinoave.

"This was a good asking. When the heart is warm and the thoughts deeply stirred, one ascends without difficulty to the Friend-of-the-Soul-of-Man and all things accord with our interests. 'I wish a song so pleasing,' said Cinoave, 'that all men hearing it will say, "Surely this is a Coyote Song." This was said in flattery, for he knew, having thrown him a tule root to taste, that Old Man Coyote would not go away without his belly full. Also he wished to make sure that it would not prove a Coyote giving. That is a saying to our fathers for a gift that is taken back again when the giver is so minded.

"Cinoave threw him a fat, sweet root and when it was eaten he said, 'Swear to me it will not be a Coyote giving.'

"Coyote swore by the pelt of his mother, 'So long as the song is used for what it is given, to warm the hearts of the tribe and stir up their thoughts within them, it will not be taken away.'

"Then Cinoave threw him the bag of roots and they were well pleased with the bargain.

"That year at the feast of the Piñon Harvest when the tribes came together, Cinoave sang his song and the people were astonished, saying, 'Surely this is a Coyote song?' In every camp there was talk of it, and the pride of Cinoave swelled like a young gourd in the rain. Everywhere he went singing it, their hearts were warmed and their thoughts stirred up within them. So it went until the feast of the Grass-on-the-Mountain. Then the tribes and the sub-tribes came together at the place called Corn Water and there was no one who could sing equal to Cinoave. They had him sing his Coyote Song over and over, and as he listened to the talk and the hand-clapping he changed the words of the song so that those who heard it should say, 'This is the Song of Cinoave.'

"It was now some months since he had bought the song of Coyote, and the song and the praise of it had entered into his bones. He thought of nothing but being praised and remembered for the power of his singing. So he sang it until he and the people were all wearied, and fell into the deep sleep of exhaustion. But because he had forgotten that the song could only be sung for the purpose for which it was given, Old Man Coyote came in the night and stole the song away. When the people awoke, it was discovered that not one of them could remember a word of it.

"Thus it has become a custom among the Paiutes, when it is remarked that a man warms the hearts of the tribe by his singing and stirs up their thoughts within them, we do not praise him much. For who knows but it may turn out to be a Coyote Song? And when a song is used for other than the purpose of the giving, may not the giver of it take it away?"

As the Amerind says, "Thus shortens my chapter."

III

Bibliography

BOOKS

Adamson, Thelma, *Folk Tales of the Coast Salish*, Memoirs of the American Folk-Lore Society, G. E. Stechert and Company, New York, 1934.

Alexander, Hartley Burr, *The Mythology of All Races*, Vol. X, "North America," Marshall Jones Company, Boston, 1916.

Arnold, Oren, *Wild Life in the Southwest*, Banks Upshaw and Company, Dallas, 1935.

Austin, Mary, *The Land of Little Rain*, Houghton Mifflin Company, Boston and New York, The Riverside Press, Cambridge, 1903.

Austin, Mary, *Land of Journey's End*, The Century Company, New York, 1924.

The Coyote: Animal and Folk-Character

Austin, Mary, *One Smoke Stories*, Houghton Mifflin Company, Boston and New York, 1934.

Bailey, Vernon, *Mammals of New Mexico*, Bulletin 53, Biological Survey, United States Department of Agriculture, Government Printing Office, Washington, D. C., 1931.

Bailey, Vernon, *Destruction of Wolves and Coyotes*, Circular 63, Biological Survey, United States Department of Agriculture, Government Printing Office, Washington, D. C., 1908.

Barker, S. Omar, *Vientos de las Sierras*, S. Omar Barker, Beulah, New Mexico, 1924.

Bayliss, Clara Kern, *Old Man Coyote*, Thomas Y. Crowell and Company, New York, 1908.

Beckwith, Martha Warren, *Mandan and Hidatsa Tales*, Vassar College, Poughkeepsie, New York, 1934.

Beechey, F. W., *Narrative*, H. Colburn and R. Bentley, London, 1831.

Benedict, Ruth, *Tales of the Cochiti Indians*, Bulletin 98, Bureau of Ethnology, Smithsonian Institute, Government Printing Office, Washington, D. C., 1931.

Boas, Franz, *Chinook Texts*, Bulletin 20, Bureau of Ethnology, Smithsonian Institute, Government Printing Office, Washington, D. C., 1894.

Boas, Franz, *Kathlamet Texts*, Bulletin 26, Bureau of Ethnology, Smithsonian Institute, Government Printing Office, Washington, D. C., 1905.

Boas, Franz, *Kutenai Tales*, Bulletin 59, Bureau of Ethnology, Smithsonian Institute, Government Printing Office, Washington, D. C., 1918.

Brinton, Daniel G., *The Myths of the New World*, Henry Holt and Company, New York, 1876.

Brinton, Daniel G., *Essays of an Americanist*, Porter and Coates, Philadelphia, 1890.

Burlin, Natalie C., *The Indian's Book*, Harper and Brothers, New York, 1907.

Compos, Ruben, *El Folklore Literario de Mejico*, Wec. de ed., Pub., Mexico, 1929.

Chapman, Wendell and Lucy, *The Little Wolf, A Story of the Coyote of Our Rocky Mountains*, Charles Scribner's Sons, New York, 1936.

Charencey, H., *Le Mythe d'imos Traditiones des Peuples Mexicains*, Ser. 1., Vol. I, No. 7 and Ser. 1, Vol. II, No. 7, and Ser. 27, Vol. I, No. 14, Mexico.

Cronyn, George W., *The Path of the Rainbow, The Book of Indian Poems*, Boni and Liveright, New York, 1918.

Cushing, Frank Hamilton, *Zuni Folk Tales*, Alfred A. Knopf, New York, 1931.

Coyote Wisdom

Dale, Edward Everett, *Tales of the Tepee*, D. C. Heath and Company, New York, 1920.

De Huff, E. W., *TayTay's Memories*, Harcourt, Brace and Company, New York, 1924.

De Huff, E. W., *TayTay's Tales*, Harcourt, Brace and Company, New York, 1933.

Densmore, Frances, *Mandan and Hidatsa Music*, Bulletin 80, Bureau of Ethnology, Smithsonian Institute, Government Printing Office, Washington, D. C., 1923.

Densmore, Frances, *Yuman and Yaqui Music*, Bulletin 110, Bureau of Ethnology, Smithsonian Institute, Government Printing Office, Washington, D. C., 1932.

Densmore, Frances, *Papago Music*, Bulletin 90, Bureau of Ethnology, Smithsonian Institute, Government Printing Office, Washington, D. C., 1929.

Densmore, Frances, *Pawnee Music*, Bulletin 93, Bureau of Ethnology, Smithsonian Institute, Government Printing Office, Washington, D. C., 1929.

Dixon, Joseph, *Control of Coyotes in California*, Bulletin 320, College of Agriculture, Berkeley, California, 1920.

Dobie, J. Frank, *On the Open Range*, The Southwest Press, Dallas, Texas, 1931.

Dobie, J. Frank, (Ed.), *Puro Mexicano*, The Texas Folklore Society, Austin, Texas, 1935.

Dobie, J. Frank, *Tongues of the Monte*, Doubleday, Doran, and Company, Inc., Garden City, New York, 1935.

Dodge, Richard Irving, *The Hunting Grounds of the Great West*, Chatto Windus, London, 1878.

Dodge, Richard Irving, *The Plains of the Great West and Their Inhabitants*, G. P. Putnam Sons, New York, 1877.

Frachtenberg, Leo J., *Alsea Texts and Myths*, Bulletin 67, Bureau of Ethnology, Smithsonian Institute, Government Printing Office, Washington, D. C., 1920.

Gifford, E. W., *The Kami of Imperial Valley*, Bulletin 97, Bureau of Ethnology, Smithsonian Institute, Government Printing Office, Washington, D. C., 1930.

Goddard, P. E., *Myths and Tales from White Mountain Apaches*, The Trustees, American Museum of Natural History, New York, 1919.

Goddard, P. E., *Myths and Tales from the San Carlos Apaches*, The Trustees, American Museum of Natural History, New York, 1918.

Goddard, P. E., *Indians of the Southwest*, American Museum of Natural History, Government Printing Office, Washington, D. C., 1913.

Greeley, Horace, *An Overland Journey from New York to San Francisco*, C. M. Saxton, Barker, and Company, New York, 1860.

The Coyote: Animal and Folk*Character

Grinnel, George Bird, *By Cheyenne Campfires*, Oxford University Press, London, 1926.

Harrington, John P., *Karuk Indian Myths*, Bulletin 107, Bureau of Ethnology, Smithsonian Institute, Government Printing Office, Washington, D. C., 1932.

Hornaday, Dr. W. T., *American Natural History*, Charles Scribner's Sons, New York, 1924.

Hornaday, Dr. W. T., *The Minds and Manners of Wild Animals*, Charles Scribner's Sons, New York, 1922.

Ingersoll, Ernest, *Wild Neighbors*, Macmillan Company, New York, 1897.

Jacobs, Joseph, *The Most Delectable History of Reynard the Fox*, Macmillan Company, London and New York, 1895. (First Edition. Il. by W. Frank Calderon.)

Jaeger, Edmund C., *Denizens of the Desert*, Houghton, Mifflin Company, Boston and New York, 1922.

Jardine, James T., *Coyote-Proof Inclosures*, Government Printing Office, Washington, D. C., 1911.

Kroeber, Alfred L., *Handbook of the Indians of California*, Bulletin 78, Bureau of Ethnology, Smithsonian Institute, Government Printing Office, Washington, D. C., 1925.

Knibbs, Henry Herbert, *Riders of the Stars*, Houghton Mifflin Company, Boston and New York, The Riverside Press, Cambridge, 1916.

Lafrentz, F. W., *Cowboy Stuff*, Il. by Henry Ziegler (original etchings), G. P. Putnam's Sons, New York, 1927. (Author's Autograph Edition).

Lampman, Herbert Sheldon, *Northwest Nature Trails*, Il. by Quincy Scott, Metropolitan Press, Portland, Oregon, 1933. (Sponsored by Oregon State Game Commission).

Lantz, David E., *Coyotes in Their Economic Relations*, Bulletin 20, Biological Survey, United States Department of Agriculture, Government Printing Office, Washington, D. C., 1905.

LeNoir, Phil, *Rhymes of the Wild and Wooly*, Phil H. LeNoir, Santa Fé, New Mexico, 1920.

Linderman, Frank B., *Kootenai Why Stories*, Charles Scribner's Sons, New York, 1926.

Lindeman, Frank B., *Old Man Coyote*, The John Day Company, New York, 1931.

Lummis, Charles F., *Pueblo Indian Folk Tales*, The Century Publishing Company, New York, 1910.

Matthews, W., *Navaho Legends*, Memoirs of American Folk-Lore Society, G. E. Stechert and Company, New York, 1897.

Merriam, Dr. C. H., *Revision of Coyotes*, Biological Society, Washington, D. C., 1897.

Coyote Wisdom

Mills, Enos A., *Watched by Wild Animals*, Chapter VII, "The Clown of the Prairie," Houghton Mifflin Company, Boston and New York, 1932.

Mills, Enos A., *Wild Animal Homesteads*, Chapter III, "A Coyote Den by the River," Houghton Mifflin Company, Boston and New York, 1932.

Mourning Dove (Hu-mis-hu-ma), *Coyote Stories*, The Caxton Printers, Ltd., Caldwell, Idaho, 1934.

Penafiel, Dr. Antonio, *Nomenclatura Geografica de Mexico, Atlas*, Fototipa de la Secretaria de Fomenta, Mexico, 1895.

Penafiel, Dr. Antonio, *Nomenclatura Geografica de Mexico Etimologias de los Nombres de Lugar*, Secunda Parte, Oficina Tipografica de la Secretaria de Fomenta, Mexico, 1897.

Ramirez, Roman, *Coyotes O Lobos del Campo*, Government Bulletin, Mexico, 1909.

Robelo, Cecelio A., *Diccionario de Aztequismos*, Imprenta del Autor, Cuernavaca (Cuauhmahuas), Mexico, 1904.

Robelo, Cecelio A., *Diccionario de Aztequismos*, Nueva edicion, prenta del Museo N. de Arqueologia, Historia, y Etnologia, Mexico, 1912.

Robelo, Cecelio A., *Nombers Geograficos Indigenas del Estado de Morelos*, Impresor L. G. Miranda, Cuernavaca, Mexico, 1897.

Robinson, Will H., *Under Turquoise Skies*, The Macmillan Company, New York, 1928.

Roosevelt, T., *Ranch Life and the Hunting Trail*, The Century Company, New York, 1902.

Roosevelt, T., *Hunting Trips of a Rancher*, Review of Reviews Company, New York, 1904.

Sarett, Lew, *Slow Smoke*, Henry Holt and Campany, New York, 1925.

Seton, Ernest Thompson, *Wild Animals at Home*, Grosset and Dunlap, New York, 1913.

Seton, Ernest Thompson, *Wild Animals I Have Known*, Charles Scribner's Sons, New York, 1924.

Seton, Ernest Thompson, *Lives of Game Animals*, Vol. I, Part II, Doubleday, Doran and Company, Inc., New York, 1929.

Seton, Ernest Thompson, *Lives of the Hunted*, Charles Scribner's Sons, New York, 1930.

Simeon, Remi, *Dictionnaire de la Langue Nahuatl ou Mexicaine*, Imprimerie Nationale, Paris, France, 1885.

Spence, Lewis, *Myths of North American Indians*, Farrar and Rinehart, New York, 1932.

Spence, Lewis, *The Myths of Mexico and Peru*, Farrar and Rinehart, New York, 1931.

Stefansson, V., *Adventures in Error*, McBride, New York, 1936.

The Coyote: Animal and Folk*Character

Teit, James, *Folk Tales of Salishan and Sahaptin Tribes*, Memoirs of American Folk-Lore Society, G. E. Stechert, New York, 1917.

Teit, James, *Traditions of Thompson River Indians*, Memoirs of American Folk-Lore Society, G. E. Stechert and Company, New York, 1898.

Thompson, Stith, *Tales of the North American Indians*, Harvard University Press, Cambridge, Mass., 1929.

Thompson, Stith, *European Tales Among North American Indians*, Colorado Springs, 1919.

Twain, Mark, *Roughing It*, Harpers, New York, 1871.

Underwood, John Curtis, *Trail's End, Poems of New Mexico*, New Mexican Publishing Corporation, Santa Fé, New Mexico, 1921.

Van Dyke, John C., *The Desert, Further Studies in Natural Appearances*, Charles Scribner's Sons, New York, 1930.

Webb, W. P., *The Great Plains*, Ginn and Company, Boston, 1931.

Zitkala-Sa, *Old Indian Legends*, Ginn and Company, New York, 1901.

Periodicals

1. Magazines

All the Year Round
    Holder, C. F., "Coyote Hunting, a Sketch," 34:462, 1875.
American Magazine
    Mara, W. A. and Canfield, E. M., "New Ways of Keeping the Wolf from the Door," 114:66, October, 1932.
Catholic World
    Rakes, L. W., "Shaggy Fellow," 125:217-21, May, 1927.
Colliers
    Stearns, M. M., "Black Coyote," 81:23-4, February 25, 1928.
Current Literature
    Anonymous, "Chased by Coyotes," 34:69, January, 1903.
    Holder, C. F., "Don Coyote," 27:261-2, March, 1900.
Delineator
    McIlvaine, C., "How Coyote Got His Marks," 67:207, February, 1906.
Field and Stream
    Faile, Edward G., "Wolf, Fox, or Dog," August, 1920, p. 401.
Forest and Stream
    Brooks, Allan, "Northerly Range of the Coyote," 71:812-13, November 21, 1908.
    Carney, Emerson, "Wyoming Vermin Bounties," 52:145, February 25, 1899.
    Grinnell, G. B., "About Wolves and Coyotes," 47:511-12, December 20, 1896.

Coyote Wisdom

Grinnell, G. B., "A Coyote Partnership," 48:104, February 6, 1897.

Meacham, A., "The Coyote as a Strategist," 60:48, January 17, 1903.

Pellett, Frank C., "The Prairie Wolf in Iowa," 76:450, March 25, 1911.

Wilmot, Lew, "Coyotes Hunting in Bands," 48:284, April 10, 1897.

Good Housekeeping
Squier, E. L., "Coyote Who Talked with God," 77:30-1, December, 1923.

Illustrated World
Nelson, L. A., "Hunting Down Mad Coyotes," 25:508-9, June, 1916.

Land of Sunshine
Holder, Charles Frederick, "Don Coyote," 4:179-80, March, 1896.
Lummis, C. F., "The Coyote," 3:215-7, October, 1895.

Literary Digest
Anonymous, "Giving the Coyote a Good Name," 92:61, March 26, 1927.
Anonymous, "Sixty Hounds in a Coyote Hunt in Texas," 84:70-2, March 28, 1925.
Anonymous, "His Hand was Quicker than a Wolf's Jaw," 114:23-4, September 3, 1932.
Anonymous, "Go East, Young Coyote, Go East!" 112:41-2, January 16, 1932.
Anonymous, "Lone Wolf," 122:14-5, December 19, 1936.
Donahue, Ralph J., "Coyote," 122:27, December 19, 1936.

Mentor
Finley, I., "Wild Dog of the Desert," 12:28-9, August, 1927.

Nature Magazine
Bailey, Vernon, "Mammals of the Lone Star State," December, 1930.
Finley, William L. and Irene, "Skeezix, a White Coyote," 15:227-9, April, 1930.
Humphrey, Imogene, "Kiyi, a Coyote," 22:83-4, December, 1933.
Squire, L., "Hunt of the Coyote," 22:151-4, October, 1933.
Squire, L., "Coyote of the Plains," 17:162-7, March, 1931.
Stevenson, E., "The Case of Reddy—a Coyote," 27:140-2, March, 1936.

Outdoor Life
Hall, E. Raymond, "Coyote and His Control," April, 1934.

Outing
Chapman, A., "Pariah of the Skyline," 44:131-8, May, 1904.
Fenton, D. W., "Coyote Hunt," 33:572-5, March, 1899.
Holder, C. F., "Don Coyote," 54:692-6, September, 1909.

The Coyote: Animal and Folk-Character

Laing, H. M., "Wanted, a Coyote," 66:316-26, June, 1915.
Reed, John S., "The Coyote Song," 14:1, 1889.
Steele, J. W., "The Figurehead of the Frontier," 50:407-10, July, 1907.
Outlook
Lambert, P. L., "Coyotes and Their Habits," 115:568, March 28, 1917.
Shoemaker, T., "Kiote," 101:679, July 27, 1912.
Overland
Cobb, M. S., "Coyote Hunt," 57:380-3, April, 1911.
Harte, Bret, "Coyote," 3:93, 1869.
Kipe, L., "Coyote Canyon," 9:27, 1872.
Kroeber, H. W., "Navajo's Fairy Tale," 54:456-8, November, 1909.
Millard, F. B., "Coyote—That—Bites," 18:471, 1891.
Sabin, E. L., "Story of Coyote," 21:274-9, May, 1908.
Sedgwick, C. B., "Hunting the Coyote for Scalps," 19:192, 1891.
Popular Science Monthly
Ingersoll, Ernest, "Coyote, the Hound of the Plains," 30:306, 1887.
Readers Digest
O'Connor, J., "Furry Gangsters of the Desert," 28:47-9, June, 1936 (Condensed from *Field and Stream*, April, 1936).
Recreation
Hulse, J. W., "Woodland Tragedy," March, 1899, p. 220.
Greenwood, Charles, "Coyotes," September, 1897, p. 233.
Saturday Evening Post
Bulger, B., "Catching the Coyote," 206:84-5, September 23, 1933.
Evarts, Hal G., "Spread of the Coyote," 196:44, December 15, 1923.
Yore, C., "Coyote Danger," 201:205-6, October 13, 1928.
Scientific American
Anonymous, "Coyote Move East by Modern Methods," 152:328, June, 1936.
Von Blon, J. L., "Commercializing on Coyotes," 122:246, March 6, 1920.
Scribner's
Roosevelt, T., "Wolf Hunt in Oklahoma," 38:513-32, November, 1905.
Seton, E. T., "Tito, the Coyote that Learned How," 28:131-45, August, 1900.
St. Nicholas
Gleeson, J. M., "Coyotes at Home and in Captivity," 31:606-7, May, 1904.
Sunset
Young, S. P., "Senor Yip-Yap," 61:28-30, December, 1928.

Coyote Wisdom

Temple Bar
Anonymous, "Adventures with Coyotes in Central America," 23:
66, 1867.
Woman's Home Companion
Baynes, E. H., "My Young Coyote, Romulus," 32:16, March, 1905.

2. Newspapers

The Dallas Morning News, Magazine Section, "This Week," October
18, 1936.
Dilly Herald, February 5, 1937.
The New York Times
1922, Oct. 21, 15:2. Riverton N. J. farmers kill coyotes that had
been robbing chicken roosts.
1923, Je. 3, I pt. 2, 5:7. Boy bitten at Bronx Zoo by Coyote.
1924, S. 20, 17:2. Hunting party organized to hunt them in N. J.
1926, S. 23, 24:5. Ed. on feud between homesteader of Harney Co.,
Oregon, and "Coyote" Bill Snyder, over latter's trapping activities.
1926, Ap. 3, 2:5. Airmail beacons drive them away from sheep
ranges, but light keeps sheep awake.
1926, M. 15, 6:3. "Old Renegade," credited with having done
$14,000 damage to flocks in Orleans Co., N. Y., hunted in
vain by gunners and dogs.
1926, M. 28, 21:2. Hunters shoot 3 in Orleans Co., N. Y.; get
$900 bounty.
1927, Jl. 15, 2:7. Mrs. R. Sanders to give baby one to Mrs. Cool-
idge.
1928, Mr. 11, V 25:1. Hunting them on Western plains.
1928, Mr. 18, X, 10:2. New Mexican rancher protects sheep from
them by barbed wire.
1928, N. 25, 11, 1:7. Alaska wars on them as serious threat to game.
1929, Jl. 6, 20:3. Alaska legislature appropriates $30,000 for cam-
paign against them.
1930, Mr. 3, 14:7. Aviator kills coyote with his plane, Anchorage,
Alaska.
1930, Ap. 30, 24:4. Ed. on preservation.
1930, Jl. 20, 19:4. Kan. officials charge bounties are collected on
scalps from other states.
1930, Jl. 27, III, 6:6. Kan. discovers "racket" in scalps brought
in from other states.
1931, F. 11, 30:4. Escaped mascot of Cal. Univ. crew hunted as
marauder at Princeton, N. J.
1931, Mr. 29, III, 5:8. Kansans have new sport, chasing them in
planes. Dodge City.

The Coyote: Animal and Folk-Character

1931, Jl. 19, III, 5:4. House cats used to lure them.
1933, F. 19, IV, 6:8. Coyotes overrun Kansas Farms.
1933, D. 21, 14:2. One reported caught in New Jersey.
1934, Ja. 21, IV, 5:6. Seen in Pa. Letter.
1934, J. 28, IV, 6:4. Pa. state Game Warden H. Meiss loses bet that they were found in Washington County, to H. R. Mallon.
1934, May 6, IV, 5:8. Letter on Pa. fight against them.
1935, Ja. 20, II, 2:6. Women join coyote hunt at Lawrence to rid area of animals.
1935, Me. 16, IV, 12:5. Migration to Central and Eastern part of state laid to rabbit hunt. Kansas.
1936, D. 29, 16:3. All night hunt, Trenton, N. J.
1937, F. 10, 25:5. Kill deer in streets of Cordova, Alaska.
1937, J. 8, 21:5. Coyotes hunted by riders and hounds, in Idaho.
1937, Ja. 11, XI, 11:2. Comment on coyote and jackrabbit hunting from autos.
Waco News-Tribune, November 12, 1936, p. 11.
Waco News-Tribune, May 31, 1937, p. 1.

Annual Reports

Annual Report of the Bureau of American Ethnology to the Secretary of the Smithsonian Institution, Government Printing Office, Washington, D. C.

*Vol. I (1879-1880), Powell, J. W., "Sketches of the Mythology of the North American Indians," pp. 17-56.
Vol. 2 (1880-1881), Cushing, F. H., "Zuni Fetishes," pp. 3-45 (26).
Vol. 8 (1886-1887), Mindeleff, V., "A Study of Pueblo Architecture: Tusayan and Cibolo," pp. 2-228 (Coyote Kiva, 116).
*Vol. 11 (1892-1893), Powell, J. W., "Report of Director," pp. xxi-xlvii; Stevenson, M. C., "The Sia," pp. 3-157.
Vol. 14 (1892-1893), Hoffman, W. J., "The Menomini Indians," pp. 3-328 (205).
Vol. 17 (1895-1896), McGee, W. J., "The Seri Indians," pp. 1-128, 129-344; Hewitt, J. N. B., "Comparative Lexicology of Serian and Yuman Languages," pp. 299-344.
Vol. 19 (1897-1898), Fewkes, J. W., "Tusayan Migration Traditions," pp. 573-633 (467-468).
Vol. 21 (1899-1900), Fewkes, J. W., "Hopi Katcinas," pp. 3-126; Hewitt, J. N. B., "Iroquoin Cosmology," pp. 127-339 (14, 111, 112, 125).
Vol. 24 (1902-1903), Culin, S., "Games of North American Indians," pp. 3-809 (794).

Coyote Wisdom

*Vol. 26 (1904-1905), Russell, Frank, "The Pima Indians," pp. 3-389; Swanton, John R., "The Tlingit Indians," pp. 391-485.
Vol. 28 (1906-1907), Fewkes, Walter, "Casa Grande, Arizona," pp. 25-179 (44).
*Vol. 32 (1910-1911), Curtin, J. and Hewitt, J. N. B., "Seneca Fiction, Legends, and Myths," pp. 37-813.
Vol. 41 (1919-1924), Boas, F., "Coiled Basketry in British Columbia," pp. 119-484 (223).
*Vol. 43 (1925-1926), Harrington, J. P., and Roberts, Helen H., "Picuris Children's Tales, with Texts and Songs," pp. 289-447.
Vol. 45 (1927-1928), Teit, James A., "The Salishan Tribes of the Western Plateau," pp. 23-396.

The Journal of American Folk-lore, published for the American Folk-Lore Society, by Houghton, Mifflin and Company, Boston and New York, 1888-1910; by G. E. Stechert and Company, New York, 1911-1937.
Vol. 1 (1888), p. 166.
Vol. 2 (1889), pp. 174, 188.
Vol. 3 (1890), pp. 211, 212, 297.
Vol. 7 (1894), p. 195.
Vol. 8 (1895), pp. 128, 318.
Vol. 13 (1900), pp. 166, 168, 189, 267.
Vol. 14 (1901), pp. 123, 161, 184, 186, 195, 240-251, 252-285.
Vol. 15 (1902), pp. 38, 63, 137, 178.
Vol. 16 (1903), pp. 32, 42, 49.
Vol. 17 (1904), pp. 8, 61, 83, 154, 187, 219, 232.
Vol. 19 (1906), pp. 31-51, 56, 59, 60, 67, 134, 136-139, 158, 251, 259, 313, 322.
Vol. 20 (1907), pp. 42, 49, 82, 121-126, 177, 224, 226, 227.
Vol. 21 (1908), pp. 13-22, 91, 92, 93, 99, 103, 110, 124, 126, 127, 149, 159, 161, 162, 163, 165, 166, 169, 170-176, 230, 231, 237, 238-241, 244, 245, 273, 274, 288, 305, 308, 309, 313, 321, 323, 333, 338, 339, 345, 347, 348.
Vol. 22 (1909), pp. 265-267, 269, 270, 273-281, 284, 287, 339-342, 350, 351, 373, 431-433.
Vol. 23 (1910), pp. 13-20, 22-37, 205, 296, 297, 299-317, 335-349, 351, 352, 355, 358, 362, 369, 370, 457, 461-466, 470, 471.
Vol. 24 (1911), pp. 238, 419, 423.
Vol. 25 (1912), pp. 95-99, 103, 200-203, 205-207, 236-238, 247, 257, 260, 290, 304-309, 327, 350, 357, 358, 368.

---

*Volumes starred are especially fruitful. Page numbers in parenthesis indicate the part of the article pertaining especially to the coyote.

The Coyote: Animal and Folk Character

Vol. 27 (1914), pp. 23, 38, 39, 134, 139, 143, 150-153, 163, 204, 206, 217, 218, 227, 359, 387, 388, 395, 396, 399.
Vol. 28 (1915), p. 356.
Vol. 29 (1916), pp. 549-551.
Vol. 31 (1918), pp. 215-245, 451-470.
Vol. 32 (1919), pp. 346-348.
Vol. 33 (1920), pp. 47-49.
Vol. 36 (1923), pp. 135-162, 163-170, 305-367, 368-375.
Vol. 37 (1924), pp. 1-242, 345-370. (The latter are written in modern Nahuatl).
Vol. 41 (1928), pp. 232-252, 253-261.
Vol. 42 (1929), pp. 1-84.
Vol. 43 (1930), p. 46.
Vol. 44 (1931), pp. 125-132, 137.
Vol. 45 (1932), pp. 400-494.

University of California Publications in American Archaeology and Ethnology, The University Press, Berkeley, California.
Vol. 1, No. 2 (1903-1904), Goddard, P. E., "Hupa Texts," pp. 154, 155, 167-168, 225.
Vol. 4, No. 4 (1906-1907), Kroeber, A. L., "Indian Myths of South Central California," pp. 169-250.
Vol. 5, No. 3 (1907), Goddard, P. E., "Kato Texts," pp. 71-238.
Vol. 9, No. 1 (1910), Sapir, Edward, "Yana Texts and Myths," pp. 6-234.
Vol. 12, No. 8 (1917), Gifford, E. W., "Miwok Myths," pp. 283-338.
Vol. 14, No. 1 (1918), Mason, J. A., "The Language of the Solinan Indians," pp. 1-154.
Vol. 16, No. 1 (1919), Barrett, S. A., "Myths of the Southern Sierra Miwok, pp. 1-28.
Vol. 19, No. 1 (1924-1926), Radin, Paul, "Wappo Texts," pp. 1-147.
Vol. 19, No. 2 (1924-1926), Loeb, E. M., "Pomo Folkways," pp. 149-405.
Vol. 22, No. 1 (1925), Reichard, G. A., "Wigot Grammar and Test," pp. 1-215.
Vol. 29, No. 3 (1932) Gifford, E. W., "The Southwestern Yayapoi," pp. 177-252.
Vol. 29, No. 4 (1932), Kroeber, A. L., "The Patwin and Their Neighbors," pp. 253-423.
Vol. 34, No. 5 (1936), Steward, Julian H., "Myths of the Owens Valley Paiute," pp. 355-440.

Pueblo Versions of Old World Tales

By ELIZABETH WILLIS DeHUFF

Finding kinships between tales constitutes a considerable part of the science of folk-lore. The scientific folk-lorist has no active interest in a tale as a tale, in the tale-teller, in the tale-listener, in folks. His business has come to be very much like that of the clever machine that packs sardines into a can. The sardine-packer fits tails to heads; the scientific folk-lorist fits tales under their proper heads.

Now, Elizabeth DeHuff is emphatically not a scientist. She is a tale-teller. However, in suggesting that the Pueblo Indian story of the Turkey Girl is but a version of the very old and widespread Old World story of Cinderella, she has touched on a theme of endless ramifications and sharp dispute. The same could be said of almost every other story she tells.

The late Mary Austin had wonderful insight, an oracular manner and a fine scorn for "that curious obsession of the American scholar which leads him to regard all aesthetic considerations as 'embellishments,' 'figures of speech,' 'emotional interpretations.'" In her Introduction to Frank Hamilton Cushing's *Zuñi Folk Tales* (1931 edition), she says: "Recently there has been an effort to classify the story of the Turkey Girl as a modern adaptation of the Cinderella motive, in which I cannot concur. The Turkey Girl is a favorite in all Pueblo fiction," etc. Aurelio M. Espinosa, who has traced the Tar-Baby story around the world and back again, would no doubt take the other side. Probably he has already taken it. Meantime the stories live on.—J. F. D.

Taytay's (Grandfather's) face is like a dried-up apple, full of kindly wrinkles mingled with crafty lines. He is a Pueblo Indian. He wears long, pear-shaped pieces of the bluest turquoise hanging by strings from stretched holes in his ears, dancing jigs upon his bronze cheeks, tapping against them, and twisting coquettishly as he talks, especially when he jerks his chin forward to point with his lips. Entwined in plaited strips of red and blue felt, his black hair hangs in two long braids over his shoulders. On the outside of his cotton trousers, fashioned like a Chinese coolie's, hangs the tail of his shirt, belted in about the hips with a leather thong laced through big silver medallions, while below the shirt tail, in front and back dangle the ends of a red loin cloth. On gala days, he changes his trousers for yellow buckskin leggings reaching to the hips, upon the outer side of which ripple and flap deep, full fringes of split buckskin colored to match. Whenever he goes out of doors, even in summer, he wraps about himself either a cotton blanket or a warm Navajo one, which, being as old as himself or older, has softened in color to beautiful pastel shades.

On cold winter days I have found Taytay in his adobe house keeping himself warm near the blaze from upright sticks in his quarter-of-a-dome mud fireplace, with a far-away expression in his eyes. He either sits in a bent chair, with hands folded and feet precisely together upon the dirt floor, or, in order to absorb more of the heat, he may be seated with feet doubled under him upon a goat skin on the floor. If I catch him in the right humor he will sit there for hours telling me tales of the "long time ago," but if the mood is not right, no amount of teasing will bring a single story, only the promise, "Some time, other day, I tell story!" Among the many tales that he has told me are some which produced an especial thrill, because they have universal or familiar themes: a Cinderella story, one of Beauty and the Beast, Bluebeard, Jack the Giant Killer, Romulus and Remus, a version of the Tar Baby story, many accounts of how rabbit-boy or other animals and birds outwitted the coyote or the fox or of how one predatory animal gets ahead of another.

The Turkey Girl

First was the Cinderella story. Castañeda, who made an *entrada* into this country with Coronado in 1540, and who

kept such an accurate account of everything that he saw
that it is said Coronado had him imprisoned when they
returned to old Mexico—he had told too much—wrote,
"There are a great many native fowls in these provinces,
the cocks with great hanging chins," and later, in 1581,
Hernan Gallegos, who visited here, recorded that the Indian
families each had a flock of about one hundred tame turkeys, which they tended like sheep and kept in separate
corrals at night, using the feathers for ceremonies and the
flesh for food.

The Cinderella story is based upon this custom and concerns the little turkey-girl, who tended the flock of turkeys
belonging to her step-sisters, the two Corn-maidens. This
was long, long ago when there were no other turkeys in
the world, except this flock belonging to Blue-Corn and
Yellow-Corn, girls who were magicians, and with whom
lived a little adopted sister or step-sister (evidently a little
slave girl).

Every day the little turkey-girl drove the flock of turkeys from their corral and tended them as they grazed, and
at sundown brought them home again, to eat for her supper
only the crumbs that the Corn-maidens had left.

The day approached for a great corn dance in a nearby
village, and the Corn-maidens began preparing to go,
making themselves new moccasins and new costumes and
washing their long hair. When the little turkey-girl begged
to go, she was told that she had to stay and look after her
turkeys, and that besides she had no ceremonial garments
to wear.

At dawn on the morning of the *fiesta*, the little turkey-
girl went out with her turkeys singing dolefully, "Kee-nah,
o-la thay-lay! Kee-nah, o-la thay-lay, e-ah-e, e-ah-e,
e-ah-e!" "We are going into the hole in the rock! We are
going into the hole in the rock; e-ah-e, e-ah-e, e-ah-e!"
(The hole in the rock means the Underworld, where one

goes after death). The turkeys, not caring to die and feeling sorry for the little girl, asked her why she was so sad.

"I am crying because I cannot go to the *fiesta*. I have no clothes and no moccasins good enough to wear and there is no one else to take care of you; so I shall take you into the hole," replied the turkey-girl, who continued her singing.

The turkeys then held a council, after which they said to the little girl, "We will give you a *manta*, a belt, and moccasins to wear and we will take care of ourselves while you go to the ceremony, but be sure to come back before sundown to put us into the corral so that coyotes cannot devour us." So one turkey dropped the *manta*, the blanket-dress; another dropped a woven belt; while a third and fourth each dropped buckskin moccasins. Happily the little turkey-girl donned them and skipped away to the *fiesta*.

All day she danced and feasted and in her joy she forgot all about the turkeys, until suddenly she looked toward the horizon, where she saw the sun sinking into his western *kiva*. Quickly she turned and ran, but it was too late. Her manta fell off, turned into a deer, and leaped away. Her sash became a snake, which wriggled off, and each of her moccasins became green scum upon a pool that was at hand. When finally she came in sight of the turkeys, they divided into four bands and flew away to the four cardinal points, calling back to her as they left, "Since you deserted us, Turkey-girl, we are now leaving you, chow, chow, piu, piu!" And that is why later turkeys have been found wild all over this country.

Beauty and the Beast

Though the thermometer was low, the sunshine gave comfort as it concentrated on the bronzed mud walls. Taytay was here, squatting upon his moccasined heels

Coyote Wisdom

against the sunny mud wall of his house. Crouching beside him, I offered him a cigarette, and after smoking in silence for a while, he waved his arm toward the Pajarito plateau, west of Santa Fé, and told me the Beauty and the Beast story.

In an old pueblo on the Pajarito plateau, named Otowi, a youth with a hideous face lived alone with his grandmother. His grandmother was a magician, but the boy did not know it. She had given him magic arrows for his bow.

Whenever the Youth went out to play with the other Indian children, they pointed their fingers in scorn at his ugly face, laughed derisively at him, and ran away; but whenever they went hunting, Ugly-boy brought back many times as many rabbits as anyone else, so that the other boys became jealous of him and despised him the more. Hence poor Ugly-boy led a lonely life.

One morning the old *cacique*, the spiritual leader of the village, had the crier announce from the highest housetop that all the men and boys must go out with their bows and arrows upon a communal rabbit hunt. None of the other people would allow Ugly-boy to hunt near them, but while they found no rabbits all day, Ugly-boy ran from one hole to another pulling out game.

He had just killed two rabbits at once and was chasing a third to its burrow, when he heard a voice near him. He looked around, but could see no one until the voice had called the fourth time; then he saw a beautiful girl standing beside him.

In the dialect of the Pecos pueblo, she asked him what he was doing, running so fast. Pointing to his belt, from which hung as many slain rabbits as he could carry, he told her of the hunt. She invited him to go home with her to Pecos, and there she gave him food. This signified a proposal of marriage, and Ugly-boy by eating it declared his acceptance of the offer. Then the girl gave him a ceremonial *manta* as a present to his grandmother, and after filling a basket with cornbread and strips of dried venison, they set out for Otowi.

When they neared the pueblo, people watching from the housetops jeered at him because of jealousy, for the girl was beautiful, and he came loaded with rabbits while they had none. But when Ugly-boy offered to share his rabbits, they refused to accept any. Unmindful of their taunts, Ugly-boy and his bride went on to his grandmother's house at the edge of the village.

At the hatchway upon the roof, Ugly-boy paused and, looking down, called, "Grandmother, I am coming bringing a wife to help you with the work of the house."

"Poor, my son," replied the old woman, "you are so ugly I fear no one can really care for you!" For she thought the lonely boy was teasing.

To prove that he had told the truth, Ugly-boy then threw down into the room, the *manta* and his belt of rabbits. The old woman, being overjoyed, called to them to enter. When they came down, the Grandmother sprinkled spring water and sacred corn meal over the boy's head, and then, catching hold of his hair, she lifted from him the ugly mask, revealing him as a handsome young Indian.

"This mask I made you wear, my grandson," she said, "so that you would not marry a deceitful witch wife. Now you do not need it any more, for I know that this girl is good or she would not have married you for your good traits instead of your handsome face."

Cliff-Dweller, the Blue Beard

What a joy it was to discover Beauty and the Beast! No less pleasurable was it to find that the Indians, too, have Blue Beard, only his name is always Cliff-dweller, and he is a giant in size. I knew from Taytay's serious expression throughout that the tale was to him an historical fact.

The pathway leading up to the house in the otherwise unscalable cliffs where Cliff-dweller lived was so cleverly concealed that it was known only to himself. Down this he would go to the Indian pueblos seeking pretty girls to take home to become his wives; as soon as he would tire of one wife, he would force her to do something to displease him, thus giving him an excuse to shut her into a big cave to starve. Then he would fare forth to find another.

Thus he had treated many wives, when one day he saw Flower-petal making pots in the sunshine. With promises of many gifts, he persuaded her to climb upon his shoulder and let him take her to receive them and to be his bride.

Every day, after that, Cliff-dweller would leave Flower-petal at home to work, while he went out to hunt.

Soon he tired also of Flower-petal and wanted an excuse to get rid of her. Now in his house were four huge store-rooms. The one to the east was half filled with ears of white corn; that to the south was full of ears of blue corn; the room on the west side, twice as large as the two former, was full of corn with red kernels; and that to the north, also large in size, was brimming full of ears of corn of mixed colors.

Leading Flower-petal to the room half filled with white corn, he commanded: "When I return this evening, I shall expect to find all of this corn ground into meal, or I shall punish you!" And then he went away.

For a moment Flower-petal stood looking at the impossible task. If she ground an armful only of the corn during the day it would be a good day's work. She sat down and wept. Soon she heard a voice at her feet.

"*Hist, hist!*" it said. "Do not weep, my grandchild. Tears will not help, and while you weep you waste your time. Come, come, I shall help you.

Drying her tears and looking down, Flower-petal saw Spider-old-woman. "How can you help, Grandmother?" asked the doubting girl. "You are even smaller than I."

"I will bring my magic turkeys and as we shell the corn, they will grind it into meal." So Spider-old-woman hurried away and brought a flock of magic turkeys, and shortly before Cliff-dweller returned at sundown, the room to the east contained only a pile of cobs and baskets of snow white corn meal, neatly piled.

When Cliff-dweller saw that the task had been done, he was angry instead of pleased; and he began to wonder what kind of woman Flower-petal really was. Next day, he led her to the room on the south and gave her the same commission with the same threat of punishment. Again Flower-petal sat down and wept, for even with the help of Spider-old-woman and her turkeys on the day before, they had ground only half as much meal as was now required, and the grinding had taken them all day.

"*Hist, hist!*" came the voice of the spider. "Have I not told you not to weep? I shall bring twice as many turkeys today and we shall work twice as fast." And so they did. At sundown, Cliff-dweller once more found the task he had assigned completed, and he roared with anger. "Tomorrow," he stormed, "you shall grind all the corn in both the room to the west and that to the north, or I shall kill you as a trifling wife!" And Flower-petal spent the night in tears.

Next day, Cliff-dweller had scarcely gotten out of sight, when once more came the noise of "*Hist, hist,*" and Spider-old-woman was there with double the number of magic turkeys. Flower-petal worked so fast that her fingers ached, and before sundown the corn was all ground into meal and neatly piled in baskets. Cliff-dweller, as before, flew into a fury. "You are a witch," he cried. "No human being could have ground so much in a day. I shall kill you for a witch!"

Coyote Wisdom

But knowing that he had not proved that she was a witch, he could not kill her. "Tomorrow," he added, "you must take a jar and go to the White Lake in the east and bring me a jar of its water." Since no human being could go to the far-distant White Lake and back in one day, Cliff-dweller went to sleep in a happy frame of mind. "Now," he felt, "I shall have reason to put her into the cave!"

But after he had gone next day, Spider-old-woman came us usual. This time she brought with her a long ball of spider web. "Be not sad, my grandchild," she said. "Since you cannot go to the lake, I shall bring the lake to you. Close your eyes until I tell you to open them."

Flower-petal did as she was bidden, and when she was told to open her eyes again, there was the water of the lake lapping the ground beside her feet. Stooping down she dipped up a jar of water, and immediately the lake disappeared.

Cliff-dweller, of course, was again angry, for when he tasted the water, it was the bracken water of White Lake; so he commanded that on the following day Flower-petal should go twice as far to the south to bring him a jar of water from the Blue Lake.

The end has come, thought Flower-petal, for surely Spider-old-woman could not bring a lake so far.

"*Hist, hist,*" came the voice of the spider. "Today Cliff-dweller will look for your footprints. Take off your moccasins and give them to me, and also give me your water olla. Thousand-legs will wear your moccasins and bring back the water." And so it happened.

When Cliff-dweller sought the moccasin prints, he found them; but since he could think of no more impossible tasks for Flower-petal, he determined to put her into the cave anyway.

"You are a witch!" he charged. "Four days from today I shall return to kill you!"

Pueblo Versions of Old World Tales

While Cliff-dweller was away, Spider-old-woman spun a long web. Then, leading Flower-petal to the edge of the cliff, she bade her close her eyes, after causing her to sit in a carrying basket. "Do not open your eyes until you feel ground beneath your feet, or you will fall and be killed," warned Spider-old-woman. Flower-petal obeyed this injunction until she was almost down, but, feeling the wind whistling in her ears, she opened her eyes, and down she tumbled to earth. Fortunately she was almost there, so that the fall only stunned her. Getting up soon, she ran in the direction that Spider-old-woman had pointed out to her.

She had not gone far when she heard heavy footfalls behind her, and without looking back she knew that it was Cliff-dweller in pursuit. Looking around for a place to hide, Flower-petal could see nothing better than a tiny hole in the ground. She ran to the hole and called down, "Who is there? Can you help me?"

To her surprise the "*Hist, hist,*" of Spider-old-woman came to her from below. It was the home of the spider. "Put your foot upon the doorstep and enter!" she called.

"But I cannot enter, Grandmother," replied Flower-petal in despair. "I am big and the hole is little."

"Put your foot upon the doorstep," repeated Grandmother Spider. And Flower-petal did as she was told. Immedaitely the hole expanded large enough for her to enter, and then closed again, so that when Cliff-dweller reached the spot he could see nothing but a tiny hole. He thundered down the hole, "Come out, you witch, or I shall dig up the earth and find you!" But though he hammered and dug with his stone axe, he could not even make a dent in the roof of Spider-old-woman's house, for it was lined with magic pitch and covered with magic clay.

Finally when Cliff-dweller had grown so tired that he had to sit down to rest, Spider-old-woman slipped out and stung him with her magic arrow head, and he fell dead on the spot. Immediately he turned into stone, and if you know where to look, you can see the great stone now out on the mesa.

The Giant-Killer Twins

In the story of Jack the giant-killer, Jack is usually in the form of supernatural Twins—Youth and Fireboy—children of the Sun-father and the Corn-maiden, of miraculous conception, who grew to manhood in four days. Though they sometimes slay a man-eating giant, they more frequently slay a group of witches, who are also cannibalistic. These tales are numerous, and although they differ widely in detail the plot is essentially the same, showing great courage upon the part of the Twins, who are either handicapped in size or in numbers. An example is the following story:

Long, long ago the children of Pojuaque pueblo, on a tributary of the Rio Grande, were so bad that neither their parents nor the Old Men could make them behave. Finally a council was held to decide what to do with them, and among the men at the gathering was a wizard. He told the people that if they would shut him in an underground room and feed him raw deer meat for four days he would then punish the bad children. The name of this wizard was *Tsah-ve-yoh*.

The Indians did as suggested, and at the end of the fourth day when they went to let out *Tsah-ve-yoh*, he had grown so large that even though he was doubled over, he filled up the entire big room, and in order to get him out the Indians had to tear off all the building above. As soon as he got out, he ran away to Black Mesa to live in a cave. Having developed an insatiate appetite for fresh meat, every day he took four steps to Pojuaque and caught the bad children one by one, sometimes bringing them back and baking them in his oven, but often sitting upon his stool (the head of the eroded camel-formation along the highway between Santa Fé and Pojuaque) and eating them alive.

When he had eaten all the bad children, he caught the good ones, and nothing could stop him. Finally, having devoured all the children, he began to eat the grownups, one by one, until not a single Indian was left in Pojuaque.

Then with four steps he went each day to eat the children of San Ildefonso pueblo. The frightened people covered their children within the walls of their houses and plastered them into their adobe ovens, but the *Tsah-ve-yoh* brought a cane, for by tapping the walls he could always tell from the hollow sound where the children were. Tearing open the walls, he would pull them out and carry them away.

The despairing Indians held a council to discuss how they might kill the giant, and they decided to appeal to the little Twin War Gods, living not far away with their Grandmother, who had made for them magic arrows and bows.

In order to gain the good will of the twins, each clan offered to give its greatest treasure as a gift: the *cacique* and his clan donated sacred meal; the Buffalo clan gave

"THE INDIANS HELD A COUNCIL"

tobacco; the Shell and Turquoise clans gave beads; the Rain Chief gave a ceremonial skirt; and the Deer clan gave buckskin robes and moccasins.

Wrapping all the gifts in the ceremonial skirt, the old *cacique* took them to the home of the twins. When he knocked upon the door, the happy twins were playing and laughing so that they did not hear him.

"Are you here?" called the *cacique* at the top of his voice.

"Yes, we are here. Come in!" replied the twins.

Entering, the *cacique* presented his gifts and explained the troubles of his people.

"How many children have you left?" asked the twins.

"Only one boy and one girl!"

"We will go with you," and the twins took down from the wall their bows and magic arrows. After bidding goodbye to their grandmother, they went with the *cacique* to call a council of all the Indians.

"Watch at all times from the tops of your houses," said the twins, "and whenever you see smoke coming out of Black Mesa on the East, Chimayo on the West, Pajarito Plateau on the North, and the mesas on the south, you will know the giant is dead.

Standing on their housetops the people saw the *Tsah-ve-yoh* upon the summit of Black Mesa. With four great strides, he came to the village and picked up their last boy and girl and the twins. Before he reached home he had swallowed them alive.

As soon as the twins were inside the giant, they strung their arrows and began to explore. First they found a convulsing wall.

"What is this?" they called to the giant.

"It is my stomach!" thundered the giant. "Leave it alone, you are making me sick!"

Pueblo Versions of Old World Tales

Moving on inside, the twins found another very dark and very hard object. "What is this?" they called.

"It is my liver, which will soon digest you."

Again the twins searched. "What is this?" they asked.

"We hear the wind whistling through it."

"That is one of my lungs," bellowed the giant, making the people in San Ildefonso tremble.

"Then the heart is nearby," whispered the twins. Soon they came upon a great throbbing wall, thumping like an Indian drum.

"What is this?" they cried.

"It is my heart!"

At that moment the twins let fly their arrows through the giant's heart. He fell dead with his mouth open, and the twins came out leading the little boy and girl.

Because the giant was a wizard, the twins cut out his heart to burn it so that it might never again become a witch. Into his stomach they stuffed cacti, the real food for witches, and then, having put the giant's body and his heart into his own oven, they built a fire and burned them up.

Immediately there was great rejoicing on the housetops of San Ildefonso, dancing and the beating of drums, for the Indians saw smoke issuing from Black Mesa, from Chimayo, from Pajarito Plateau, and from the mesas to the south, and they knew that the *Tsah-ve-yoh* was dead.

When the twins returned home to their grandmother, after the Indians had showered them with gifts, prepared for them a feast, with an elaborate dance ceremonial, the grandmother gave them a new heart for the *Tsah-ve-yoh*.

"Go back," she said, "and put this new heart into the body of the *Tsah-ve-yoh*. His wicked witch heart is gone. Let him come back to life with this new heart. Then he will no longer eat anything but bad children. He will like bread and all the food of good people."

» 117 «

Coyote Wisdom

The twins did as they were told, and the *Tsah-ve-yoh,* no longer so big as he was originally, still lives on Black Mesa. He visits the pueblos each Christmas, carrying a long whip with which to punish all the children who have been bad. The mothers of the good children give him bread so that he will not whip their children, and the children are generally hidden, so that the *Tsah-ve-yoh* must look for them.

The Pueblo Tar Baby Story

The tar baby in Pueblo Indian stories becomes the piñon gum baby, and the most popular version of this theme is the trapping of rabbit-boy for stealing the coyote's water. In this arid land where water is a most treasured possession, many contests have ensued over some spring or other water supply. The story goes that Coyote-man had a spring during a very dry year when there was no other water in the country. Rabbit-boy kept watch, and every time Coyote-man left his spring, where he spent most of his days and night on guard, to seek food, Rabbit-boy *loppity-lopped* to the spring for a drink.

Upon his return each time, Coyote-man noticed that some one had been drinking from his spring, for the supply of water would be lower. The spring barely trickled. Finally, when the water was so low in the basin that he feared it might soon be exhausted, causing him to perish of thirst, Coyote-man determined to find out who was the culprit. So he made a search around the spring for tracks in the mud. Sure enough, there were tracks—the footprints of Rabbit-boy. Knowing Rabbit-boy's friendly disposition, he gathered a lot of pine gum from a piñon tree and fashioned it into a baby animal, which he set close beside the spring. Then, pretending that he was going away in search of food, he circled around behind a clump of brush to watch.

Pretty soon, here came Rabbit-boy to drink. Seeing the stranger, he greeted him; but the strange baby would not reply, and, just as in Uncle Remus' Tar Baby story, Rabbit-boy stuck himself to the pine gum animal and tumbled into the spring.

Coyote-man sprang forward and pulled him out, crying, "Now I have found the thief who steals my water! And since I have caught you, I shall eat you!"

"All right, Coyote-man," replied Rabbit-boy, "you can eat me, but first you should take a drink before someone else drinks up your spring."

"Yes," said Coyote-man, "I will take a drink first. Then I shall eat you." But all the time the Coyote was drinking Rabbit-boy was rubbing himself and the pin gum animal in the sand to free his hind legs, and when Coyote-man stopped drinking and had his mouth open licking the water from his lips with his tongue, Rabbit-boy thrust the gum

"HERE CAME RABBIT-BOY"

animal into his mouth and gagged him. That is why coyotes have such black noses and black streaks down the sides of their jaws.

The Coyote's Moon-Child

The desert wolf, the coyote, takes the place of the wolf in the Romulus and Remus theme. The Indians of the Pajarito village, one and all, went out to camp on the piñon flats to gather the pine nuts in the fall. During their stay a young girl secretly gave birth to what we would call an illegitimate baby boy. She feared the displeasure of her maternal uncle, who is always a child's special guardian; so when she returned to the pueblo, she left the baby there among the piñon trees.

Not long after that Coyote-woman in passing by heard the infant crying. Going to it, she lifted it carefully in her mouth and carried it to her den, where she had a litter of whelps. Here she nourished the human child, who grew with the coyotes for nine years, learning to eat their food, to follow their ways, and to understand all the languages of different animals.

When the child was nine years old, the Indians from that same pueblo again came to this same piñon flat to gather nuts, for once more there was a big harvest of them. By accident a group of men came upon several coyotes with an Indian child, naked, wild, and with hair unkempt, in their midst. Calling the whole clan together, the men told of their strange find and begged anyone knowing aught of this child to speak. Then the young mother told about her deserted baby.

After much discussion the Indians decided that since the child was one of them, he should be caught and brought up as an Indian and not as a coyote. Forming a great circle, which gradually closed in, they trapped the child, who in fear fought savagely. When they took him back to the pueblo, they confined him in a room beneath the underground *kiva* until he could be tamed and taught to eat cooked food and to speak the Indian's tongue. Then he was freed and brought up with the other children of the village. Later this lad became a great *cacique* among his people, for the magic he had learned of the animals aided them in their hunts. Knowing the language of the animals, he could prophesy the weather, prepare for dry years, and for the great flood, and live with wisdom. He bore the name of "The Fox."

Fox-Woman and Bear-Woman

Taytay was busy painting a bow for his son to sell to tourists in the city, when I went in one day. By the way he pointed with pursed lips towards a chair and nodded his head, I knew he was inviting me to be seated. We sat quietly until he had completed the red snake, with sharp ears and a zigzag tongue, which he painted with vegetable stain, before we asked after each other's families, commented upon the weather and the crops. Then he began the story of how the fox outwitted the bear. (I have changed his broken English but not the tale.)

"Long time ago, Fox-woman had two children, and one day she went out to look for some food for them, but all she could find was choke cherries.

" 'I like meat for myself and my children,' growled Fox-woman; 'berries are for bears!'

"So Fox-woman went to the home of Bear-woman and knocked upon the door.

" 'Come in,' called Bear-woman.

" 'I bring you good news, Bear-woman,' exclaimed sly Fox-woman. 'I have found a bush of ripe choke cherries. I know how much you like them; so I have come to take you there so that you can get some for your dinner.'

" 'Thank you for your thoughtfulness, Fox-woman, but

Coyote Wisdom

I cannot go. I have no one to take care of my babies while I am away!'

" 'Oh, then I shall tell you where to find the cherries, so that you can go while I stay to take care of the little bears for you!' offered Fox-woman, with a grin that she tried to make into a smile. Then she told the bear just where to go to find the choke cherries.

"Bear-woman did not want to go and leave her babies; but she was very hungry and the cherries sounded too delicious to miss. So she got her pot to fill. Then, suddenly remembering that it was time to cook dinner, she shook her head slowly and told Fox-woman that she could not go because she had to cook dinner.

" 'I will cook dinner for you, too,' suggested Fox-woman, watching the hungry Bear-woman out of the corner of her eye. 'The cherries are now ripe, and if you wait, someone else may get them.'

"Bear-woman hesitated a moment, but her mouth was watering for those delicious cherries. In a moment she walked to the wall, took down a sheep's rib hanging there, and gave it to Fox-woman to boil for dinner. Then off she went in search of the choke cherries, following the path that Fox-woman had directed."

Taytay picked up a cottonwood branch from a pile lying beside him and began skinning it with his knife for an arrow shaft. For a moment all was silence except the scrape of his knife blade upon the soft wood. At length he continued:

"As soon as Bear-woman was gone, Fox-woman boiled that sheep's rib and ate it herself. Quickly she grabbed the baby bears from their cradle, chopped off their heads, skinned their bodies, and dropped the bodies into the boiling pot.

"The Fox-woman took the little bears' heads and placed them carefully back in the swinging cradle. Then she pulled up the cover just as if those little bears were still sleeping.

"When Bear-woman came back with her Indian pot full of choke cherries, she looked toward the boiling pot and invited the Fox-woman to stay and have dinner with her.

" 'No, thank you!' replied Fox-woman, 'I must hurry back to my own children.' She rushed out, not even waiting for Bear-woman to thank her for cooking the dinner and telling her about the cherries.

"After Fox-woman had gone, Bear-woman went to the cradle to get her babies, but she found only their heads. She was so angry that her eyes turned red like this fire." Taytay pointed with his pursed lips at the blazing wood, standing upright in the tiny fireplace before him, for his hands were busy with the arrow shafts.

"Very mad like that, Bear-woman ran after the fox. But Fox-woman saw her coming and ran into a cave where the floor was all fine white clay. Quickly she spat upon the white dust there and made a paste; and, smearing the paste all over and all around her eyes so that she looked as if she were blind, Fox-woman stuck her head out of the cave door just as Bear-woman was passing.

"Bear-woman came puffing along as fast as she could run. She saw the strange blind person sitting beside the cave door, sticking her head outside.

" 'Blind-woman,' " she called, 'did you hear a fox trotting by?'

" 'No,' replied a voice that sounded like a fox's, and yet not exactly like a fox's either, 'no fox has passed this way!' And Bear-woman hurried along, running as fast as she could go.

"Fox-woman rolled in the white dust with laughter and rubbed the paste from her eyes. Then she began to feel hungry, for there had been little meat on the sheep's rib;

so out she went in search of more food. Finally, after a long hunt, she went to White Rock.

" 'White Rock,' she asked, 'can you tell me where to find something to eat? I am starving!'

" 'Get a sharp stick,' replied White Rock, who is like an oracle, and knows everything. 'Go over this hill and there you will find my patch of Jerusalem artichokes. You will know them by their yellow flowers, like tiny sunflowers. They are all mine. Dig as many as you need!'

"Fox-woman found a sharp stick and went over the hill. Sure enough the valley was covered with yellow flowers, as White Rock had said. She dug up one and tasted the tubular root. It was delicious. Then she dug and dug and dug and ate and ate and ate until there was not an artichoke left, not even one for seed. After such stuffing, she felt thirsty, and trotted to a spring not far off. There she drank and drank, but she did not seem able to quench her thirst.

"The water caused the artichokes inside Fox-woman's stomach to swell and swell, until she ached with a pain that made her feel as if she would burst. She started home for medicine, holding her swollen stomach with one paw. Her path passed by White Rock.

"When White Rock saw Fox-woman coming holding her stomach, she knew that the greedy fox had eaten all of her artichokes, not even leaving her a few for seeds. So when Fox-woman came near, White Rock gave her a good hard kick, which sent Fox-woman flying up into the air like a big balloon. High up against a mountain top she struck with such force that she blew away in a dozen pieces, scattering the artichokes to seed among the valleys on all sides. And that was the end of the greedy fox!"

Slowly Taytay unfolded himself and got up. He went to a wall of the room where a bunch of soft eagle feathers were hanging from a peg. Taking these down, he returned with them to finish his arrows.

Pueblo Versions of Old World Tales

In studying these applications by the Indians of universal story themes, one cannot help making certain deductions. The Indian does not romance about life. He accepts it as it is, believing in cause and effect. The little turkey girl does not find a Prince-Charming. She gets her deserts. Not having kept her bargain with the turkeys, the story shows, she deserved nothing better than rags. In life, according to the Pueblo Indian, one usually gets as much or as little as he earns.

Because of superstition, or perhaps a code of politeness, one—either Indian or animal—must accept all invitations and all challenges to contests, even though he may fear the host or feel unqualified to compete. This fact runs through all their stories.

Destruction of life has no horror to the Indian. The cooking of the baby bears does not make an Indian child cringe, because the Indian child knows, according to his beliefs in immortality, that one does not harm the spirit of the animal by slaying his body. The animal is only inconvenienced, for he must go and find another body-house. A great dual creative force, male and female in one, permeates everything—men, animals, birds, insects, rocks, clouds, and hand-crafts—and this force is indestructible, going from this world, when its material body is destroyed, to the Underworld, where there is perpetual summer-time and continuous food supply. It is a heinous crime, followed by dire consequences, for any being to eat his own children.

Almost every story bursts into song at least once, often many times. If an animal or person is supposed to sing as he journeys along, the Indian story-teller does not say that the "animal sings as he goes," he will repeat the same song over and over, saying, perhaps, "The fox, he go 'long to that piñon tree and he sing this song. [He sings the song.] The fox he reach that big rock and he sing. [The song is sung again.] The fox go to that arroyo and he sing. [The song is again repeated.]"

There is much that I have gained from my friend Tay-tay besides the pleasure of drinking in the warmth from fireside or sunshine, at his adobe home in the sunbaked, mud-pie pueblo.

Navajo Creation Myths

By Elizabeth Willis DeHuff

Coyote the Sly Trickster

IT TOOK many mornings and evenings for Nasuit to tell me the Navajo creation myth, which truly ranged from the sublime to the ridiculous. There were descriptions of "mirage figures," "glittering moss," "reflected sun-red," "sun ray and sunlight glittering in color," "skyblue and evening twilight," "folding dawn," "folding twilight," and much more beautiful imagery, and then there were the truly absurd antics of the giant Coyote, variously called the "Roamer," and "Scolder," and the "Youth Folded in Dawn." Sometimes the detailed imagery continued for so long a time without interruption that my mind felt confused, and often I wanted to laugh at the Coyote; but to Nasuit one part was as sacred and important as another, so that neither the one could be shortened or slurred nor the other laughed at. Often with effort I listened, trying to attend or to smother my amusement.

In the second of the four worlds upward, through which the first living things climbed, First Man—a superhuman, not a real man—placed a piece of white shell, the size of a woman's comb, in the East; a piece of turquoise in the South; abalone in the West; and jet in the North. Rays from the shells in the East and West would slowly rise, causing daylight. When they met above it was midday; then they would recede and other rays from the turquoise and jet would come up causing the darkness of night. One of Coyote's first tricks was to sneak over to East and West and "tie down" these light rays, leaving the animals, insects, and supermen in darkness. That was, no doubt, the first eclipse. There Coyote kept the rays tied until First-Man and First-Woman made a proper sacrifice to him.

In each world Coyote was up to some devilment, until finally, in this last world, he caused the Grand Canyon and the Flood that almost destroyed the world and everything on it.

One of the early supermen was Fire-boy, who used his magic for the good of mankind. Noticing that when the moon was not shining at night there was not enough light upon the earth, Fire-boy gathered up a buckskin bag of mica dust and stepped up into the clouds. There he made stars and placed them in symbolic designs. Before he had finished his task, however, Coyote found out about it. Softly he sneaked along over the clouds behind Fire-boy, and when the giant boy was not looking he snatched up the mica dust and blew it across the skies. We call the result the "milky way." Then Coyote turned to run away; but he stumped his toe and fell to the earth, cracking it open. The Grand Canyon is that crack.

Now the Indians, according to their traditions, migrated for a long time before coming to the lands in which they live; and these super-creatures who lived before them had also roamed a long distance. During the travels of these former people, they came to a wide river. While rafts for crossing it were being made under the direction of First Man, the insect and animal people, who were the only beings created at that time except the few giant men, camped beside the stream. Here they built houses of dark moss, blue moss, yellow moss, and white moss. They then dug ditches and farmed.

Big Trotter (the Wolf) planted white corn to the east; Mountain Lion used yellow corn to the westward; Blue Fox planted blue corn on the south side; and Badger dug holes for black corn on the north.

Nàtli (Hermaphrodite), the first one in existence, had charge of the grinding and cooking. He taught the maidens to grind, and as they ground upon the colored stone metates, Blue-fox, Yellow-fox, Badger, and Weasel beat upon basket drums as they sang a song of rhythm for the grinding. During this ceremony, the maidens would frequently take pinches of the corn meal and sprinkle it upon the heads of the singers, who would forthwith return the compliment in like manner.

Since this was the first time that the early people had really labored, they found need of a sweathouse. When it was built, Owl made for its doorway the usual four blankets: the first was a white one of dawn; the second was yellow, made of evening twilight; the third, the blue of sky-blue; and the fourth black of darkness. When the men would come home from the fields, they would cleanse themselves in the sweathouse and then play games, which the women also learned to play. They played the hoop and pole game, three kinds of dice games and the bounding stick game.

Most of the time the men were busy in the fields, so that their time for play was limited; but the women began to neglect their housework and everything for these games. Particularly neglectful was the wife of Blue-fox, and when he mildly complained she flew into a rage with him. Day after day this truant behavior went on, until poor Blue-fox could stand it no longer. [This, you see, is a man-made myth!] So Blue-fox called a council of all the men and they decided that, since the crops had been gathered, they would move across the river and leave all the women behind. This news was received with taunts and rejoicing by the women.

Coyote Wisdom

Dividing the corn and other seeds equally, the men and boys took their share and crossed the river upon a raft. Nátli went with the men and continued to look after the culinary department. For months after the move had been made, whenever a boy baby was born to one of the women, she would go to the river's edge and call to the men to come and get it; and Nátli gathered milk from the stem of the milk-weed and cared for these infants successfully.

The first year, the men worked industriously and filled their granaries. Then they cleared more ground for extended crops. But, as before, the women spent most of their time singing, dancing, and playing games, so that the weeds choked their corn and they had poor crops.

The second year was a repetition of the first, with increased harvests and greater acreage cleared for the men and poorer harvests for the game-loving women. At the end of the fourth year, the men had more food than they could consume for years, and the poor women had nothing. They were starving. They grew as thin as skeletons, ate all the wild things they could find, and began to lie down one by one and die.

Seeing this distress from across the river, the men's hearts were filled with forgiveness and compassion, and they called across the river offering to take back their wives and feed them. The women accepted this offer immediately with rejoicing. They danced and sang for the first time in many moons. And so the raft was once more put into use to row the women and girls across the river.

Coyote enjoyed the trip back and forth across the water, and so every time the raft left shore, he sneaked upon it.

Upon the last crossing, two little girls fell overboard and descended down into the house of the Water Spirit. Cyote watched them from above, and in watching he saw a beautiful baby down there, the child of the Water Spirit. He determined some day to steal it.

This was the first and last time that men and women ever tried to live apart, for it was found that women could not take care of themselves; they needed the men.

"Was that coyote like the coyotes of today?" I asked Nasuit, as he wiped his moist brow against his shirt sleeve.

"No, he was bigger. All those animals was big when the world was young. But that coyote he is the great grandfather of all those coyotes we have now."

The Creation of the Navajos

As the tale of the creation of man and domestic animals was told to me one autumn day, when a fall of wet snow, which festooned the scantily-leaved trees and shrubs and the last courageous stalks of blossoming chrysanthemums with a soft drape of billowy whiteness, bending them into graceful rhythms, and which even transformed weeds into lacy, branching white coral, I could easily imagine the blankets of dawn, darkness, sky blue and evening twilight about which Nasuit, my Navajo friend, talked.

Since his tale was long drawn out, with its over-burden of detail, such as how the dark wind glittered as it was forced into the dark mirage figure (in making the first horse) and how the blue wind glittered as it was forced into the blue mirage figure (in creating the first sheep), etc., I shall condense the story and tell only of the creation of the Navajos, though under other blankets at the same time were formed and given life the Pueblo Indians, white man and woman and horses, sheep, goats, chickens, cattle, and pigs. These, of course, were made of substances of lesser value than the Navajos.

Long ago when the "world was young," according to the legend, it was only peopled by giant insects, birds, animals that are now classed as "wild" and superhuman beings, all of whom had come up by slow stages and much magic from the four underworlds to this one in which we now live.

The most important giants were First Man and First Woman. It was First Man who threw a circular piece of abalone shell up into the sky to form the sun's disk and later threw up a piece of white shell, which is the moon. It was First Woman who created Navajos and this is how it was done, with the help of the Sun Spirit!

Upon the ground First Woman spread blankets of mist, five of them. Upon the first two were created the two Navajo clans, a man and a woman on each; upon the third were Pueblos; upon the fourth "Americans;" and upon the last the domestic animals. Then upon each of the first two blankets she placed two ears of corn, one black and one white. Beside these she laid abalone shell for toe and finger- nails; white shell for bones; red-white stone for flesh; darkness for hair; dawn for skulls; rough white shells for brains; smooth white shell for the whites of the eye; col- lected sky waters for tears; shaken-off mica and rock crystals for the pupils of the eyes; red-white stone for ear lobes; white shell oval beads for the ears; more abalone for noses; white shell in strips for esophaguses; more white shell for teeth; straight lightning for tongues; rainbows for arms; and plants of all kinds for pubic hairs and skin pores. All of those things she placed from the east side. Then stepping to the west side, she spread on the corn greasy white and yellow water. The greasy white water was to form marrow in the bones and the greasy yellow water made sinews.

Now that all of the ingredients were ready, First Woman spread over them four sheets or blankets: the first was of dawn; the second, a blanket of darkness; the third was of sky blue; and the fourth was of evening twilight. She then stepped over the two groups of materials from east to west and from south to north. After that, one by one, she drew back the covering blankets. The one of dawn she drew back toward the east; the blanket of darkness she drew toward the south; the sheet of sky blue she threw back westward; and the blanket of evening twilight, toward the north.

There, upon the mist spreads, lay four inert forms. Into the first man on the first spread she sent a blue wind and into the other form she blew a white wind. Then going to the second spread, she placed in the first form a yellow wind and into the second a dark wind. Her tasks being completed, First Woman called to the Sun Spirit.

Answering her summons, the Sun came and filled his jet pipe with tobacco. After lighting it with rock crystal, he blew the smoke over the still forms, blowing it from each side of the spread of mist; first from the east, next from the south, then from the west and then from the north, and finally he blew it from above. Next he repeated this process by blowing the smoke from his turquoise pipe. After that he filled his white shell pipe with tobacco and blew its smoke in the same way, and at last he blew in like manner smoke from his pipe of abalone. Immediately the people sat up and spoke the Navajo language and they were the first people of the two great Navajo clans.

The other people were made in like manner at the same time by Begochidi, a giant of lesser importance than First Woman. When the Sun finally blew smoke over them they could not talk; so First Woman took a dark bow about three feet in length, with a bowstring of rainbow, and upon this string she placed the other people, who could not speak Navajo, and also the animals. She shot them up into the air four times, and then far up in the air the sound of "*mal, mal*" could be heard. She blew upward four times upon them and they landed beyond the ocean. One of these people became the god whom the "Americans" worship, and the others were first the "Americans," then the cliff dwellers, the Pueblos, the Mexicans and "other people." Of these some were male and some were female, so that later they increased to make the people of the world.

At the same time, in similar manner, Begochidi made the domestic animals upon the fifth spread of mist, but the materials out of which they were made were different. These are the things he used: striped mirage formed their feet and hoofs; red arrow-point and dark mirage were used for their soles; their tails were made of dropping rain; their ears of plants of all kinds and their mane of a certain plant; their bodies were of dark clouds; their "moving power," or legs, of zigzag lightning; their eyes, of big stars; their teeth, of white shell; their lips, of big beads; their tongues, of straight lightning; while black, blue, yellow and white winds were given them to tell them things. These little winds travel hidden in their ears.

During the telling of the long tale, the warm autumn sunshine had been shining through a rift in the clouds, slowly melting the white world without, with a musical *drip, drip,* in our ears. So that when Nasuit had finished there were only a few patches of snow upon the north side of things. First Woman had lifted her blankets. Into the stubble of the alfalfa patch in front of my house strayed two horses and a burro.

"Look, Nasuit," I exclaimed, "the blankets have been drawn back and there are the animals created!"

There was a responding twinkle in Nasuit's eyes.

Trubble, Brudder Alligator, Trubble

By E. A. McILHENNY

E. A. McIlhenny lives at Avery Island, Louisiana, and is responsible for the extraordinary bird sanctuary there. As a child he and his brothers issued a kind of plantation magazine with Uncle Remus stories in it as told by the plantation darkies. Many years later the boy who had collected Negro folk tales became one of the foremost naturalists and conservationists of bird life in the South, his interest in the lore of the land having kept apace. When his intensely interesting book, *The Alligator's Life History*, appeared three years ago, the editor of the Texas Folk-Lore Society wrote him asking if there were not in the swamp lands of Louisiana a kind of alligator culture, a cycle of tales about alligators, a body of alligator lore analogous to the coyote, the rattlesnake, or the jackrabbit lore found elsewhere. The tale that follows is a part of the response.

In de ole time days, all de beasts en de birds en tings, dey could talk to each udder jis like folks, en dey used to have meetin's en rallies en tings jist like folks do. En each en every kind could unnerstan' de talk uv de udder kind. Dey wuz all frien'ly enough en didn't pester each udder none wen dey wuz togedder, but all de same, most uv 'em wuz er watchin' fer to see dat de udder didn't git de fus chance fer a breakfus er dinner off'n him wen he warn't lookin'.

Der wuz two uv dem beasts wut kep dey eyes on each udder more den de rest. Dese wuz Mister Rabbit and Mister Alligator. Mister Alligator he wuz always layin' roun de edge er de bayou hopin' to get er chance fer to make his dinnuh off'n some uv Mister Rabbit's fambly wen dey cum down to de water fer a drink. En many a time he gits his chance en knocks a nice, fat, young rabbit wid a swif' flop uv his tail, right down he throat en in ter he dinnuh bucket.

Coyote Wisdom

Now, Mister Rabbit ain't got no way fer to git even wid Mister Alligator, caise he don't eat no alligator meat, but every spring he slip roun tru de rushes in de marsh en find whar ole Mrs. Alligator done bilt her nest, en he watch. In time she done lay a big passel uv eggs; den he run quick en call Mister Coon and Miss Possum to cum see, en he show de nest to dem and dey digs out all de eggs en eats em! But dat don't do Mister Rabbit so much good, caise tain't Mrs. Alligator but Mister Alligator wut done him so much dirt.

Well, de time slips 'long en Mister Rabbit ain't seen Mister Alligator fer de longest, caise most uv his days is spent in dodgin' ole Marse Johnny's houn' dawgs, wut mos' every mornin' puts dey nose on Mister Rabbit's track, whar he done been in de white folks' kitchin garden de night befo, feastin' heself on all de best garden truck wut's growin' dere. Now wen dem dawgs starts dey music on his track, tain't nuttin' fer Mister Rabbit to do but git to de biggest briar patch wut he kin find, en lemme tell you he is got ter do sum tall dodgin' fer to keep fum givin' dem dawgs er breakfus!

Well, dis mornin' wut we is tawkin' bout, Mister Rabbit done lose dem houn' dawgs, en bein' putty well hot en tired, he tink he'll go down to de bayou fer to git heself a drink er water. So off he slip tru de tall marsh rushes en jis befor he hits he bayou he run slap bang in ter ole Mister Alligator wut's done hawl heself back in de rushes fer to kotch heself er little nap.

Wen Mister Rabbit seen Mister Alligator wuz snoozin', he pass 'roun en gits in front uv him; den he break heself one uv dem long roseau canes en he 'gins fer to tickle Mister Alligator on de nose. Mister Alligator tinks it's er fly wut's pesterin' him; so he open his mouf wide-like so de fly kin walk in, but he ain't open his eyes. Wen Mister Rabbit see ticklin' uv de nose don't wake up Mister Alli-

Trubble, Brudder Alligator, Trubble

gator, he push de roseau cane kinder hard-like against Mister Alligator's tongue. Wid dat Mister Alligator brung he jaws togedder *ker wap*, en he smash dat roseau cane all to smithereens. Wen he jaws hits de roseau cane, dat wake Mister Alligator up, en he riz he head en open he eyes. En dere he see Mister Rabbit jis crackin' he sides laffin'.

Wen Mister Rabbit seen Mister Alligator done wake up, he say perlite like: "Howdy, Brudder Alligator. How is you ter-day, en how is all de little 'gators? Is you got er right smart crop uv 'em at your house?" Mister Rabbit he knowed good en well dat Mister Coon en Miss Possum done et up all de eggs wut Mrs. Alligator done laid, en dey ain't gointer be no little alligators, not dis summer nohow.

En Mister Alligator seein' as how Mister Rabbit was standin' right befo him out er reach of his jaws en dey warn't no chance fer to hit him a wop wid his tail, he made perlite answer, en he say: "Howdy, Brudder Rabbit. I'se fine, tank you, en we sho' is got a right smart crop of youngsters at us house dis summer. I disremember jis how many Mrs. Alligator tole me dere wuz, but somewhere round forty er fifty. En how is you fambly, Brother Rabbit, dat is, wut is left uv dem dat de houn's dawgs ain't et up?"

"Wut is you talkin' bout, Brudder Alligator?" sez Mister Rabbit. "Don't you ever tink I'se gointer let no lazy houn' dawgs ketch none er my youngsters. Naw, sur, not me! Time dem houn' dawgs' 'gin ter push one er my youngsters, I cuts cross de trail slow-like en den dey takes after me, en in no time I done loss 'em in de briar patch, dat's wut I does. Gives me er lot us trubble, but don't give no houn' dawg no breakfus."

"Dat's fine, Brudder Rabbit," sez Mister Alligator. "I'se shore proud to hear you all gettin' on so fine, but I jis don't unnerstan' all wut you say. Wut is dat you call trubble? I ain't nebber meets up wid no sech ting."

Coyote Wisdom

"You ain't nebber had no trubble, Brudder Alligator?" sez Mister Rabbit. "You's sho you don't know wut trubble is?"

"No, Brudder Rabbit," sez Mister Alligator, "I ain't know wut trubble is, en I sho' wish I has sum, caise it must be mighty good ef you's got so much uv it."

"So!" sez Mister Rabbit, "you wants trubble, does you? Well, you jis lay right whar you is, Brudder Alligator, en trubble will cum to you mighty quick." En wid dat Mister Rabbit he slips off tru de long grass, en back to sleep goes Mister Alligator.

Well suh, long 'bout tree 'clock dat afternoon wen Mister Rabbit knowed Mister Alligator would be sleepin' hardest, here cum Mister Rabbit jis er-lopin' down fum de white folks' yard, en in he hand he had a splinter er light wood wut he done stole fum de white folks, en de end er de splinter er light wood wuz jis er-sputterin' en blazin', caise Mister Rabbit done stuck de end in de fire at de white folks' house, en he run so fast and hold dat light wood splinter so high dat de fire nebber had no chance to go out.

Den Mister Rabbit gits to de marsh whar he knowed Mister Alligator wuz a-sleepin' in de long tall grass wut's mighty dry about now. He slips easy-like en fast in a big ring roun Mister Alligator, settin' fire to de grass ev'ry few jumps.

Wen de ring er fire wuz all set, Mister Rabbit he run to de edge er de grass, en he hollers, "Wake up, Brudder Alligator! Wake up! Trubble done cum."

But Mister Alligator wuz a-sleepin' en he ain't answer him nuttin'. Den Mister Rabbit he hollers more louder, "Hey! Brudder Alligator, wake up—trubble done cum!"

Dat time Mister Alligator he wakes up, en he looks all round, but he don't see no trubble; all he sees is er little smoke risin' out er de grass, en dat don't cause him to worry, 'caise he done seen marsh fires every fall since he

Trubble, Brudder Alligator, Trubble

was 'bout er foot long—en dat's er mighty long time ago!

En he made answer en he holler back, "I'se awake, Brudder Rabbit, en I'se look all round, but I don't see no trubble."

"Dat's all right," Mister Rabbit hollers back. "Dat's all right, Brudder Alligator. You sez you wants trubble, an I'se done brung it to you! Cain't you heah it poppin' in dose dry roseau?"

En Mister Alligator he make reply, "Shore I heahs de roseau poppin', Brudder Rabbit, but dat ain't no trouble. Dat's nuttin' but er little marsh fire, en I done seed dem every year fer de longest. Wut fer you didn't bring me sum er dat trubble wut you wuz tellin' bout?"

Jis den er good breeze sprung up en starts de fire errorin', en Mister Rabbit he jumps up en he cracks he heels togedder en he hollers: "Yo trubble is comin' now, Brudder Alligator! En it's comin' on de win'." En wid dat Mister Rabbit he pulls out jis er-lopin' fer de briar patch.

Now as de win' riz, it push de ring er fire wut Mister Rabbit done sot roun Mister Alligator, en de ring er fire close in on Mister Alligator. Den Mister Alligator tinks it's time to move heself, en he starts crawlin' towards de bayou, but he goes only a few feets en he meets up wid de fire. Den he tries er-nudder way en he meets up wid fire dere, en every way he turns—dere is fire! En putty quick-like, de fire 'gins to skotch he tail. Den Mister Alligator he don't know wut ter do, en he turn heself dis way en dat, en he don't seen no openin' in de fire ring.

Den he hollers, "Trubble, Brudder Rabbit, trubble! Trubble, Brudder Rabbit, trubble! Cum er-runnin' en help me, Brudder Rabbit. I'se got trubble!"

Mister Rabbit heered Mister Alligator hollerin', but he ain't answer him nuttin! He jis set in he house in de middle er de briar patch jist crackin' his side er-laffin'.

By en by de fire ring round Mister Alligator gits so hot

he cain't stand it no mo', en he takes a runnin' start, en he buss right tru dat fire, en in ter de bayou he goes! But he back en tail wuz putty well singed, en he ain't feelin' none too good.

Cum nix Sunday mornin', heah cum Mister Rabbit all dress up in he best Sunday-go-to-meetin' close on his way to de meetin' house. En as he goes he pass er long piece out er his way so he can have a laff at Mister Alligator. En he pass long de aidge uv de bayou, en dere he see Mister Alligator layin' 'way out in de stream wid nuttin' but he eyes en nose 'bove de watter. Mister Rabbit ain't knowed it, but Mister Alligator's been lain' dat way ever since de fire done singe he back, hopin' ter git a chance fer to git even wid Mister Rabbit, caise he suspisshun Mister Rabbit is de one wut puts de ring er fire round him en singe him all up.

Now Mister Rabbit he ain't let on dat he tinks dere's anything de matter wid Mister Alligator; so he take off he hat en he makes Mister Alligator er deep bow en he say: "Mornin', Brudder Alligator. How is you feelin' dis mornin'? Is you found out wut's trubble yit?"

"I sho is, Brudder Rabbit. Trubble done kotch up wid me, en it ain't none too good, en dat's er fack," sez Mister Alligator. "Is you had any more trubble lately, Brudder Rabbit?"

"No, Brudder Alligator," sez Mister Rabbit, "trubble done pass me by uv late, en I'se sho' glad, caise it ain't no fun, is it, Brudder Alligator?" sez Mister Rabbit.

"You right fer dat, it sho' ain't!" sez Mister Alligator. "I sho' feels sorry fer you havin ter dodge dem dawgs all de day long. I don't wonder you is gittin' so poor en skinny. I tell you wut, Brudder Rabbit," sez Mister Alligator, "de nix time trubble gits atter you, you runs down to de bayou en I'll git trubble fum you. Now I know wut trubble is, I'll help my bes' friend git away fum it enny time."

"Tank you kindly, Brudder Alligator," sez Mister

Trubble, Brudder Alligator, Trubble

Rabbit, "tank you. I shore will 'member wut you sez, en de nix time I gits in trubble I suttinly will cum to you fer help." En wid dat Mister Rabbit he lope off ter de meetin' house.

Well, cum de nix mornin', Marse Johnny's houn' dawgs, time dey wakes up dey goes to de veg'table garden ter pick up Mister Rabbit's scent, fer to try en git dem sum fresh meat fer breakfus. Sho nuf, dey finds Mister Rabbit's trail right in de cabbage patch, en it's jis ez fresh ez de mornin' air; de dew ain't even off it yit. So off dey starts wid dey mouf wide open hollerin' loud as dey can, "Heah we cum, Brudder Rabbit, heah we cum fer our breakfus."

Dat ain't skeer Mister Rabbit none, caise he done heah dat sort er dawg talk dese many days, en he knows all he got to do is slip into de big briar patch ter git shut er dem houn's, caise dem houn' dawgs' legs is too long fer to let dem pass under de briars. So he took de dawgs fer a little race up en down de big woods fer to limber up he legs en digist he breakfus. Dere's one ting wot puzzle him though. En dat is, wen he makes er swing roun' dem hounds en is a doublin' on his back track, bless God ef he ain't run most plum in-ter er little low speckle dog wut he ain't nebber seen befo, en dat little low dog is so fer behin' dem big dogs dat dey done mos' loss him, but he's stickin' to de trail jis like dem houn's, only he don't give no big mouf bark, jis a little sort er whinin' yip.

Wen Mister Rabbit seen dat little dog, he is sorter puzzlefied, en he scratch he head en say to his self, "I wonder wut dat little piece er dog meat's adoin' ramblin' dese woods? I'se er mind ter give him er swif kick en run him home." But it warn't long befo' Mister Rabbit knowed why en wut fer dat little fiest dog wuz runnin' wid de houn's. Dem houn's done got tired er Ole Man Rabbit slippin' off in de briar patch, whar dey cain't foller, time dey 'gins to push him right hard en wen dey tinks breakfus is mos ready. So dey goes down to de quarters, dis mornin' wut we is talkin bout, en dey gits one er dem short-legged nigger fiest, de kind de niggers take wen dey goes rabbit huntin', caise dey ain't no briar patch low enough en thick enough ter keep a fiest fum followin' er rabbit enny whar he go. But Mister Rabbit he ain't know dat.

By en by Mister Rabbit 'gins ter git sorter tired en lets de houn's most come up ter him, en wen dey tinks dey got him, he slips in ter er big briar patch, en sit down ter blow en rest heself.

Bout de time he 'gins ter git he wind back, he heahs a noise wut 'sturbs him, en dat is not fer from him in de briars. Wut he hears is dat little fiest yippin' en a-crawlin' under de briars, gittin' closter every minute, en putty soon dat little low-down fiest done cum right under de briars smack to whar Mister Rabbit wuz a-settin'. Den twarn't nuttin' fer Mister Rabbit ter do but to make tracks away fum dere, or be kotched by dat fiest. So way he went, en atter him cum de fiest jis-a-yippin', en de houn's on de outside er de briar patch, wen dey heered de fiest goin' way towards de udder side er de briar patch, dey runs round en gits to de udder side jis as Mister Rabbit slip out en takes down de big woods again. En away dey goes atter him, givin' full tongue.

Mister Rabbit run he best, but he done run a lot his mornin' en he belly is mighty full er white folks' cabbage; so he cain't run es fas es he used to, en he see mighty quick dat he is got ter find sum way fer to git round den dawgs, er he's sho' nuf a goner.

Jis den it cum to him wut Mister Alligator done tole him, en dat wuz, dat now he knowed wut trubble is, if Mister Rabbit ever gits in trubble jis cum ter him en he will help him. So away he went tru de woods to de marsh, en tru de marsh to de bayou, en every jump he makes in de marsh, he hollers.

Trubble, Brudder Alligator, Trubble

He jis holler en holler, "Trubble, Brudder Alligator, trubble! Trubble, Brudder Alligator, trubble! 'Member your promise, Brudder Alligator! I'se got trubble!"

Atter he done holler dat same ting tree or fo' times, all de time er-unnin', he cums to de bayou en dere he sees Mister Alligator layin' side er de bank like he is waitin' fer him, en he sez, "You done heered me, ain't you, good ole Brudder Alligator?"

En Mister Alligator he make answer, en he say, "You's got trubble, has you, Brudder Rabbit? Well, whar it is? I don't see no trubble. Ef you is got trubble, show me; den I'll help you." Dat's wut Mister Alligator sed, jis like dat.

En Mister Rabbit he talk fas' caise dose dawgs is gittin' mighty close, en he say: "I cain't show you my trubble, Brudder Alligator, caise ef I waits to show it to you dem houn's gointer kotch me. Cain't you hear dem gittin' closter en closter?"

"Shore, I hears 'em," sez Mister Alligator, "but ef dem houn' dawgs is wut you is feered of, wut fer you don't jump in de bayou en swim across? You know dern well no houn' dog gointer try en swim no bayou, not wile I'm heah, nohow! Jump in, Brudder Rabbit, en leave you trubbles on dis side er de bayou."

"No, Brudder Alligator," sez Mister Rabbit, "I won't jump in caise I cain't swim, en I'd jis as soon de houn' dawgs would kotch me es git drowned."

"Well, Brudder Rabbit," sez Mister Alligator, "ef you cain't swim, jis jump on my tail en I'll ferry you across de water."

En wid dat Mister Alligator riz he tail a little bit out er de water, en time he done dat Mister Rabbit jumps on, en Mister Alligator starts swimmin' er cross de bayou.

Now wen dey gits a little piece fum shore, Mister Alligator lets he tail sink down slow like till de water wets Mister Rabbit's foots. En he say, "Step up on my back,

Brudder Rabbit. You is too heavy fer me to carry you er-cross on my tail."

So Mister Rabbit he moves up Mister Alligator's tail en he spraddle he-self on Mister Alligator's back. Bout dat time dey is half way cross de bayou, en Mister Alligator 'gins ter settle he back down in de water slow-like en de same time he rize he head a little mo higher, en he say to Mister Rabbit, "Step up on my neck, Brudder Rabbit. You is putty heavy fer my back, en de water is so deep here, you is got me mos sinkted. Ef you step up on my neck, I tink I kin make it er-cross."

So Mister Rabbit he steps up on Mister Alligator's neck. Time he got dere Mister Alligator sink heself a little mo low in de water, en Mister Rabbit foots 'gins ter git wet ergin.

Den Mister Alligator sez, sez he, "You is mighty heavy fer my neck, Brudder Rabbit. Walk out on my head, en I'se shore I can git you er-cross."

So Mister Rabbit he walks out on Mister Alligator's head. But he's watchin' mighty close—caise he tinks Mister Alligator gointer play a trick on him. Now wen Mister Rabbit walks out on Mister Alligator's head, dey wuz most to de udder shore. But Mister Alligator he ain't nebber had no mind ter let Mister Rabbit git to de bank, en time Mister Rabbit gits on he head Mister Alligator throws he head high in de air en open wide he big mouf, speckin' Mister Rabbit gointer fall right down he throat. But Mister Rabbit was a-watchin', en time Mister Alligator throwed up he head, dat's de time Mister Rabbit gives a big jump, en he lands most six feet up de bank on de udder shore.

Den he hollers, "Tanks, Brudder Alligator, fer gittin' me outer trubble."

En dat's de way Mister Rabbit gits de best er de hound dawgs, en Mister Alligator, en Ole Man Trubble, all de same time.

Philosophy in Folk-Lore

By Radoslav A. Tsanoff

MY TOPIC may remind some reader of the learned treatise on Snakes in Iceland, which boiled down to the statement that there are no snakes in Iceland. So, is there any philosophy in folklore? If by philosophy we understand only the elaborate systems of analysis and theory dealing with the ultimate nature and organization of reality, the origin and criterion of knowledge, the character and the implications of value, then certainly it would be futile to look for that sort of philosophy in folklore. Philosophy thus regarded, like science, is not the expression of the childhood or even of the adolescence of human consciousness, but of its maturity; some say, of its old age. So Hegel told us that "the owl of Minerva takes its flight only when the shades of night are gathering."

But surely it would be pedantic to assume that men had to wait until they had achieved technical mastery of analytical methods, of experiment and theory, before they could have any sense of the problems of life and nature. On the contrary, it was just because men had a dim presentiment of the world-enigmas, only because they perceived certain basic truths which life teaches all of us, that they came to demand and to achieve the fuller perfection of the mind as an instrument of understanding. We cannot afford to neglect this truth. It is a dull parent that fails to recognize the real problems and pleas which children's minds are trying to express in their untutored ways. Equally dull and uncomprehending is so much of our sophisticated dismissal of popular traditions as old wives' tales, of religious belief and ritual as superstition, of persistent attachment to certain ways of thought and conduct as the stiff bigtory of ignorance. Really mature intelligence is marked not only by perfection of criticism, but also by tolerant insight. The folk-mind is untutored but it is not at all stupid; its answers and theories may well be misguided, but this need not mean that its questions and problems are unreal or can be loftily brushed aside. The obscurity of early thought is not infrequently the obscurity of unfathomed depths; but modern sophistication should guard against the clarity which is due to mere shallowness of perception.

Primitive man, conscious of his zeal for knowledge, his abysses of mystery, his longings and joys and sorrows, might devise incredible fantastic notions of his soul or shadow or the elusive spirit that in him and in others performs all the marvels of experience. These notions may well be repudiated by the more critical thought of civilized man. But this gain in detail becomes a basic loss in understanding, if we ignore the essential problem in active intelligence and — like a certain type of so-called scientific psychologist — declare that human thought is simply a certain kind of gurgling in the larynx. So again it would be possible to extract from the history of religions an array of unspeakable ideas which men have entertained of Deity. But it was no doubt a learned fool who, brushing all this superstition aside, settled the whole matter and said in his heart, "There is no God."

I trust that I shall not be misunderstood here. I am not reading a brief for superstition, but rather a plea for a more tolerant recognition of untutored folk-wisdom, so that while we transcend old errors, as we must, we may not lose the sense of deep problems which puzzle and confuse the folk-mind, but which may not be set aside, lest we be left, as so much modern learning is left, with a stock of propositions incontrovertible but also trivial.

So this, in the first place, is the philosophy that may be found in folklore: a feeling of the problems of life and nature, confused, uncritical, but genuine and fertile. The historical sense which the early nineteenth century achieved has made it possible for us to understand and appreciate beliefs which we cannot share. In our more learned maturity of culture we may be enabled to experience again the wonder and the deep creative perplexity of the childhood and adolescence of mankind. We are both chastened and reassured when we recognize, beneath the crust of ancient error, the radical problems with which we ourselves are grappling.

It would be out of the question to develop at all adequately here the theme which I am suggesting. We can only, by way of illustration, glance along one or two paths of inquiry that could be pursued to advantage.

Early thought is deficient alike in analysis and in synthesis. Primitive man, vaguely perplexed but unable to formulate his problems, ascribes the most various potencies to particular things and acts. So in the beliefs and ritual of taboo may be found, in almost indiscriminate confusion, the elements of practical everyday caution, wariness of contagion, poison, or other lurking dangers, moral scruple and vigilance, unquestioning conformity to traditional ways of respecting the dread powers that are believed to control human life. To take an instance: regarding blood as above all things taboo, primitive man may at first shrink from the slayer as from one smeared with a fatally contagious taint, not distinguishing clearly between the deliberate murderer, the innocent blood-shedder, or even the blood-bespattered object of whatever sort. In the course of time more mature reflection comes to distinguish objects and causes of horror: not the bloody smear itself but the mur-

derous act; so men come to discriminate between killings
that call for revenge, and mere fatal accidents. In the distant prospect the blood-taboo may be seen as yielding the
lofty idea of the inviolable sanctity of human life and
personality. Or again, at first the ritual of taboo prohibitions may be unmotivated and unanalyzed: simply one
must on no account do this or that. When in the development of religion the idea of God comes to dominate man's
outlook, taboos themselves become divine prohibitions, and
the transgressions of them, sins. But then, as men's ideas
of deity mature, a time comes when more critical minds
realize the inappropriateness and indeed the absurdity of
certain prohibitions. So the taboos of tradition are revised
to meet the demands of a progressive conception of God.
The prophetic reformation of the popular religion of Israel
illustrates this sort of advance from the folklore of tribal
monolatry to the sublimities of ethical monotheism.

By another more secular path of advance, the primitive
mind, while respecting in practice the verdict of tradition
that certain transgressions are inexorably followed by suffering and by death, might not venture to question the
taboo potency, but may yet become curious about the
manner of its operation. How or why does so slight a contact have such dire consequences? Persistent observation
here would lead to the noticing of negative instances, to
the critical revision or to the dismissal of certain beliefs. In
this process the development of causal thinking in the more
routine experiences of men invades and takes possession of
taboo areas also. Men's success in explaining little things
leads them to attempt larger issues, and even dread perplex-
ities yield to expanding inquiry. What remains, however,
is the basic note of ultimate wonder and cosmic uneasiness
which first moved the primitive mind to its strange specu-
lations, but which are also bound to characterize the deep-
est thought of scientist and philosopher.

Philosophy in Folk·Lore

Sometimes the savage mind, in its effort to explain some calamity, private or public, may stumble accidentally upon the right track, but, lacking trained intelligence, is unable to develop its idea or carry it through advantageously. Then civilized man with his scientific nose for implications comes along and realizes the possibilities of the primitive notion. But the sophisticated contempt for savage superstition may lead the modern mind to dismiss offhand traditional ideas of great value. An instance illustrating this point came to my notice recently. In his book *First Footsteps in East Africa*, Sir Richard Burton, the translator of the *Arabian Nights*, describes his travels and adventures in eastern Ethiopia in 1854-55. The work is of timely interest in its account of the physical environment, customs, dwellings, food habits, and many diseases of the natives in the country recently subjugated by Mussolini's troops. Speaking of the native tribesmen's partiality for the bats which keep off flies and mosquitoes, the plagues of the Somali country, Burton observes: "Flies abound in the very jungles wherever cows have been, and settle in swarms upon the traveller. Before the monsoon their bite is painful, especially that of the small green species; and there is a red variety called 'Diksi as,' whose venom, according to the people, causes them to vomit. . . . The mosquito bites bring on, according to the same authority, deadly fevers: the superstition probably arises from the fact that mosquitoes and fevers become formidable about the same time." So here, in an immemorial traditional belief, was the secret of malaria and yellow fever and other pestilences, waiting for modern science to grasp and solve it to the advantage of mankind. But Burton's civilized scorn leads him to cast it aside in a footnote as savage superstition, and the world has to wait decades before medical science reaches the same fruitful suggestion and utilizes it in research and in medical application. This example is cited to illustrate the

Coyote Wisdom

importance of the right kind of tolerant attitude towards the ideas and mental processes of simple folk. They may turn out to be on the right track in other subjects besides those of flies and mosquitoes.

Perhaps we may trace, however briefly, another path of folk-wisdom, which finds expression in the prayers of men and nations. In the evolution of prayer, which has been surveyed by Farnell and others, men's changing ideas of their relation to God and to the world-process are revealed. In primitive incantations men might undertake to work a magic, regarding the course of events, especially of human events, as subject to a certain necessity which they themselves may control and direct by their spells. Sooner or later disabused of their conceit, magician and medicine-man join their former votaries in imploring the cosmic powers which had proved unyielding to magical compulsion. But, while thus the prayers of entreaty and supplication succeed the incantation-spells, a further two-fold process may be observed in operation. On the one hand in the field of religion, as men's ideas of divinity are perfected, they come to realize that prayers of unworthy ends are insults to God and impious. So this truth is expressed with peasant irony in a proverb: "If God were to listen to the crows' praying, there would be dead horses lying about right and left." The prayers of men come to represent a progressively more refined spiritual perception. But on the other hand, as expanding experience reveals the range of human effort and accomplishment, practical self-reliance and moral responsibilty replace much elaborate praying. Men perceive the operation of natural causes and effects; the understanding of the necessary order of nature frees the soul of much of its earlier futile supplication and needless anxiety. The rain falls on the just and on the unjust; and, rain or no rain, as an old saying has it, "a rocky vineyard does not need a prayer but a pickaxe." The right conclusion of a prayer, so we hear in a number of popular proverbs, is in a person's firm resolution to undertake and carry out that for which he prays. So the Bulgarian peasant concludes: "It is not enough to say, Our Father; one must also say, Amen."

Not accidentally have proverbs crept into this brief paper. For folk-wisdom does not find expression in systematic doctrines. It engages the imagination, sees truth and principles concretely, and is communicated in tale or parable or more concisely in proverbs. This is the second type of philosophy in folklore which I should like to consider. The wisdom of life which we can learn from popular proverbs is one of thousandfold observation, reflection, irony. There is, of course, as radical a difference between real folk-proverbs and those made by philosophers and men of letters as there is between the folk-tale and the literary fairy-tale. The folk-proverb does not harp on the same note; it is a whole little orchestra of moods and motives and slants on life. I have been reading lately a collection of more than three thousand Bulgarian proverbs on all conceivable themes, often with many variants of the same wisdom running the change of emphasis from mild to tart irony; it is rarely more than tart. They are marvels of conciseness; not only is all irrelevant and stodgy argument spared, but also all lame qualifying clauses, and likewise all the flunkey words of mere grammar that do not count in the meaning. It is as if, after a long and tedious discourse, the conclusion and upshot of the whole matter had been uttered in one telling sentence, four words perhaps, four hammer-blows. Are we all engrossed today by the conflict of Great Powers for world-supremacy, in which conflict small nations serve as pawns and are trampled down?—the Balkan States, Belgium, Ethiopia? The Bulgarian peasant takes this distressing topic of international affairs, glances ironically over his pasture or stable, and sums it all up in

a word: "The stallions stamp, the donkeys get the kicks."
But the least change of phrasing, and we have a sardonic
chapter of social-economic philosophy, only without justi-
fication or protest or propaganda, just the bare statement
of the facts: "The stallions prance about, and the donkeys
work to death." You and I might learnedly advocate an
international policy of conciliation and mutual concession,
or else in individual relations urge the advisability of a
spirit of common understanding and tolerance; but the
folk-mind does not need so many long words. It declares
more simply: "Two sharply pointed stones grind no flour."
Our journals are full of discussions of hours of labor, a
living wage, and the price-index of various basic commodi-
ties, the subtleties and refinements of men speaking for
capital or for organized labor. The peasant settles one side
of this argument very neatly: "Nine livers for a penny are
still too high for Uncle Lackpenny." We remember that
Rome was not built in a day; the village sage has not been
to Rome, but he scratches his head and reminds us, "In
twenty-four hours, a louse can become a patriarch." So in
proverb after proverb. Do these three need any commen-
tary? Judge for yourselves:—"Even in Paradise, living all
alone would be hell." "God does not pay wages every Saturday." "Back from Holy Land, the pilgrim donkey's ears
are just as long as ever."

Folk-wisdom is not one-sided. Sometimes two turns of
the same proverb state both sides in balanced irony. Should
we elaborate at length that a man's worth of character is
better than pretentious external polish? The village-mind
expresses it in one whiff: "On golden platters — rancid
butter." But often a vulgar exterior or a disagreeable manner may spoil the career of a really honest and competent
man. The peasant gives us a variant proverb: "Perfect butter, packed in a dog's skin." And then, as if both of these
truths had to told as one, with double-edged irony cutting

Philosophy in Folk-Lore

and correcting each other, the story is told of two thieves robbing a church. One of them sees a golden lamp hanging above the altar and climbs up to reach it. "Fie, fie," the other thief censures him, "take off your sandals when you climb on the altar." "Don't worry," the first robber answers as he unhooks the golden lamp, "God does not care for clean sandals but only for a clean heart."

I barely mention this last wisp of a folk-tale, and at once other tales crowd into your mind and mine: tales with much deeper treasures of wisdom or perplexed meaning. You recall the old English story of Childe Roland: how his sister Helen was stolen by the fairies and carried away to the Dark Tower of the King of Elfland, how his two brothers one after the other sought to release their sister from her enchantment, but because they did not prove loyal to all their duties failed in their quest and were themselves enchanted, and how when Childe Roland finally essayed to save his sister, his task was made the more grievious by the failure of his two brothers. This eternal story of the good suffering for the evil, the innocent for the guilty, was used by Josiah Royce as the parable of the Christian mystery of the atonement. Or shall I recall to you the folk-tale motive of stories in which builders of mighty towers or wide-spanning bridges, to assure solid and abiding construction, bury a human soul in the foundations, preferably the soul of a maiden or of a young bride? This folk-theme has inspired story-teller and dramatist in many lands, and in faraway China Lafcadio Hearn found it, the tale of the bell-founder in whose crucible a lovely maiden was melted with the metal, his own daughter in devotion to her father's art, to give the great bell the deep resonant wail of the human life that was in it. This tale with all its variants has expressed to men the profound truth of ethics and social philosophy that all abiding achievement and all beauty and loveliness in life are rooted in the heart and souls of men, that human life and character is the source and basis of all real value. Some of the greatest works of literature had their germs in such folk-tales: the myth of Prometheus, the story of Job, and in the days of the Renaissance, the Faust-saga. It is a great poet who can hear in the simple accents of folk-speech "the still sad music of humanity," and give it fuller and more mature utterance. But I am touching here on sublime themes that should be treated fittingly or not at all.

One might say: "A little of this and that and the other thing: but where is the philosophy?" So a Bulgarian peasant told me once, when I was trying to gather new proverbs from him: "You must be hard up for wisdom, my lad, with all your learning, to be gathering crumbs from me." And then he summed me up in a proverbial grunt, me and many other philosophers and system-makers: "Gathering horse-nails, to make him a horse."

Comic Exempla of the Pioneer Pulpit

By Mody C. Boatright

ONE of the most remarkable of many remarkable men who have left their impress upon American culture is Francis Asbury, who came to America in 1771 to propagate the faith of John Wesley. He was greatly handicapped in his work by the stand which Wesley had taken on the American Revolution, and after the war, by the deism of men like Franklin, Paine, and Jefferson, dominant not only among the statesmen who launched the new government, but also among the frontiersmen, in whose minds any sort of priesthood represented the kind of special privilege against which the Revolution had just been fought.

Asbury was fortunate, however, in having a theology well adapted to frontier needs; for the borderland farmers, even before Concord sages, had revolted against the teachings of John Calvin, and were demanding that the gates of heaven be opened to men in buckskin shirts and coonskin caps. But Asbury's success was due chiefly to his own genius — his genius for organization and his genius for picking men. The circuit-rider system, which he originated and which other denominations adopted, is too well known to require explanation here. The success of the system depended upon its personnel. Knowing that the frontiersmen would not tolerate a priestly class, Asbury turned to the laity. The typical frontier preacher, regardless of denomination, was a man who had practiced some other profession or trade, and who had been called to the ministry from among the folk whom he served. For example, Peter

Cartwright, perhaps the most famous of all circuit riders, had not been bred up in the church. When he was sixteen years old his father gave him a deck of cards and a race horse by way of a start in life. Jack Potter, Texas Methodist, before his call, had followed the profession for which the elder Cartwright had destined his son. H. K. Stimson, who carried the Baptist standard into Kansas, was driving a stage coach when it was borne in upon him that he must preach. Wilson Pitner, Methodist, who rode circuit in several western states in the early years of the nineteenth century, was formerly a hunter and scout. William Cavens, a Paul Bunyan among the early circuit riders, was at one time a Virginia stone mason. William Winans, one of Asbury's personal appointees, was a blacksmith. W. S. James was one of several Texas cowboys who felt the call to wrangle souls.

Some frontier preachers were relatively well educated; most of them undertook some course in reading under the direction of the presiding elder or some older minister. Many of them, however, hardly got beyond the Bible and the church discipline. "They had," says one observer, "about as much theological learning as that a man must mend or the devil will have him."[1] Even so, they had, as a rule, enough to serve the needs of the time. Bishop Asbury urged those of his faith upon going into the field to "leave all your vain speculation and metaphysical reasoning behind."[2]

But if their theology was not that of the Yale, Harvard, and Princeton divinity schools, and if their syntax sometimes fell below the requirements of a college entrance board, they knew the people whom they were sent to teach, and they could speak the language of the backwoods and the plains. The preaching of the frontiersmen, wrote

[1] W. H. Milburn, *Ten Years of Preacher Life*, New York, 1859, p. 358.
[2] J. B. Finley, *Sketches of Western Methodism*, Cincinnati, 1856, pp. 97-98.

Comic Exempla of the Pioneer Pulpit

Henry Fowler, "is by no means thin. It has body, and that of great power. The sermon has been built up day after day, by reflection on horseback, study in cabins, and practice through its growth three or four times a week. All the varied experiences with nature, with people, in conversation, by anecdote, on the road, in the cabin, through the field, are made to contribute to its life; and thus when finished, it is like its robust originator, hearty and elastic, full of vitality . . . and electricity, instead of being pale and abstract like the dyspeptic clinger to rocking chairs and book encircled rooms."[3]

The idiom of the frontier is frequent in the memoirs of the early western preachers; it must have been even more frequent in their sermons. Wilson Pitner once felt as if his soul "were running horse races on the great plains of divinity."[4] John Grenade used to represent the devil as an armed man gunning for the righteous. By prayer the Christian could bend the barrel of his gun; by faith he could knock off the hind sight. Once in a sermon he exclaimed that he felt like breaking the trigger of hell, giving emphasis to his statement with a stamp that broke a floor joist.[5] Peter Cartwright once angered his hostess by holding prayer in her house. "I saw in a minute," wrote Cartwright, "that she was mad and the devil was in her as big as an alligator."[6] When J. W. Anderson, Texas cowboy who turned preacher and afterwards wrote his life, came to tell of his courtship, he burst into the following interesting combination of western idiom and Hebrew melody:

"I soon said in my heart, 'She is mine
I would bridle a comet if possible for her;
I would muzzle a cyclone for her heart and hand.'"[7]

---

[3]Henry Fowler, *The American Pulpit*, New York, 1856, p. 130.
[4]H. W. Milburn, *op. cit.*, p. 77.
[5]John Carr, *Early Times in Middle Tennessee*, Nashville, 1857, p. 121.
[6]Peter Cartwright, *Autobiography*, New York, 1856, p. 305.
[7]J. W. Anderson, *From Plains to Pulpit*, Houston, 1907, p. 84.

Coyote Wisdom

But it was by the use of anecdote more than by the use of folk idiom that the frontier preacher held his audience and expounded his text. In 1844 when Z. N. Morrell was preaching in Huntsville, Texas, he was repeatedly disturbed by men and boys who had gathered on the outside and were telling anecdotes and laughing. Finally Morrell went to the door and invited them in for a contest. He told them that if he could not beat them telling anecdotes, he would take his signs down and listen to them. They accepted the challenge and came inside. Morrell told about a party of Tories (Mexican sympathizers) who at the beginning of the battle of San Jacinto shouted for Santa Anna, but who soon shouted even louder for Houston. He made application and surrendered the floor. The leader replied, "You have the floor, sir; proceed; we give up."[8]

At all times a frontier preacher needed a good stock of anecdotes. The first generation of western preachers drew on their own amusing experiences; the second generation added to their inherited repertoire. Some of the anecdotes, I am sure, would have seemed irreverent to Jonathan Edwards or to Ellery Channing, but not to the robust ministry of the frontier. It was a Texas preacher of indubitable piety who recorded the story of the man who crossed the Sabine River going west with a posse at his heels, and who rode out of range of his pursuers' guns remarking that "The Sabine River is a greater Savior than Jesus Christ ever was. He only saves men when they die from going to hell; but this river saves living men from going to prison."[9]

One larger cluster of exempla centers around the theme of religious ignorance. Such ignorance was a frontier reality. Men to whom churches were a necessity did not move to regions where churches were not. The intelligensia of the frontier — army officers, lawyers, and doctors — if we

[8]Z. N. Morrell, *Flowers and Fruits*, fourth edition, Dallas, 1886, p. 205.
[9]Morrell, *op. cit.*, pp. 29-30.

may trust the memoirs of the pioneer preachers, were largely deists, or infidels, as they are more frequently called. Among the folk there was widespread indifference, and many frontier children grew up with no religious instruction at all. The historian of pioneer Kentucky estimates that when that state was admitted to the Union, two-thirds of its people were without church affiliation.[10] At the beginning of the nineteenth century Cartwright found the state a "Tower of Babel."[11] Learner Blackman reported in 1805 that the vast majority in Natchez were "decided opponents to the Gospel of Christ."[12] Thirty years later J. H. Ingraham questioned some of the people of Natchez "on the simple principles of religion and education which every child is supposed to know, and found them wholly uninformed."[13] When Timothy Flint was called to St. Charles, Missouri, in 1818, he found that "religion was considered contemptible," and suspected that he had been sent for to promote a real estate speculation. "A minister — a church — a school," he wrote, "are words to flourish in an advertisement to sell lots."[14] When T. A. Morris came to Texas in 1844, he was entertained in the home of one of Austin's colonists who during his first ten years in Texas had not heard a sermon,[15] and Mrs. Dilue Harris knew a young man who, in 1837, had never heard one.[16] Early western preachers complain of a scarcity of Bibles, Timothy Flint estimating that not more than one immigrant family in fifty brought a Bible with them.[17] As late as the 1870's it was said in Kansas that there was no Sunday west of Junction City and no God west of Salina.

---

[10]R. S. Cotterill, *History of Pioneer Kentucky*, Cincinnati, 1917, p. 243.
[11]Cartwright, *op. cit.*, pp. 220-221.
[12]J. B. Finley, *Sketches of Western Methodism*, Cincinnati, 1856, pp. 218-219.
[13]J. H. Ingraham, *The Southwest*, New York, 1835, II, 172.
[14]J. E. Kirkpatrick, *Timothy Flint, Pioneer Missionary*, Cleveland, 1911, p. 293.
[15]T. A. Morris, *Miscellany*, Cincinnati, 1852, p. 336.
[16]"The Reminiscences of Mrs. Dilue Harris," *Texas Historical Association Quarterly*, IV, 102 (October, 1900).
[17]Kirkpatrick, *op. cit.*, p. 102.

Coyote Wisdom

As serious as religious ignorance was to the earnest preachers, they often saw the humor growing out of it, and they enlivened their sermons with anecdotes illustrating it. In 1779 Garrettson, an early associate of Asbury, was riding his circuit in the Cypress Swamp district, Delaware, when he encountered a man singing at the top of his voice. Garrettson, supposing that the song was a hymn, thought he had found a Methodist brother. He soon discovered, however, that the man was singing a profane song. Shocked, he rode up to the traveler and asked:

"Do you know the Lord Jesus Christ?"

"Sir," replied the man, "I know not where the gentleman lives." Garrettson thought surely he had been misunderstood and repeated the question, but the traveler replied in all innocence, "I know not the man."[18] A few years later in Clarksville, Tennessee, according to a tradition recorded by James Ross, a Methodist minister was describing hell in the most lurid colors he could command and exhorting his hearers to reform and escape its tortures, when a man in the audience rose and said, "Parson, I don't think there is any such place as that, or somebody would have heard of it before now."[19] In Tygart's Valley, on the westward slope of the Alleghanies, at the beginning of the nineteenth century, William Cavens came once to a log cabin where a German woman was preparing dinner. She remembered having heard a sermon once in Pennsylvania when she was a girl. She called her husband from the field, and Cavens preached to the family and a few neighbors in the cabin. He took for his text, "Ye must be born again."

After the sermon the woman remarked, "Vell, I dinks I shall not."

---

[18]Herbert Asbury, *A Methodist Saint*, New York, 1927, pp. 117-118; Abel Stevens, *History of the Methodist Episcopal Church in the United States of America*, New York, 1864, I, 364.

[19]James Ross, *Life and Times of Rueben Ross*, Philadelphia, 1888, p. 261.

Comic Exempla of the Pioneer Pulpit

Asked what it was that she would not do, she replied that she would not be born again. For seven long years, she said, she had carried the corn to mill on her back, and she thought she had "borned a plenty."[20]

From experiences like these has descended a host of anecdotes, which were frequently used to spice sermons. The application could be made that he who hears and heeds not is spiritually more ignorant than he who has not heard.

A preacher approached a man and said, "My dear man, don't you want to be a laborer for the Lord?" "No thank you," was the reply, "I have a job."

A preacher called at a backwoods cabin and asked a woman what her faith was. "I hain't got no faith," she replied. "John is sech a liar I can't believe anything he says."

"You must know that Christ was crucified for you."

"No, I hadn't heerd nothing about it. This is sech an out-of-the-way place that nobody ever comes here to get crucified."

A preacher found a woman groaning from having eaten too many green cherries. Thinking that she was laboring under conviction of sin, he sought to comfort her by saying, "You know that Jesus died for you." She replied, "Is he dead? I didn't even know he was sick."

In another version the question is, "I suppose you know who died for you?" The layman replied, "Yes, God."

"No, not God," corrected the preacher, "but Jesus, the son of God."

"Oh," exclaimed the backwoodsman, "it was one of the boys, was it? I thought it was the old man."

A cowboy, seeing a crowd gathered in a public building, came in and took a seat in the rear. After his exhorta-

[20]J. B. Wakely, *The Bold Frontier Preacher*, New York, 1869, pp. 68-72.

tion, the preacher called upon all who were Christians to stand. Nobody rose.

"What?" exclaimed the minister, "not a single friend of Jesus in this house!"

The cowboy then stood, the preacher rejoicing to find at least one Christian in the community.

"Stranger," said the cowboy, "I don't know who this man Jesus is. I never heard of him before, but I'll stand up for any man who hasn't got any more friends than he has."

Another cowboy heard his first sermon. The next day he walked up to the local Jewish merchant and knocked him down.

"What's the matter with you?" asked the Jew.

"Wasn't it your people that killed Jesus Christ?"

"If it was," replied the Jew, "it was over eighteen hundred years ago. You are a long time resenting it."

"Well," explained the cowboy, "you see I didn't hear about it till last night."

Anecdotes of this sort, having their ultimate roots in the experiences of early frontier preachers, tended to cluster together to form the sort of backwoods story of which "The Arkansas Traveler" is the best known example. The following one was current in Texas twenty years ago:

A Presbyterian home missionary came to a cabin and engaged a woman in conversation.

"Are there any Presbyterians in this country?" he asked.

"Now, I jest couldn't say about that," replied the woman. "These woods is full of all kinds of varmints, but I ain't paid much attention to 'em. My husband, he's out with the dogs now. If he was here, he'd know. He keeps his hides on the south wall of the cabin. You might go around there and see if he's got any Presbyterian hides nailed up. I know he's got foxes and bars and painters, and

I know if there's any Presbyterians in the country, he's caught some of 'em before now."

"My good woman, you seem to be in the dark."

"Yes, I been after my old man for months to saw me out a winder."

"You don't understand. Have you any religious convictions?"

"Naw, nor my ole man neither. He was tried once for hog-stealing but he warn't convicted."

Misapplication of scripture, a specific kind of religious ignorance, has its quota of exempla. Peter Cartwright is my authority for the following incident. Wilson Lee, in Kentucky about 1813, preached on the text, "Except that a man deny himself and take up his cross, he cannot be my disciple." When Lee left the meeting, he overtook a German settler carrying his wife on his back. When asked why he was doing this, the man replied that he was carrying out the injunction of the text. His wife was the greatest cross he had to bear.[21]

Another frontier anecdote on the same theme tells of a merchant who gave his clerk a Bible and told him to follow its teachings in all dealings with his customers. Soon afterwards the clerk charged a purchaser two prices for a pair of shoes, and reported the feat to his employer, expecting to be commended. Instead, he was reproved.

"Didn't I tell you always to follow the teachings of the book I gave you?" demanded the merchant.

"I did," replied the clerk. "He was a stranger and I took him in."

Then there is the story of the woman who, when advised by the preacher to heap coals of fire upon the head of her

[21]Cartwright, op. cit., p. 43.

inconsiderate husband, substituted hot water, thinking it would be just as effective.

A series of exampla concerning insincerity and lack of faith in prayer seem also to date back to early western missionary acitivity.

James Ross was told the following story by a man who lived at New Madrid, Missouri, at the time of the great earthquake of 1811. On the banks of the Mississippi there lived an old woman whose husband and children had died of malarial fever and had left her poor and lonely. One day, being in an especially disconsolate mood, she went out to a place by a high bank and knelt and prayed the Lord that if it was His will, she might be taken from this world of sin and sorrow to a better one where she would be at rest. While she was thus engaged, a slight shock occurred and some of the bank fell off and struck her on the back. She jumped up, brushed off the sand, and exclaimed, "Well I do declare. What's this world coming to? Now-a-days everything a body says is taken in yearnest."[22]

Lorenzo Dow, who despite his passion for martyrdom, had a sense of humor, is said by oral tradition to have tested the sincerity of one of his fellow preachers who used to end his sermon on the joys of heaven with the cry, "Hurry up, Gabriel, and blow your horn." Dow hired a boy to hide himself in a treetop and blow his hunting horn in response to the prayer of the minister, who, thinking that the day of judgment had in sooth come, began praying for mercy. In one version of the story, he exclaimed, "Lord, you ought to know that I don't mean everything I say."[23]

---

[22]Ross, *op. cit.*, p. 208.

[23]Comic anecdotes concerning prayer were common among both whites and negroes. See "At the Prayer Tree," in J. Mason Brewer's collection of slave tales, "Juneteenth," Pub. No. X of the Texas Folk-Lore Society, Austin, 1932.

Comic Exempla of the Pioneer Pulpit

I suppose no exemplum had wider currency in the frontier pulpit than that of the woman who, encouraged by a sermon on the text, " . . . whosoever shall say unto this mountain, be thou removed and be thou cast into the sea, and shall not doubt in his heart . . . he shall have whatsoever he saith," prayed that a hill which rose in front of her cabin and obstructed her view might be removed. The next morning she went out early to view the results of her faith, and finding the hill still there, turned away in disgust, saying, "Yes, just as I expected."

A franker sort of scepticism is illustrated by the following anecdote current in West Texas. The country was suffering from the most severe drouth in two decades. Spring had come but the grass had not greened. The mesquite had not budded. Streams were drying up. Cattle were dying by the thousands, and the prairie dogs, in the absence of vegetation, were eating their carcasses. The preachers arranged for a series of meetings to pray for rain. At one school house near Fort Griffin the people had assembled. The preacher read scriptures on the benevolence of God and the power of prayer. His exhortation finished, he said, "Now let us pray." An old rancher, whose knowledge of West Texas weather was greater than his faith, rose and said, "Bretheren, there ain't a bit of use in praying for rain as long as the wind is in the west."

A part of the technique of the frontier revival was the use of lay "Christian workers," that is, church members who interviewed "sinners" to induce them to be "saved." The following anecdote illustrates the necessity of tact on the part of such workers.

The town barber, newly converted, volunteered to speak in private to some sinner within the following twenty-four hours. As the day wore on, customer after customer was shaved and shorn without being spoken to. The barber

would think of various ways of opening the subject, but
each seemed wrong. It was nearly closing time, and he
had not redeemed his promise. Just as he was about to lock
the door, a customer came and apologetically asked the
barber to shave him even though it was closing time. The
barber felt that this was his heaven sent opportunity, if he
could only think of a way to begin. He stropped his razor
for a long time in silence, examined the edge carefully, and
stropped it some more. With the razor poised in his hand,
he said solemnly, "Prepare to meet thy God." The customer
did not wait for the shave.

The pioneer preacher was always ready to defend the
faith that was in him. Doctrinal debates were characteristic of frontier religion. "Contrary to my natural inclination," wrote Z. N. Morrell, "I had often by the force of
circumstances been compelled to meet Indians and Mexicans on their invasions into the country from the West,
and aid in repelling force by force, and now, equally contrary to my inclination, I was compelled by a sense of duty
to the cause of my great Master to confront, and if possible
beat back, this advance guard of heretics invading the
country from the east." Specifically, he felt called upon to
oppose T. W. Cox, fellow Baptist, who "clearly taught
the errors embraced in the system commonly known as
Campbellism."[24] What exempla Morrell used in his debate
with Cox he does not record, but we may be sure that
anecdote was employed by both to drive their points home.

My father once heard a Methodist preacher make the
following refutation of the doctrine of apostolic succession:

A traveler lost his way in the backwoods country. While
wondering which path to take, he heard the breaking of
twigs in the underbrush, and presently there emerged an

------

[24]Morrell, *op. cit.*, p. 145.

overgrown boy with a rifle on his arm. By way of opening conversation, the traveler remarked, "That's a good looking gun you have."

"Yes," replied the youth, "this was grandpap's gun. He carried it through the Revolutionary War."

Surprised by this statement, the traveler looked at the gun more closely. "Why, the barrel," he said, "seems shorter than those of the Revolutionary period."

"Yes," said the boy, "Pap had a new barrel put on."

The traveler continued his examination of the gun. "That looks like a new stock," he observed.

"Yes," said the boy, "pap had that put on."

"The lock can't be very old either," observed the traveler.

"Pap had that put on too," said the boy.

"Then you must have a new gun."

"No," said the boy, "it's the same old gun grandpap carried through the Revolutionary War."

Most money-raising exempla are hardly less serious than funeral sermons. James Tooley, however, who had little difficulty in financing his revivals, used to tell the following story before sending around the collection plate.

During a period of drouth a ranchwoman pledged two dollars to the church. Her husband reproved her, saying that they did not have two dollars in the world, that they were operating on credit, and that if it did not rain soon, they would be completely ruined.

The wife replied that she knew all those things were true, but that she had prayed the Lord to send her the means to redeem her pledge, and that she had it borne in upon her that the money would be forthcoming.

The next day her husband came in from the pasture very melancholy and reported that their cattle had begun dying. He had found a dead cow.

Coyote Wisdom

"I told you so," exclaimed the wife. "I knew the Lord would answer my prayer. The hide will pay my pledge."

Among the many deathbed stories there are a few that are consciously humorous. The following is from the repertoire of Elder Horn, pioneer North Texas disciple of Alexander Campbell.

A certain ranchman and his partner had a way of putting their brand on calves and yearlings without being too particular about the ownership of their mothers. Their herd increased at the expense of their neighbors, some of whom were war widows. Eventually Bill, the older of the men, came to his deathbed. Jim, the junior partner, came to see him, taking along a friend, Dave. Asked how he was feeling, Bill said he guessed he was a goner this time.

"Say, Jim, [he continued] der ye mind them widder-wimmin's calves en yearlin's we branded in times gone? De ye reckon I could kinder square it up with the Lord 'fore I have ter meet Him? I've been layin' here tryin' ter count up how many——.' His voice trailed off.

Jim turned to Uncle Dave. "I say, Dave, we'd better be a-goin'; we'd better be gittin' along now. His mind's a-gettin' flighty! He don't know what he's sayin' no more. Let's be movin' along, Dave, fore he goes crazy ontirely."[25]

If by confining my discussion to the comic exempla of the pioneer pulpit I have left the impression that the typical frontier preacher was a mere showman, given to clowning in the house of God, I have done him an injustice. In high seriousness, in the desire to know the will of God and to make that will prevail, he was the peer of Matthew Arnold. In his perception of the ludicrous he was Arnold's superior. His aspirations were heavenward, but he dwelt near enough to earth to hear the robust laughter of the frontier.

---

[25]Robert C. Horn, *The Annals of Elder Horn*, New York, 1930, pp. 188-189.

Running down the Fool Killer

By Ralph S. Boggs

"What do you mean by 'self-evident?'" asked President
Webster of Union College of his mental philosophy class.
"I don't know, sir," replied the student.
"Well, I will try and illustrate," said the president. "Speaking
about mythology—suppose I should ask you if there ever was
such a person as the 'fool killer?'"
"I should say I don't know. I never met him."
"That is self-evident," said the Doctor.—From *Kings of
the Platform and Pulpit*, ed. by Melville D. Landon (Eli Per-
kins), 1896, p. 540.

IN *Publications* of the Texas Folk-Lore Society, Number
VIII (1930) appeared an enquiry by Ernest E. Leisy
into the identity of and activities of a personage known as
Jesse Holmes the Fool Killer. The data assembled consists
of (1) a quotation from the *Southern Literary Messenger*,
which opens, "Jesse Holmes is the name of the 'Fool Killer'
employed by the Milton (N. C.) *Chronicle;*" (2) a quotation from one of O. Henry's surprise-ending extravaganzas,
in which the Fool Killer's fame is said to be perpetuated in
an adage, "Down South whenever anyone perpetrates some
particularly monumental piece of foolishness everybody
says, 'Send for Jesse Holmes'"; and (3) a letter in which
R. R. Clark, of Stephenville, N. C., recalls the reputation
that the Fool Killer and the editor of the Milton *Chronicle*
enjoyed about 1880.

Upon examining the fragmentary files of the Milton
Chronicle, published by C. N. B. Evans, in the libraries of
University of North Carolina, Duke University and the
North Carolina Historical Commission, at Raleigh, I found

several issues, mostly from the 1850's and 1860's, containing Jesse Holmes' material. Two of the articles bear the same pictorial head: the Fool Killer, with upraised club, grasping in his other hand the lapel of a fool whose fingers are spread wide in terror, whose hair stands on end, and whose hat is on the way to the ground. Both articles, which are in the form of letters, conclude, "Yours foolishly, Jesse Holmes the Fool Killer."

A Letter from the Fool Killer.

Sitting on the Right side of the R & D. R. R.,
Marci., 1859.

The earlier of them is headed, "Sitting on the Right side of the R. and D. [Richmond and Danville] R. R.," March, 1859, and the other, "Down about Norfolk, Va., June 1861." The Fool Killer took the subjects for his "maulings," as he called his pointings-out of folly or cupidity, where he found them—whether along a railway track or in a military encampment. The Civil War afforded him a scope for his powers far beyond his previous run of post office scandals, corrupt legislatures, consultors of witches, and unscrupulous courters of women with property. In his "slatherings" of "black republican wretches," slackers, "the prince of fools elected to the Presidential chair" (in 1860), "patriots" in "soft places," and profiteers, he was at his bludgeoning best. Nor did he spare personal reference.

Jesse Holmes had none of the suavity of an Addison dissecting with light wit a beau's head and a coquette's heart, but delivered blows with the wide arm-swing afterward adopted by H. L. Mencken while editor of the *American Mercury*. The tone, if not the subject, of the following sounds peculiarly familiar:

> Passing by Bethel Church in Person County, and discovering that preaching was going on, I peeped in and descried a cloven-footed, box-ankled, bandy-shanked lark with his head thrown back, mouth open and full of flies, snoring so loud as to disturb the whole congregation. One tap of my club landed him on the other side of Jordan.

Apparently all wars show up the same brands of selfcare and cupidity. In satirizing these human follies during the Civil War, Jesse Holmes wielded the full force of his club.

> Down in Suffolk I noticed entirely too many young bucks displaying their *gallantry* in the wrong way. Instead of arming themselves with the musket and entering the tented field to defend Virginia's booty and beauty, too many of these "nice young men" preferred to remain at home and *arm* the girls about in evening promenades.
>
> Out upon the man that cries "party" now—down with him who would say, give this man a fat office because he was an immediate secessionist—deny office to that man because he was not. Down, I say, with all such party spit-licks, and ask the editors of the "Journal" [Raleigh *State Journal*] how it happened that they are ensconced outside of the battle field? Tell them that in this field every Southern man can find an office—

to pull the trigger at the enemy. Let them, then, and their office-seeking friends hie to it in haste. Let their language be *come* and not *go*, boys!

I think I shall go from here to Todd's Point, at the junction of Paygan and Jones Creeks with James River, where the Milton Blues and Ronaldsburg Riflemen are quartered in charge of a Battery with four guns mounted. I understand a very benevolent old friend resides there, and that there is no limit to his hospitality—he sends our troops buttermilk and only asks eight cents a quart for it! Besides, he actually opened his heart and presented the "Blues" with three or four fishing lines! But he can afford to be generous.

Some of the Suffolk people treated the troops kindly and some again didn't hurt themselves by their kindness. They know how to charge the poor soldiers two or three prices for everything they buy in and around Suffolk. And I want you to inform the young man who keeps the post office there, that I think he would make a good-looking soldier. An old gent, or a trundle-bed boy could attend to the post office. I also descried a few lawyers sitting at their office doors like so many spiders inviting flies to "walk into the parlor" who would have looked better to my eyes in the tented field.

Mr. Clark wrote concering Evans, editor of the Milton *Chronicle* during the Fool Killer's lifetime[1]: "He was very outspoken and independent and his paper, for a small paper in a very small town, attracted attention. He was evidently quite original. His stuff was much copied and when he wrote anything that went the rounds he would say that 'it had legs'. " Of all his "stuff" Jesse Holmes the Fool Killer traveled farthest. He traveled on his own legs to adjacent counties and across the Virginia state line. But O. Henry gave him his longest ride. O. Henry wrote in his story "The Fool Killer," " . . . few and happy are the households from the Roanoke to the Rio Grande in which the name of Jesse Holmes has not been pronounced or invoked." But the

---

[1]Leisy, Ernest E., "Jesse Holmes the 'Fool Killer'," *Publications* of the Texas Folk-Lore Society, VIII, 1930, pp. 152-154. For a full sketch of Editor Evans, see "Charles Napoleon Bonaparte Evans," by Jay B. Hubbell, *The South Atlantic Quarterly*, Vol. XXXVI, 1937, pp. 431-446.

reader, observing that Guilford County, North Carolina, in which O. Henry's birthplace, Greensboro, is situated, corners on Caswell County, of which Milton is an unimportant town, suspects that the Fool Killer was not far from home when O. Henry heard his name invoked and that he himself did more than anyone else to exalt a newspaper fiction into a folk personage. At any rate Jesse Holmes has attained that best of all assurances to longevity —he belongs to the folk.

Every known contemporary reference to Jesse Holmes the Fool Killer assigns him to the Milton *Chronicle*. An 1880 issue of the Danville (Va.) *Times* recites a "foolish" conversation and comments, "We don't know what to do about it unless we send the case to the fool-killer of the Milton *Chronicle*." Likewise the *Southern Literary Messenger* speaks of Jesse Holmes as "employed by the Milton *Chronicle*."[2] This is exactly the sort of character that an editor "outspoken and independent" would be likely to create, though why Mr. Evans chose the name Jesse Holmes instead of some other is a secret that probably died with him.

---

[2]Leisy, *op cit.*

Legend Making on the Concho

By Fannie E. Ratchford

LEGENDS, like a commoner and less respectable form of
folk fiction, travel swiftly and far, and are often more
interesting for their origin, range, and mode of travel than
for their subject matter. Many of our legends are so old
that their origin can only be guessed, and so widespread
that they seem to have been carried on the wings of the
wind. Others there are whose beginning and dissemination
can be traced with historical accuracy. Many of us, no
doubt, have been present at the fabrication of some yarn,
watched it pass from mouth to mouth, and become more
or less firmly fixed in popular belief—a legend. This paper
is concerned with the last group.

The most common of all local legends and the easiest to
classify are those that have been transplanted from other
localities, either knowingly and deliberately or through a
confusion of geography. The adaptation of legends for the
purpose of propaganda finds its classic example in the
widely spread Montezuma legend of New Mexico. According to evidence collected by Dr. Adolf F. Bandelier, a docu-
ment connecting the unfortunate Aztec Montezuma of
the Conquest with the Pueblo Indians of New Mexico was
concocted by the Mexican Government and skilfully circulated at the beginning of the War with the United States,
in 1845, for the purpose of holding the inhabitants of the
territory loyal to the mother country. Although the expedi-
ent failed to save New Mexico, the legend has become one
of the most widely spread and deeply rooted of Pueblo
Indian stories.

Legend Making on the Concho

The transfer of legends from one locality to another, however, is usually made unconsciously and more subtly, so that it is difficult, if not impossible, to determine just when or how it took place. There is hardly a mountain point or river bluff in Texas that does not have its "lover's leap" story, all, perhaps, going back to one real incident, though few communities know how or when the legend became attached to their own landmark.

Near Paint Rock, Texas, there is a long bluff of rocks running parallel with the Concho River, about a quarter of a mile from its banks. The region was once used as a camping place by the Comanche Indians, as is shown by Indian pictographs covering the face of the bluff, giving it the name Painted Bluff. At one point a spring gushes out from two ledges of rock and goes cascading to the foot, pouring itself into a rocky basin. Near the basin, watered by the spring, there formerly stood several large pecan trees.

A great many years ago a letter addressed to "An Old Settler, Paint Rock, Texas," was delivered to my father. The writer inquired if there were in that locality a group of pecan trees at the foot of a spring coming out of a bluff. The letter gave definite measurements indicating the relative positions of the trees to the bluff and to each other, which my father listed one day, while surveying near the spring. If allowance were made for the change of terrain over a number of years, the bluff, spring, and trees might be said to fit the description contained in the letter; so my father wrote the inquirer.

A second letter came promptly. The writer had a map showing the location of a treasure buried near the spring. He proposed that Father undertake the search on shares. This letter was not answered, and no more was heard of the matter.

Coyote Wisdom

Later, a young man named Dave Ransbarger, who lived on the Colorado River about fifteen miles from town, brought in a bar of dark metal taken from the gravel of an abandoned crossing on the Colorado. The bar was melted down and found to be lead. The local assayer could detect no trace of silver. Of course, there was much speculation as to how the bar came to be embedded in the gravel, and as the crossing where it was found lay on the old Spanish road to the San Saba Mission, someone suggested that it must have been dropped by a mule train carrying metal from the San Saba mines.

As a child I heard these two incidents mentioned by older members of the family, who certainly had no thought of connecting them. Yet in recent years they have been combined into a typical buried treasure story of wide circulation: mule train of silver bullion from the San Saba mines, pursuit by Indians, hasty burial of treasure, battle with the Indians, escape of a sole survivor, etc. No circumstantial detail is wanting, except an explanation of how the Spanish mule-train carrying the treasure came to be at the Painted Bluff, which is fifteen miles or more off the San Saba road.

It often happens that a story offered originally as a mere hypothesis, or even as a frank joke, through much repetition, gains currency as a reputable legend. One of the favorite local stories among the children of my generation was that of Uncle Rich Coffee's escape from the Indians by hiding in the cave at the Painted Bluff. Now this cave is hardly more than an angle in the bluff enclosed by a fallen rock. We could never understand why the Indians, who must have known the cave quite as well as we did, did not find him. This question was put one day to an older friend who had taken us to the Painted Bluff for a picnic. I well remember his teasing smile as he said, "Oh, I guess Uncle Rich must have crawled through the crack in the back of the cave into another cave that runs so far back the Indians couldn't find him."

Now, we knew that the crack in the back of the cave was too small for any one of us to wriggle through, and Uncle Rich Coffee, according to tradition, was a tremendously big man. We knew also from our own investigation that the crack did not lead into a second cave. But the suggestion was too fascinating to reject on the mere ground of facts, and it has become an interesting and orthodox part of the Uncle Rich Coffee story.

Several years ago, in the course of a terrible drouth in West Texas, I was teaching in the high school of a small town in the stricken section. By the time the third winter without grass or feedstuffs of any kind had rolled round, many of the stockmen were without resources or credit for buying feedstuff, and the miserable cattle in the pastures were left to die of starvation.

Day by day the unclouded sky became more and more thickly dotted with buzzards, which hung over the country like the spirit of drouth itself. The children on the school ground amused themselves, first, by trying to see who could count the greatest number of buzzards during one recess. From this simple sport, the high school children passed on to the more complicated game of working out a set of superstitions that would cover every possible grouping of the birds in the sky. One buzzard seen alone was bad luck; groups of even numbers were bad luck; odd numbers were good luck. If one caught sight of a buzzard over his left shoulder he must find one on his right to balance it before he took his eyes from the sky. When four buzzards were seen symmetrically placed at the four cardinal points of the compass with one directly overhead the drouth would be broken.

These signals, made up purely out of the imaginations of the older girls, were accepted without question by the younger ones, and came to be half-believed even by their authors. I have no doubt that a visitor to that community twenty years hence will find distinct survivals of this game in the luck beliefs of the people.

The most fertile source of legends on the Concho was the Old Ostrander House. Sometime in the early or middle '80's a man named Ostrander, from Syracuse, New York, came out as head of a ranching company, enclosing with wire fence a large stretch of land lying between Paint Rock and San Angelo. Part of the enclosed land was bought outright, but much of it was state school land. The pastures were stocked with fine horses and cattle; barns and stock sheds were built over the ranch; and on a hill overlooking Kickapoo Creek was erected a large stone ranch house, called Thornfield, the wonder of the country round. The whole was a mere speculative bubble. This was the period of investment of foreign capital in western ranches, and it has been supposed that Ostrander hoped to unload on some innocent English or Scotch younger son with more money than judgment. Before a victim was found, however, the passage of the Texas Alien Land Law ruined his plans. Suddenly Ostrander, with his wife and daughter, took French leave—so suddenly, indeed, that, according to tradition, they left the evening meal they were eating unfinished, and took with them only the clothes they were wearing.

For fifteen years or more Thornfield stood unoccupied and uncared for, the resort of picnickers and sightseers, when suddenly one day Ostrander reappeared and sold off such furniture as he could find buyers for in the neighborhood and again vanished.

Out of the many surmises concerning the sudden departure of the Ostrander family has arisen a cycle of legends, most of them having some basis in fact, but the story that has gained the widest circulation is fiction pure and simple.

Legend Making on the Concho

It arose after this fashion. When I was a child, about twelve years old, I went one day with friends who were taking a visiting relative to see the Ostrander House. The visitor was an old lady of a fluffy, romantic turn of mind, who firmly believed that she had the gift of prophetic dreams. As we walked around the house to the flag-stone porch at the back, she caught sight of a half fallen-in cistern curbing.

"Just exactly as I saw it in a dream!" she exclaimed, and then she related with dramatic gusto a dream which had for its climax the drowning of a beautiful young girl in this very cistern. Whether the tragedy of the original dream was suicide or accident I have forgotten. I have since heard both versions told as legends. But I well remember being tremendously impressed with the story she made of it, and I have no doubt I did my part in spreading it.

I had forgotten the incident until a few years ago, when I read a feature story concerning the Ostrander House. In this account, published in one of the Texas daily newspapers, the ghost of the drowned girl played a spectacular part. Through the name of the writer I was able to trace the story to the source I have indicated. Only a few months ago, while at home on a visit, I sought information concerning the actual operations of the Ostrander Ranch in its heyday. An old-timer whom I approached said, "For heaven's sake, don't go telling that yarn about the ghost of a drowned girl again."

"How do you suppose such a story got started," I asked.

"I'm sure I don't know," he answered, "but it is told everywhere now, and half the people in this country believe it."

The last and most interesting class of local legends are those peculiarly the product of a region's individual life and conditions, reflecting a folk reaction to natural or social phenomena. The Old Ostrander House has given to the Concho community a group of real legends of this kind, far more significant than the imported ghost story. One has it that the elaborate pretense of ranching was but a blind to cover the operations of a far-flung chain of robbers and that the house was a depot for stolen goods. This theory was based on the lavish supply of food and dry goods found in the house after the Ostrander family had taken flight. One woman who had known the house well in her childhood told me that she was inclined to believe the story, because she could remember seeing whole closets packed full of blankets, linen, piece goods, and even knitting wool and artificial flowers.

When I was small, if one of my brothers wanted to hurry me in what I was doing, he would likely say, "Get a Canterbury move on you!" The admonition meant nothing to me until I read Chaucer. Here, I thought, was an explanation of the expression, for I knew my brothers' fondness for turning their classics into household slang. But when I proclaimed my discovery to the family I was laughed to scorn. In the early days of the town there lived here a young man of some social pretensions by the name of Canterbury. One night while at a dance in the Court House, he met with an accident to his trousers which caused him to flee precipitously from the ball room. "A Canterbury move" was merely reminiscent of our local speed record.

The most individual of all our Concho legends are those concerning the Kilpatricks, who have wanted only a competent biographer to give them a place in the brilliant galaxy of Texas desperadoes along with Sam Bass, John Wesley Hardin, and Ben Thompson. It may be that these local celebrities will yet come into their own.

Even in the democratic society of our little western village the Kilpatricks were completely without the social and moral pale. Though they lived hardly more than two hundred yards from us, as we then measured distances, we had little contact with them, and they had for me all the fascination of legendary figures. From my mother's indignant denunciations of the Kilpatrick boys for robbing her turkey nests, I conceived a most enviable picture of heroic figures squatting over a campfire on one of the hills back of our house roasting turkey eggs.

My mother was a very busy woman and it often fell to the lot of one of my older brothers to put me to bed at night. If I was sleepy and impatient of the undressing and bathing process, he would ask severely, "Do you want to sleep in your clothes, like the Kilpatricks?" Though I never found the courage to admit it, this was exactly what I did want, and I secretly dreamed of running off to live with the Kilpatricks a life of joyous freedom, roasting stolen turkey eggs over a campfire, and sleeping in my clothes.

My first actual contact with the Kilpatricks, that I remember, came several years later. Mrs. Kilpatrick sometimes did washing for us. One day while Felix Kilpatrick, a boy about twelve years old, was waiting on the porch for the clothes, my brother and I slipped out to hold forbidden conversation with him. His dirt-encrusted feet caught our wonderous attention, and with childish lack of tact we asked, "Why don't you wash your feet?"

"Because," he answered, "if I can get the dirt to stick thick enough, thorns won't stick in."

This was practical wisdom, and we took note. When bedtime came that night we passed it on to Mama, promising to sleep with our feet hanging off the beds if she would let us go without the usual scrubbing. One of our older brothers, hearing our plea, put in, "You bet, Mama, that's a good idea. The dirt will protect the children from snakes. Yesterday when Felix was fishing on the creek, a big moccasin bit him on the toe. He kicked it off and stuck out the other foot, asking, 'Don't you want to taste this one too?' But the snake crawled up on the bank and died."

Along about this same general period I met one of the Kilpatrick girls and was struck with envy of her long black-bordered finger nails, nail-trimming being the most painful of all my childhood afflictions. "Why don't you trim your nails?" I asked.

"I want to see how long they will grow by Christmas," was her proud answer.

When I repeated this conversation at home, my teasing brother said, "And didn't you notice how nice and black they were? That's her graveyard, where she buries all the people she slays with her tongue."

These family jokes and legends of the Kilpatricks illustrate the stories current in the neighborhood. One boy of the town, I remember, had a long popular repertoire of Kilpatrick stories which he gave in lifelike imitation of their slow drawl and outlandish English. One only I remember well enough to repeat.

One day Boon Kilpatrick was hit on the head at school by a baseball that knocked him senseless for a few minutes. George Kilpatrick, his rather weak-minded brother, rushed home to break the news to the family. Leaning against the door facing, with one leg twisted around the other, he drawled out, "Po-er Boon, po-er Boon, po-er Boon!" until his father took enough notice of him to ask, "Well, what's the matter with Po-er Boon?"

"Po-er Boon's dead, plum dead!"

"Plum dead?" repeated his father. "Air yer sure? Then I guess you'd better go get the mules and drag him off before he gets to stanking."

"And," the relator of this fanciful incident always added in conclusion, "the buzzards over the hill are playing seven-up for his eye-balls yet."

Legend Making on the Concho

The Kilpatrick boys had long been notorious for their petty thieving, which was more or less winked at by the community, before they made their formal debut into the world of crime by robbing a sheep camp near town. From a seat of vantage on our gatepost, I watched the officers bring them in under arrest — my first sight of the law in operation.

The county jail to which they were committed had not had a tenant in years. The bars were rusted from the windows, and the doors sagged on their hinges. Since the prisoners had nothing stronger than their pleasure to hold them, they took frequent recesses, slipping off to the river to fish or gather pecans, always returning promptly for meals and bedtime. Their faithfulness gave rise to several delightful dime novel stories of the sense of honor that kept them from escaping because they had given their word to the sheriff. Judging from their subsequent behavior, I am more inclined to think that they were enjoying a sense of their own importance in having their meals brought to them three times a day from the village hotel. There is a story, which I cannot recall clearly, about their moving their beds and sleeping outside the jail after they had unearthed a den of rattlesnakes inside.

I was still a small child when the Kilpatricks moved from our town to a ranch in the southern part of the county, where they maintained headquarters for a gang of robbers and counterfeiters that operated for several years before it was broken up. Two of the Kilpatricks were killed early, in bank and train robberies. A third carried through successfully one of the most daring train hold-ups ever committed in this country, but was later caught and sent to the penitentiary.

After serving out his term, he came back to our town on a visit, calling on his old acquaintances with the air of a hero returning in triumph. Only a few months later he, with a lone assistant, was killed while holding up a Southern Pacific train near Sanderson, Texas.

Out of such material as this the legends of Sam Bass and other notorious desperadoes have grown. Without some stimulating interest from the outside, such stories fade from the popular mind. But once caught up and circulated in print they multiply by the hundreds. The Kilpatricks have been overlooked by the dime novelists. Their later crimes, particularly several brutal murders, so outraged the feelings of the tolerant community, that the earlier amusing stories have been forgotten. What with the natural change of population over a number of years, I doubt if a half dozen of the once numerous Kilpatrick yarns could be recovered. The vast majority have gone to join the multitude of lost local legends.

Pie-Biter

By JOHN GOULD

THE longer I live, the less reverence I have for truth. I think truth has been grossly overrated, as a virtue. I humbly disagree with Keats in his tenet that truth is beauty. I can agree with Bryant that truth crushed to earth shall rise again, but it follows that truth is likely to be disfigured in the crushing. Too often, the face of truth is harsh and dour. Legend as distinguished from truth may not be as dignified, but it is much more interesting. It may not have the commanding presence, but it is far more likely to step out with you and show you a good time.

A lively legend can mean much more to us than a staid and proper truth. It has more blood in it.

Consider, for example, that sublime story that has come to us from the Alamo about the line that Travis drew upon the floor. It has not been authenticated and probably cannot be. As Texans, we want to believe it, and we do believe it regardless of its apochryphal quality. Would the truth, if it could be established, be any more inspiring? Could anything else have been said or done that would have been more magnificently in keeping with the Alamo's epic story? It is a legend, but it has a grandeur that the truth could not surpass.

I submit, therefore, that truth can be too stodgy, too dull, for us always to regard with reverence. Understand me, I have no objection to it in its proper place, serving its proper use. I find it quite helpful sometimes in my work, which is that of an editorial writer. But I have acquired an awareness of its limitations and its disadvantages that makes me less worshipful of it than I once was.

Pie-Biter was a man whose nickname deserves a place in Texas folk-lore because of his persistent refusal to be hampered by the bonds of truth. His real name was an undistinguished one, Jim Baker. I shall tell how he came by that name, but it is one of the least important things about him.

He was a cow-camp cook, one of that brotherhood of culinary experts who did so much to make possible the winning of the West and who have received so little credit for it. The bacon, the beans, the biscuits and the coffee that he prepared were the subsistence of men who served humbly but mightily in pushing civilization westward. Pie-Biter was a cook, a musician, a sprinter, and a teller of tall tales.

Our story begins with a game of poker. The players were using grains of corn, yellow corn, for the purpose — whatever it may be — that chips are supposed to serve. Pie-Biter's store of corn had steadily diminished, and his supply of money was also depleted. A less resourceful man would have quit the game. Pie-Biter had within him something readier than money. He excused himself on some pretext — I am told that a man whose chips are exhausted can always get excused from a poker game — and went outside. He went to the corncrib and there, in the dark, he obtained an ear of corn, shucked it, shelled it, put the grains in his pocket, and returned nonchalantly to the game.

What followed immediately was all Pie-Biter's fault. He should have remembered that nature occasionally produces an ear of red corn along with the yellow kind, just to show that hers is not a one-track mind. When an ear of red corn is shucked at a husking bee, custom prescribes that its finder is entitled to a kiss. And so when Pie-Biter reached into his pocket for some grains of corn to support some remarks he had made, and it proved to be red corn instead of yellow, the others in the game kissed him, using the butts of their pistols, the toes of their boots, or whatever else came handy. Then they bade him be gone as one whose ethical standards made him unwelcome.

And so we find Pie-Biter, astride his pony, plodding disconsolately across the prairie. He was hungry and broke, and his sadness was intensified by the thought that he had sinned and got caught at it. As his pony jogged along, he sought and found surcease in sleep.

He awakened presently to face troubles far more serious than those he had left behind. A roving band of Indians had seen him and had effected his capture before he awoke. That was in a day when the Indian had not yet fully realized that the white man's coming was a blessing. It was made known to Pie-Biter that the Amerind intention was to make an example of him.

Meanwhile the Indians had possessed themselves of his belongings: pony, saddle, and clothes. But the fiddle which he always carried with him was something new to their eyes. They regarded it with doubt and suspicion. Seeing this, Pie-Biter took the instrument from the Indian who had seized it and began to play.

As the strains of the one and only selection in his repertoire, "The Arkansas Traveler," rose upon the autumn air, he was conscious of a change in the Indians' demeanor. It seemed to him that their menacing and ferocious looks gave way to an air of softness and tenderness. Perhaps Pie-Biter had never heard that music hath charms to soothe the savage breast, but he was nevertheless ready to demonstrate that power. The braves gathered around and listened, rapt, attentive. Perhaps the music turned their minds from thoughts of scalps to the squaws and papooses they had left behind. Pie-Biter played on and on, hoping against hope that his music would somehow turn the odds in his favor.

It might have done so. He might have lulled his captors into a merciful state of mind. But the same perverse fate that had caused him to pick up red corn instead of yellow now caused the E-string of his fiddle to snap violently in two. One end of it whizzed through the air like a whiplash and struck the chief squarely in the eye. The fiddle and the bow were angrily seized and reduced to kindling-wood. And the plans for dealing rudely with Pie-Biter were resumed where they had been left off.

The first number on the program was an act called running the gauntlet. The braves lined up. I have said that sprinting was among Pie-Biter's talents, and he proceeded to give a demonstration. He ran down the line of braves so rapidly that they had no chance to strike him with their clubs and tomahawks. It was like striking at the shadow

— A "TENDERFOOT" LEADS THE RACE! —
—Drawn by Edgar Rye.

of a non-existent black cat in a dark room, so rapidly did he run. And before the startled red men were aware what was happening, Pie-Biter was gone from there, running with all his might in the direction of civilization.

They tried to overtake him, but he had too long a start. Only one of them stuck to the chase persistently enough to catch up with Pie-Biter, and that was some time later. This brave, Pie-Biter discovered, was out of breath, his mouth wide open, and his strength almost spent. But he had weapons with which to make up for this disadvantage.

Pie-Biter reached out, as the Indian caught up with him and caught the pursuer's protruding tongue in his hand. With his other hand he struck the brave very hard in the stomach, causing him to convulsively close his jaws and bite off his own tongue.

In the course of time Pie-Biter reached a cowcamp on the Burk Burnett ranch. There he was clothed and fed. As luck would have it, the outfit was in need of a cook, and Pie-Biter was employed then and there.

Setting about to prepare supper, he discovered that there was no fuel gathered and that none was readily available. The cowhands were standing around, weary after their toil, and anxious for food. It was in the fall of the year, and Pie-Biter noted that the grass was thick and dry He hit upon the plan of setting fire to the grass and cooking supper on it as it burned, carrying, of course, his skillets with him as the fire advanced.

His resourcefulness was rewarded. Presently supper was ready. But there was no one there to eat it. Pie-Biter had run with the fire as it moved and by the time everything was cooked, he was eight miles from camp.

About his name, Pie-Biter. He was very fond of sweet potato pie and would consume several pies at one sitting. His favorite manner of eating them was to stack them one above the other and bite through them all at once. From biting through two pies at a time, he advanced with practice to biting through three at once. Like most talented persons, he strove to further improve himself and before long was biting through four pies.

His exploits became known far and wide, and folks would travel many miles to see him eat pie.

There is something about fame and success, I am told, that gets into a man's blood. He is not content to rest upon his laurels but obeys that higher law which demands that he press onward and upward to new and grander heights. And so it was with Pie-Biter. There came a day when he felt the urge to bite through five pies. He made known his ambition, and there was a great gathering of the yeomanry to see him make the attempt. Someone offered to bet him that he could not perform the feat. He at once accepted and the money was put up.

"THE FIRE ADVANCED"

Pie-Biter

"HE STEPPED BRAVELY FORWARD"

In the presence of a great multitude he stepped bravely forward for the test. The pies were stacked before him, one, two, three, four, five. Women wept and strong men shuddered as the moment drew near. When Pie-Biter, opening his cavernous mouth to its fullest reach, encompassed with his jaws all five of the pies, a mighty cheer arose from the throng. Suddenly a look of dismay and then of anguish spread over Pie-Biter's features as his teeth sank inexorably into the pie. He could not make his teeth meet. Try as he might, he was unable to bite through the stacked pastry.

In a moment he abandoned the attempt, bursting into the bitter scalding tears of disappointment. And not until then did he discover that somebody had failed to remove the tin plate from under one of the pies.

NOTE: The illustration on p. 188 is taken from a special edition of *The Wichita Times*, April 9, 1909; that on p. 190 from Burton's *Cyclopedia of Wit and Humor* (I, 286), where the prairie fire story is told of Ranger Bill Dean.

The Wart Doctor

By Frank Simmons

IN SPITE of the scriptural admonition to "beware of conjurers, sorcerers and soothsayers," there are in the hills of Central Texas wart doctors who conjure warts.

A red-haired man chopping posts alongside a boy in a cedar brake of Coryell County noticed warts on the boy's hands and arms. "Let me see them warts," the red-haired man said. He looked at them silently for a little while and then added, "Leave 'em alone, and they'll go off in a few days."

I saw the warts and heard the red-haired wart conjurer. Then I decided to beard the wart doctor in his den, which was a little unpainted house on a little farm lying along one of those narrow valleys that drain down from the prairies through the limestone hills to the Leon River. The cottage had the characteristic picket fence enclosing it, the corn crib and two or three other small out-houses.

I had been searching for arrow-heads under a dull grey sky all afternoon. As dusk approached, a cold drizzling rain and northeast wind set in. Now was my time to spend a night with the wart doctor. I approached his home. A blue column of fragrant wood smoke was ascending into the gloomy skies from the chimney. The doctor, who was also a farmer, was placing another armful of wood on the porch for use in the night.

"Come in out of the rain, man. You'll die stragglin' 'round this kind of weather. Thought you knowed better."

We went into the house. I could smell the odor of boiling coffee and frying ham coming into the room from the kitchen. My appetite grew keener and keener the short while I waited for supper.

During supper I made the remark that I wished I owned his little farm and that "he had a wart on his nose." He instantly implied that he "could destroy warts." I reached the point I was driving at.

"Yes, sir, I can get rid of anybody's warts and they won't know how I done it," he continued. "I can teach one person in each family how to cure warts, but if you try to learn more than one in the family, all of them will lose the magic and none of 'em can do it." "Why only one in a family?" I asked. "Well, I don't know but it's just that way. If I tried to teach two in a family, I might lose the conjuring power myself. It's just that way for some reason or other.

"An old woman wart doctor taught me. She said it was a supernatural power some people had to conjure sick babies and warts, and cure them.

"Now there's lots of ways you can kill warts without conjuring them. You can steal a dishrag and rub your warts, then hide the rag, and when the rag rots, your warts will be gone. You can rub them with a weddin' ring. You can put wild milkweed on them. Rub some tobacco spit from a God-fearing man's tobacco on them. There are lots of ways to get rid of warts, but I had rather conjure them. Then there's no scar left, and your warts are sure gone, and they won't come back. Now I don't know exactly what conjuring is, but some of us do it anyway and cure warts.

"Let me tell you there's one thing kids ought not to do. That's play with these old warty garden toads. When they wet on their hands, it makes warts all over 'em. That makes more warts than any other one cause. The warts disfigure their little hands something ugly. They ought not to do it."

While the wart doctor thus expounded, his wife was laboring with a churn dasher to extract butter from a churn of sour cream. Suddenly the churning ceased. The good woman seized the iron poker, which stood against the jam, and thrust it among the glowing coals of the fire. She left it there until it was red hot. Then she jerked it out and immersed it in the churn. I could hear the cream and milk sizzling.

"Why are you doing that?" I asked.

"You see," she replied, "the devil has witched this churn. I've been churning till I'm wore out, and no butter yet. I stuck that hot poker in to drive the devil out. It'll oust him, too. I learned that from my old grandmammy. She came from Virginia away back yonder before I was borned. She said she always burnt the devil out when the butter wouldn't churn that way."

Traditional Nacogdoches

By R. B. BLAKE

THE history of Nacogdoches is like that of no other community in the land. Of Nacogdoches we cannot say, on this date, or that date, its foundations were laid; we can only say, as the authors of Genesis have said, "In the beginning;" or as the fablists start off, "Once upon a time."

Once upon a time there lived on the banks of the Sabine River an old Caddo chief. He had lived a long and useful life, and had taught his two sons all the wisdom of forest and stream. They had grown into strong and stalwart manhood — sure-footed, clear-eyed.

As the old chief saw his end approaching, he realized, in the wisdom of his years, that his twin sons could not both inhabit their ancestral lodge in peace and harmony, but that each should build for himself a tribal home. And so, one day he called his sons before him and told them that his end was drawing nigh. Then, placing his hand upon the head of one, he said, "Natchitoches, my son, as the dawn breaks tomorrow, turn your face toward the morning light, and for two days walk toward the rising sun. As the second sun sinks to rest in the west and you camp for the night, there build your lodge — there rear sons and daughters, and the forests and streams around you shall be yours."

Then turning to his other son, he said, "Nacogdoches, my son, as tomorrow's sunlight awakes the quail, you, too, must leave; but turn your face towards where the sun sets. For two days you will walk. Then at the end of the second day, as the sun disappears from sight, spread your camp for the night. There build your lodge and rear your increase. Along the streams and in the forests may you follow the ways of peace and plenty."

And so, in obedience to the injunction of their wise old father, Natchitoches built his lodge on the banks of Red River of Natchitoches; while Nacogdoches made his home on the banks of La Nana and El Bañito — the Nurse-Mother stream and the stream of the Little Bath.

The years and centuries passed, and Natchitoches and Nacogdoches and their children's children lived in peace and harmony. The children of Natchitoches spread out to the north, to the south and to the east, but not towards the west; while the children of Nacogdoches spread out to the north, to the south and to the west, but not towards the east. The land of Nacogdoches became the land of the Tejas — the friendly land.

The children of Nacogdoches were fair of skin, and their eyes the blue of the sky. Their hair was yellow, and sometimes ruddy gold.

Centuries passed, and among the chiefs of the Tejas there arose a leader whose name was Red Feather. Respected and loved by all the people of Nacogdoches and the neighboring pueblos, he united the tribes of his land into their first confederacy, with a central government, as a protection against the marauding tribes of the west; and it was he who first called his country the land of the Tejas.

Red Feather was tall and straight, grey-eyed and with a glint of gold in his hair. In his cap he wore a large scarlet feather, which gave him his name. His people had hitherto lived by hunting, trapping, fishing and gathering such wild fruits as they found. Red Feather taught them the arts of agriculture — taught the Tejas to dig and delve, so that when the deer and the bison should disappear from the land, they would yet have food.

Traditional Nacogdoches

He counseled his people: "Be strong, be just, be kind; plant, sow, gather, garner, give!" This was long before the Spanish and French came with their fire-water and guns, and their tales of wonders beyond the sea.

As the hand of death was laid upon him, Red Feather summoned his chiefs and his people and admonished them to live at peace, as he had taught them; to hold fast to that which was good and to cast aside the evil things that would cause their destruction. With the final blessing, he said, "Even when I am gone from your sight, I shall watch your work from the land of the Great Spirit."

With the passing of Red Feather, the sorrow of his people was great, and elaborate were the plans for his funeral ceremonies. His house was closed, and as he was laid to rest on the chief mound his people had made, a red flash soared upward in the forest. Then, as his people followed its flight with their eyes, they saw it was the first red bird. It circled in flight and alighted upon the cone-shaped top of the home where Red Feather had lived. No bird of such brilliant plumage had ever been seen before, and all the Tejas accepted it as the soul of Red Feather come to watch over them. They provided food for the bird and there it dwelt, and in its song it seemed to say: "Be strong, be just, be kind; plant, sow, gather, garner, give."

Long ages passed, and then one day history dawned. De Soto and Moscosco, in 1542, came with mailed fist and ruthless arms in search of fabled gold — and found it not.

Again the Tejas were left in peace, and in 1639 the "Angel in Blue," Mother Mariá de Jesús de Agreda, miraculously appeared from Spain, to teach the Tejas love and kindness. For more than half a century the memory of this saintly Angel in Blue lingered among the Tejas, and after Father Massanet came in 1690, he reported thus: "In times past, they say, the Tejas were visited frequently by a very beautiful woman, who used to come down from the hills, dressed in blue garments. On my asking if that had been long since, the governor said it had been before his time, but his mother, who was aged, had seen that woman, as had also the other old people."

Twenty-five years after the coming of Father Massanet, the brown-robed Franciscan friars pressed onward to Nacogdoches, and Father Margil built the Mission Guadalupe among the mounds of Nacogdoches, ministered to the needs of the simple, friendly people. When famine stalked through the land, he smote the rock on the bank of La Nana — the Nurse Mother — and the Holy Spring called The Eyes of Father Margil, gushed forth its life-giving waters. Again, as the Father was coming from the west to Nacogdoches, he was borne in the "Arms of God" away from the pursuing Apaches, across the raging torrent of the Brazos de Dios, whence that river received its name.

Then, too, along the King's Highway St. Denis pursued his journey through Nacogdoches westward across the Rio Grande in search of his Spanish bride.

Angelina, the first native missionary among the Tejas Indians, labored for the education and conversion of her people, as Mother Agreda had done more than fifty years earlier.

The tide of conflict ebbed and flowed through Nacogdoches, between French and Spanish, and then between American and Spanish. Nine flags contended for supremacy here. First, the Royal Lillies of France were borne against His Catholic Majesty of Spain; then Aaron Burr and General Wilkinson looked with longing eyes across the Sabine and used Philip Nolan as their tool; next, Magee and Gutierrez proclaimed the first Republic of Texas with the first newspaper published in Texas and almost succeeded in their undertaking, in 1813. The fixing of the Sabine as a boundary between the New Phillipines and the United States in 1819 was the signal for the formation of Dr.

Traditional Nacogdoches

Long's Republic at Nacogdoches. Next came the abortive Fredonian Republic of 1826, when Eva Catherine Rosine Ruoff met her future husband while he was a prisoner in the Old Stone Fort, condemned to be shot for treason. He survived, however, and she became Mrs. Adolphus Sterne.

Again on August 2nd, 1832, the time of war surged round the Old Stone Fort, when the flag of Bustamente was hauled down and the flag of Santa Anna raised for the Constitution of 1824. The soldiers of Piedras were driven from Texas soil, making the Texas Revolution possible.

Near the entrance to Oak Grove Cemetery, beside Hospital Street, there stood more than a century ago, a chinquapin tree of gigantic size and apparently of great age. In the early days it was called "the tree of noche triste"— of the sad night — for it was supposed that those bereaved ones who lingered here and wept out their sorrow for their loved ones would find peace and hope from the overshadowing branches of this giant of the forest.[1]

---

[1]Variant or supplementary accounts of the Nacogdoches place names treated of in this essay may be found in "Stories in Texas Place Names," by J. Frank Dobie, in *Straight Texas* (Pub. No. XIII, 1937, of the Texas Folk-Lore Society.) The legend of "The Lady in Blue," with various documentary citations, was published in *Legends of Texas,* issued by the Texas Folk-Lore Society, 1924.

The Snap Party in Mills County

By Mae Featherstone

AMONG the games mentioned by Mr. William Owens as insufficient for an evening's entertainment is Snap.[1] But the people who live in the hills of Mills County are not aware of this deficiency, for Snap has furnished them entertainment for many evenings stretching over a long period of years.

I do not know when or where Snap originated. It was brought to Mills County by the first settlers, who had played it in the older settlements along the Colorado River, Pecan Bayou, and Bennett Creek. To my knowledge, the game is still played in East Texas near Nacogdoches, in North Texas at Byers on the Red River, in West Texas at Imperial on the Pecos. But in none of these places is it played so much as in the hills of central Texas.

The country dance and the play-party have existed in Mills County since settlement, but they have never been so popular as the Snap party, partly because many Mills County boys and girls have been brought up to believe that dancing is wrong. For this reason only the "rougher elements" of society attend the dances and play-parties. Then the town of Goldthwaite has never sponsored a public dancing place of any sort, and since the rural dances have always been the rendezvous of the county's bootleggers and the scene of its most sensational murders, it is easy to see why most Mills County boys and girls do not go to dances until they go to college.

---

[1] William A. Owens, *Swing and Turn*, Dallas, 1936, p. xv.

The Snap Party in Mills County

The play-party has never been very popular in this locality, partly because of its similarity to dancing, but primarily because of the great popularity of Snap. For Snap is a game that everybody can play at the same time and that a group can keep on playing together for hours on end.

Most boys and girls do not begin going to Snap parties until they are thirteen or fourteen years old. But if there are older sisters in the family and no big brothers to take them to parties, the parents go and take the smaller children along. Since I was one of the smaller children in such a family, I started going to Snap parties many years before I was old enough to play, and I started playing the game years before I began going with an escort or "date" of my own. Thus I grew up going to a Snap party almost every Saturday night, often on Friday night, the year around, and every night during the Christmas holidays.

On account of revival meetings during the summer months, parties were usually discontinued; but very often — during that period — our parties, like the old saloon which closed on election day and opened when the polls closed, would begin after church services were over and last far into the night. In winter time, parties began about eight o'clock and broke up towards midnight; the summer parties held on longer, those that began after church services lasting until three or four o'clock.

In setting and atmosphere the Snap party is similar to the country dance and the play party. It is the game itself that is different. When a fairly large crowd has gathered, several Snap games, the number depending upon the size of the crowd, are played simultaneously. There is always one game in the "party" room, while other games proceed on the porch and in the yard.

It takes four people to play a game of Snap, the two who "hold up," the one who snaps, and the one who is snapped.

During a game, the player passes through four stages: namely, being snapped, snapping someone, holding up with the person who has snapped him, and holding up with the person he has snapped.

The original way to choose a partner was to snap one's fingers at the desired person, and from that custom the game received its name. This method of snapping, however, has been discarded in Mills County. When one person snaps another at our parties, he usually says, "Will you come catch me?" or simply "Come catch me," but often such expressions as "Let's run a race," "Get started," and "Lady, take after me," are heard. Little variation from these forms of address is permitted. One night at a party, a visiting boy from Wichita Falls went over to one of the girls and, following the coaching he had received from some local joker, said, "Come catch me, chicken. I'm full of corn." The girl answered him with a brisk slap in the face, and the boy from Wichita Falls played no more Snap that night.

The game starts with a boy and girl "holding up;" that is, they stand facing each other holding hands. Let us call them John and Mary. Another boy, say Tom, snaps a girl, Jane. Tom then walks or runs around the couple standing, and Jane chases him. When she catches him, John leaves the game; Tom holds up with Mary; and Jane snaps another boy, Henry. When Henry catches Jane, Mary leaves the game, and Tom and Jane hold up. Henry now snaps a girl, and the game continues. Thus the game goes on in an endless procession of entering, holding up with two different people, and leaving the game.

The chief action of the game comes when the couple runs around the couple holding up. The movement differs according to individual players. Some couples walk calmly and sedately through a game, but in my home community we usually played very hilariously. I have often seen the players holding up almost thrown to the floor by a runner's "swinging around the corner."

Assuming that the young folk are playing outside the house, any girl who participates is definitely associated with four different boys in the cycle of one Snap game. Let us take a girl named Jane through a game. She walks out with Tom, the boy who snapped her. She catches him and returns to the house with John, the boy who is leaving the game. She then snaps Henry and returns to the game. After he catches her, Jane remains outside holding up with Tom while Henry and the girl leaving the game go into the house together. Henry returns with another girl, and after he is caught, Jane holds up with him while Tom goes into the house with the girl Henry snapped. This girl returns with a new boy, and after he catches her, Jane, who is leaving the game, walks into the house with the new boy. During the game, then, she has been associated with both Tom, who snapped her, and Henry, whom she snapped, two different times, and with two other boys once each.

Snap may sound like a dull and uniteresting game, but it is far from that. It keeps the crowd constantly changing and moving about, and after several hours of play, each boy has had ample opportunity to talk to every girl present. The game moves with such automatic regularity that one is scarcely conscious of anything except that life is moving about him and that he is a part of it. In my heyday of Snap parties, which extended from about 1928 to 1934, they were always gay and colorful, with much laughter, talking and noise. Often the "party" room was so packed that one could hardly push through the milling throng, and the yard was usually crowded with games.

The game may progress fast or slow, according to the humor of the person who is snapping. Often an individual gets snapped in one or two other games and completely forgets the couple left standing in the corner of the yard by a lilac bush. Playing in two games at once is not at all uncommon, and sometimes one plays in three and even four at the same time. This causes long waits for some of the couples holding up, but very few of them really mind that.

Should a boy wish to be left alone with a certain girl for a while, the best way for him to manage is to snap his sister. For when brother snaps sister or sister snaps brother, it goes without saying that the snapper wishes to let the game rest. Unfortunate indeed are the boys and girls who have no brothers and sisters present at a Snap party.

Usually there were more boys than girls. At parties in my community we frequently had boys from places twenty-five and thirty miles away, while girls seldom went that far. Then the boys from town always came to our parties, but the girls never did unless some of us who lived in the country gave a party especially for our class in high school. These young men from Goldthwaite and Star and other more distant places were never popular with the home boys, and their presence often caused fights.

Among the girls at a party there were always a few whose parents forbade them to play Snap outside, and often the parents were there to enforce the rule. I have many times accompanied one of my girl friends out to the well ostensibly to get a drink but really to stand by the windmill and keep watch with a boy provided for that purpose while she played Snap. One of my best friends, however, dared not attempt this scheme, since her father, after forbidding her to play Snap in the yard, frequently did so himself. One night Jack, a boy whose father was very old and never accompanied him anywhere, snapped Sue, who, upon learning that the game was outside, replied, "My daddy won't let me play in the yard."

Later in the evening Sue snapped Jack.

"Where's the game?" he asked, and when she replied that

it was in the dining room, he drawled, "No, my daddy won't let me play Snap in the house."

At a crowded party, games may be going on in all sorts of out of the way places. I have played Snap sitting on the corral fence, on the wash bench, and on the rim of a cement watertank, and once, at a party on an old ranch, in the family graveyard. But the oddest game of Snap in which I ever played was on donkeys. Once at a party, my cousin hitched his donkey, Jennie, to one gate post, and my brother hitched Napoleon Boneparte, his Mexican burro, to the other. During the party some gay couple started a Snap game on the two animals. Instead of holding up by the gate, they got on the donkeys and took a ride while the person snapping and the person snapped waited for them. This game of taking a donkey ride instead of holding up continued until Jennie pitched the girl off in a grain field.

About 1932 a new type of Snap became common in Mills County. It was called "Swap-out," or "Car" Snap. It is played exactly like ordinary snap except that the players sit in a car instead of standing up in the yard. And instead of running around the car and catching each other, the players merely get in or out of the car. The advent of this fad caused a great deal of indignation among the older people. Many mothers thought that "Swap-out" was improper and refused to permit it at their parties. But time cures all things. Today Swap-out is the most common form of outdoor Snap in Mills County. A few enemies of Car Snap still exist, however, and their daughters are not allowed to play that form of the game.

In recent years the rural dance is becoming more popular and the Snap party is beginning to disintegrate. Play-party games are played in the house, and Snap is played outside at the same time, and the combination works very nicely. But not so with dancing. The crowd either snaps or dances. The two simply will not mix.

Snap parties in Mills County are still gay and colorful, but they are not what they used to be. In appearance they are about the same. Dress among the boys ranges from blue overalls and cowboy chaps and boots to tailor-made suits and lettered football sweaters. A sprinkling of John Tarleton and A. and M. uniforms appears at them during the Christmas holidays. Girls always dress up for a party, and to the casual observer they at first all look alike. But the colors and cut of their clothes and their hair styles mark the difference between the stay-at-homes and those who are at home only for the holidays or vacation.

The old spontaniety and unbridled gaiety are gone. The Saturday night parties break up early so that the participants can go to the midnight show. There is less laughter and more drinking. The games move slowly, couples segregating themselves more. Yet among the boys and girls there exists the same hearty degree of friendship, for they are all children of the same soil.

Christmasing with the Tarahumaras

By Robert M. Zingg

THE Tarahumaras are a tribe of some 40,000 Indians living in the Sierra Madre and occupying roughly the southern third of the State of Chihuahua, Mexico. Their culture, supporting as it does one of the largest tribal groups in North America, has been modified somewhat by the steel ax and knife, goats and cows, and certain outward forms of the Roman Catholic religion; but in essentials it remains virtually unmodified by White civilization. The Whites (Mexicans) by taking some of the richer valleys and forcing the Tarahumaras back farther into the highest and most broken areas of the rough and barranca-cut Sierra Madre of northern Mexico, have made perpetuation of indigenous Tarahumara culture inevitable.

It was among these people that Dr. W. C. Bennett and I went to live — as anthropologists, and also, perforce, as human beings. Carl Lumholtz, in his monumental work, *Unknown Mexico*,[1] left an enduring characterization of the Tarahumaras; but a more monographic treatment by Bennett and myself filled in the picture.[2]

Wednesday, December 10

Among the Tarahumaras, as elsewhere in Mexico, the Christmas season begins with the feast-day of the Virgin of Guadalupe, on December 12. The houses clustering around the church, most of which had been vacant, were already filling with people. Here and there smoke arising

---

[1]Lumholtz, Carl: *Unknown Mexico*, Vol. I, Charles Scribner's Sons, N. Y., 1902.
[2]Bennett, W. C., and Zingg, R. M.: *The Tarahumara*. The University of Chicago Press, 1935.

from a long-unused chimney announced a new arrival. Virtually all the people of the Indian community of Samachique were hastening toward the church, which is the center of the series of Catholic ceremonies always given during Christmas.

The celebrations terminate with the feast of Epiphany on January 6. But with this extraneous similarity all resemblance between the Mexican and Tarahumara festivities ends; for it is indeed in abysmal ignorance and grievous error that the Tarahumaritos celebrate the feast. They have held on tenaciously to their native ways. What they lack in knowledge of Christian customs, however, they make up for, both in the fervor of their religious feeling and in the jollity and drunken merriment that follow the sacred ceremonies.

Since the Tarahumaras have so little and such fragmentary native myth and belief, one would expect them, despite the great difficulties they present to missionaries working among them, to have learned more of the faith of the *padres*. They do not even know, for example, the name of Christ. For them Christ is Saint Joseph of Christ. He it was who was sent to earth (the sierra) to expunge the horrible conditions of cannibalism and the like which, they believe, prevailed among themselves in ancient days. As a matter of fact, the first priests in this region, such as Padre Ribas, tell of ceremonial cannibalism that accompanied the elaborate rites and fierce war customs of these Indian tribes. Be this as it may, the Tarahumaras of today think that their present social customs were inaugurated by Saint Joseph of Christ with the aid of Benito Juarez, the great leader and Indian reformer of Mexico some eighty years ago. The Huichols similarly mix up Mexican revolutionary leaders with the hierarchy of the Christian faith, Catholicism being foreign and confusing to them. This shows the close relationship existing between religion and the social order.

Most Mexican Indians, like the Mexicans themselves, believe that at one time in the distant past the mother of Christ appeared at the village of Guadalupe Hidalgo, just outside the city of Mexico. As proof of her visit she left a magic impression of her likeness on an Indian's cloak of maguey fibre. This cloak is still preserved as the most sacred relic in Mexico; and about this "Virgin de Guadalupe" has been built not only a great shrine and beautiful basilica, but also one of the most curious cults in the world. But two hundred and fifty years had first to pass, the cult grow to national proportions, and the Virgin of Guadalupe become the unquestionable "Queen of Mexico" before the Catholic Church at Rome recognized the miracle.

Today, despite anti-Catholic activity, the importance of the cult has not diminished. On December 12, Indians from all the accessible tribes of Mexico flock to Guadalupe to pray and to carry back to their tribes the sacred water of the spring nearby. *Mestizos,* as well as Indians, participate in the endless processions and observances that go on at this season. Indeed, in Mexican cities, even the upper-class Mexicans participate by dressing their children in typical Indian costume on this day in tribute to the great Indian Virgin of Mexico — as she may well be called, since in her pictures she always looks like an Indian, and she is always represented with dark brown skin.

But the Tarahumaras in their far-off mountains of Chihuahua are too far removed from Guadalupe ever to participate in this cult. They know nothing about the encounter of the Virgin with an Indian, although they celebrate the day with one of their most important ceremonies; and they are no wiser about the representation that still occupies the place of honor in the basilica — allegedly the actual cloak with the miraculous impression upon it. Of

Coyote Wisdom

course the cloak hangs so high, and has been placed behind such thick glass, that even those celebrants fortunate enough to get to Guadalupe have no chance to see it closely. However, this doesn't matter to the thousands of cultists, much less the Tarahumaras.

Among the Tarahumaras the preparations for the ceremony of Guadalupe are interesting, and more or less consistent with other tribal exercises. After a religious program of any scope and pretention, there must always be generous quantities of refreshments. Persons called *fiesteros* who are desirous of gaining social prestige volunteer, therefore, to sacrifice one of their precious cattle and much of their corn for the meat, *tortillas*, and beer with which the celebrants are regaled after the ceremony. Of such vulgar social climbing our informant, Lorenzo, despite his being *maestro*, or "master," of all these "Catholic" ceremonies, was contemptuous. In his youth he had used his wits and had learned the prayers, and thus now directed everything, sacrificing nothing save his time, which wasn't particularly valuable except when he utilized it in giving us information.

Nor would any of the rich old Philistines of this primitive community have considered sacrificing their stock so needlessly. Nothing less than their own deaths could have blasted them loose from their own prized cattle. Generally the donor of the ceremonial food and drink was some poor devil on the social fringes of the community seeking to improve his status. They got no material reward; yet their desires were always so strong that there was never any lack of volunteers for the honorary offices.

During the ceremonies of Guadalupe Day the *fiesteros* received their meed by being brought finally, though briefly, before the attention of the assembled Indians. These tribal benefactors were lined up inside the church in the presence of their friends and neighbors. Lorenzo, who was officiating, passed each of them a calabash of beer. They refrained from drinking until he had offered some of the potion to the gods of the four points.

After the *fiesteros* had thus accomplished their ambitions to be the first publicly to drink the beer, the ceremony became more complicated. Those who were relinquishing their positions as *fiesteros* folded their blankets for the new officials to kneel on, and lent them their rosaries, placing them about their necks. Then the retiring officials knelt behind their successors. The *maestro* took a lighted candle and singed the hair on the top of each new *fiestero's* head. He then gave a candle to each, and knelt before the altar to go through his meagre store of prayers.

How human these primitive people are, and what primitive human beings! In the great British Empire, but with a paraphernalia infinitely more elaborate, important social climbers are knighted in a somewhat similar ceremony as a reward for great financial or other "services to the Empire." The lesser fry have to be contented with a mere presentation at court.

In the few days preceding the ceremony the probationary *fiesteros* select from their own stock the cattle they intend to slaughter for the public benefit. When the bull-dogged animal has had its throat cut, the *fiestero* modestly announces this initial attestation of his generosity to the waiting community by touching off a giant fire-cracker.

Although this sacrifice of animals is not very exciting among the Tarahumaras, still it is definitely of a religious nature, and therefore pleasing to the gods. To the gods is offered the blood, which is carefuly saved and boiled; and small bowls of it are placed on a special altar set up in the dancing-court or "patio" with which each Tarahumara house is provided. After the gods have partaken of the spirit or essence of this offering, it is eaten by the people. The remainder of the sacrificial animal, including certain parts we would hardly think edible, is then devoured. Only the hoofs and horns are left unused.

At the ceremony we witnessed, the butchering was done so carefully that only the contents of the stomach and a few drops of blood remained. This careful slaughter was in marked contrast to the grisly slaughtering of a water-buffalo I once saw among the Ifugao head-hunters in far-away Luzon. There the animal was staked in an open place, and the warriors, charging it with their head-knives, hacked it to pieces alive. In these blood-curdling melées often the participants are themselves slashed in their wild hysteric scramble to secure portions of the sacrifice.

The women of the families of the *fiesteros* had been working for several days to prepare the corn for *tortillas* and beer. Late at night we visited one of the houses. There about a dozen women were squatting half-naked over their *metates*, their brown bodies copper-like from the light of a great, blazing fire. They had stripped themselves of their bodices in order to work without chafing their arms in their awkwardly-cut sleeve-holes. They worked happily and apparently tirelessly, laughing and joking as if the beer were already made instead of being in its first stages.

There is an exhilaration generated by communal activity or by groups of individuals each participating for the same end. Somewhat similar is the spirit brought into being by troops marching to the beat of drums and the rhythm of a band, by college rallies, by processions, and by the dancing in which primitive people take part. The movement of bodies in unison, of bodies shoulder to shoulder with others, so heightens the sense of this feeling that storm-troops, for example, will march unhaltingly with a song to certain death. Here in a little Tarahumara house, with its warmth and light contrasting with the cold and darkness outside, this same force of exhilaration was at work among the relatives and neighbors grinding corn on their *metates.* Their animation and jollity would never have been manifested otherwise, unless they were drunk.

Other preparations for the coming celebration included the annual washing of clothes. The Indians wished to look their best, or "happy," as they say. This activity was so general that it exhausted our scant stock of soap. Many of the women, however, used roots of yucca, which we call "soap-weed," fittingly enough. It makes an excellent lather. There is also an earth in the Tarahumara country which produces lather. The women washed the clothes by pounding them on rocks at the side of the river. This task seems to be theirs, though occasionally the men help.

The Indians also washed their hair, after which they began to delouse their heads — a sight that made me homesick for the Philippines. The most picturesque incident of our little village, for once filled to overflowing with Tarahumaras, concerned, however, the women's combing their husbands' hair with little, primitive, pine-cone combs. Each Indian's long hair was arranged in two long tails, often with a new ribbon braided into the ends. I have mentioned this before as one of the few evidences of affection exhibited by Tarahumara spouses.

Our contribution to the festivities to come was to consist of fire-rockets, which we had ordered a week or so in advance. We had planned on a cow, but on reflection decided that a pyrotechnic display would live longer in the memories of the Indians. The Indians were amazed by our generosity, and asked us again and again if the rockets would really be free, in fear, probably, that when they were shot off, we would try to collect for them. The Tarahumaras, like the Mexicans, are childishly elated when they can have fireworks with their religious observances. They were so enchanted with our proposal that they delayed their ceremony for several hours in order to await the arrival of the rockets. Outside of Mexico, it was only in

Coyote Wisdom

Texas that I ever saw Christmas celebrated with fireworks.

Friday, December 12
This was the great day of the Virgin of Guadalupe. The Indians postponed their ceremony until about five o'clock in the afternoon, when the rockets came. It was a welcome sight for all when our boy labored slowly into view with his heavily-laden mule. The load was a bit smashed up, as the mule had stumbled off the trail and rolled down a deep *arroyo*. Thank fortune it was not a *barranca*, for later we were to lose a mule in such a fall. The Indians were more than enthusiastic about the rockets; more pleasing to us, however, was a good supply of mail.

The ceremony got under way. About dusk the Indians began to flock to the church-yard in answer to the ringing of the bells by Lorenzo. The activities of Guadalupe Day were of two sorts. One was the procession of the women around the church-yard, following leaders who carried pictures of all the "santos" in the church, as well as small censers. Into these censers the women dropped abundant offerings of an incense made from some insect product. The censers looked like shaving-mugs, and were filled with the long-smouldering hot coals of oak fires. The Huichols use similar receptacles. This religious custom of offering incense was practised by the Indians of Mexico before the Spaniards visited the country. In those early days incense was obtained from numerous substances called *copal*, which is still used by Mexican priests in the Catholic ceremonies.

The men participate in the ceremonies of Guadalupe Day, as in other Catholic ceremonies, by their arduous dancing of the *matachines*. This dance is of mediaeval European folk origin, and, so I have read, was early danced in Italy.[3] It must have been introduced from Spain, whence

---

[3] The *Oxford English Dictionary*, however, derives *matachine*—a kind of sword-dancer in a fantastic dress—from the Arabic *mutawajjihin*, pres. pple. pl. of *tawajjaha*, to assume a mask, implying, therefore, an Arabian origin for this dance. *Ed.*

the Mexican Indians derived it. It is widely known in Mexico today, and danced by most tribes, one exception being the Huichols. During the era of the *conquistadores* it became quite prominent among many of the tribes of the American southwest. It is still practised by the Pueblo Indians; and a Jesuit padre has told me of having seen it danced by the Mescalero Apaches. In Texas, New Mexico and probably other states of the southwest Mexicans dance it.

So subdued and unimpressive are the other native dances, which we were to see later, that the complicated choreography of the *matachines*, accompanied by elaborate costuming and paraphernalia, acts as an important stimulus in Tarahumara festivities. The dance of the *matachines* is even performed, as pure swank, in certain ceremonies of death — as, for example, for rich men like Patricio.

The formation of this dance is a great deal like that of the *Virginia Reel*. Young men, who are especially honored by being regular dancers, dance to music of violins and guitars. The elders of the tribe remain quietly to one side of the dancers, and restrict their activities to shouting in unison, from time to time, during the hours that the dance continues. They are called *chapeónes*, from the Spanish word meaning the man who carries a cape in the amateur bull-fights of Spain. As one would expect, the Tarahumaras get their Spanish nomenclature all mixed up. These *chapeónes* of the Tarahumaras correspond to the *abuelos*, or "grandfathers," of some of the dances of the Pueblo Indians. One of them wears a mask on the back of his head — another instance of how poorly the Tarahumaras have assimilated certain aspects of Spanish culture.

The chief of the dancers is called the *monarco*. That the role of a "monarch" should be acted among the Tarahumaras is surprising; yet perhaps no more so than that elaborate costumes are worn for this dance by the Indians, who at other times are naked save for their clouts. The dancers wear the robes and crown of a king, a costume "gaily-colored and fancy." The robe is cape-like in design, and of bright red cloth. Trousers of a similar color are also worn. The crown is an outlandish contraption of tissue-paper, the wrappings in which cigarettes are packed, mirrors, and any other similarly glistening things that are available.

Each dancer carries in one hand a fan-like ornament decorated with paper flowers, and in the other a rattle, which is sounded as an accompaniment to the steps. The most surprising element of the entire costume, however, and one also showing a foreign provenience, is to be found in the use of shoes. Ordinarily these Indians walk bare-footed, or with their feet protected only by thin wrappings of goatskin; but for this dance they must have shoes, kept especially for this purpose.

It is a high honor indeed to be a dancer in the *matachines,* and one for which the young men vie. Many of the young men who achieve this honor are racers, and it is from this activity that they gain the endurance necessary for the long hours of dancing which they undergo. The honored elders of the community, the *chapeónes,* content themselves by shouting during the dance. Despite his poverty my friend Isidro was one of these official "shouters."

At 5:30 the dancing began. But to the Indians it was more than just the colorful spectacle it was to us; for in both their pagan and Christian ceremonies, they say that "to dance" is "to work." This "work" they will continue for hours, believing that their efforts will be construed favorably by the gods, who will then hardly deny their prayers for good health, long life, and bounteous crops.

Such is dancing at the primitive level. Our dancing in contrast is only half removed from this level, because we too participate, whereas a truly civilized people participates in nothing. A really civilized attitude toward dancing was once expressed by an old-fashioned Chinese who had visited America and was astounded to see the people dance. "You, in America, dance," he said. "In China, we hire people to dance for us."

But in America we hire specialists for almost everything else we wish done; and this is the civilized way to avoid participation. The primitive man, on the contrary, does everything for himself. Within his group there is no specialization, no classes, no diversification. Every man or every woman does everything within his respective realm. The vast cultural remove of the civilized from the primitive arises partially from the diversification of individuals into thousands of different specializations.

And although we Americans dance, we are somewhat civilized in this also, for we too hire virtuosos to dance for us. By specialization they develop their art to a plane far beyond the reach of the *Tarahumaritos*, whose dancing is essentially an exercise of propitiation of their gods. The last is the ultimate in participation; because it makes even the gods participate in the needs and cravings of the Indians. But we must return to the ceremonies of Guadalupe Day among the Tarahumaras.

About 7:30 our priceless rogue of a *maestro* suggested that it was dark enough to touch off some of the sky-rockets. Mexican sky-rockets are made from sections of reed tied on a stick. They are without fuses. Thus the trick in lighting them is first to get the end of a corn-cob glowing, and then to apply this substitute for punk to the end of the rocket, which is open. It is a dangerous method, for when the rocket leaves the hand, it spouts out a fiery trail of sparks. In addition to this peril, the Indians put their faces close to the rocket in order to blow on the glowing corn-cob. Why they don't lose their eyes

Coyote Wisdom

I can't imagine; for the rockets are poorly made. Sometimes they go down, instead of up; at other times they
shoot off sideways, and ricochet through the excited crowd.

But the Tarahumaras enjoyed it all; and the dogs, hating
the unaccustomed noise, showed their agitation and displeasure by barking and dashing around the church-yard
as recklessly as the sky-rockets; and with the entire scene
a perfect bedlam, the spectacle was a pronounced success.

When we had touched off about a dozen rockets the
women broke away from the crowd and went into the
church. They reappeared, carrying the picture of the Virgin of Guadalupe and pictures of two other "santos." They
marched around the cross set upright in the centre of the
church-yard. The men remained quietly to one side. The
musicians, with their violins and guitars, continued their
sacred minstrelsy.

After about half an hour of this, everyone filed into the
church for a prayer by Lorenzo. On this occasion of particular solemnity another man knelt and replied to the phrases
chanted by Lorenzo, as I had done when we were drunk
together. At one side knelt the woman who had had the
honor of carrying the picture of the Virgin of Guadalupe.
She was an official known as a *prioste* (a Spanish word
having an ecclesiastical significance, though very different
from our word priest, with which the reader may think
it associated) ; she had had a little training in singing. She
sang a few phrases of Catholic songs in what I thought was
a beautiful voice .

After the prayer the Indians grouped themselves around
the church door. The *gobernador* gave them the longest
sermon I had ever heard him make. Several times he must
have said "Am I right, or am I right?" for his congregation
retorted, after the manner of recitative, "You are right."

About ten o'clock the *matachines* began their dance. It
was to last all night with occasional intermissions for smok-

ing. One of my compensations for my having to study only the material culture of the tribe was that I was able to go to bed at a reasonable hour. Bennett, however, remained up all night, making a detailed account of this ceremony. He reported that at four-thirty the next morning food and beer were given to the singers, dancers, and officials, after a ceremonial offering to the four points.

Saturday, December 13

Throughout the morning everyone rested from the arduous ceremonies of the previous night. At noon the activities were continued. They began with another procession of the "santos" around the cross in the church-yard. The *matachines* then danced for about two hours. Then the festal scene passed to the houses of the *fiesteros*. With the dancers leading, everyone proceeded to these houses scattered through the "village," which had now become more important than a mere collection of huts.

At each of the houses of the *fiesteros* its court, or *patio*, had been cleared of the rubbish and weeds. In the centre was an altar, and, standing behind this, three large crosses roughly made of wood. On arriving at a house the *gobernador* and other officials made a ceremonial circuit around the altar. They crossed themselves at each of the cardinal points. Then the *gobernador* in a short speech thanked the *fiestero* for his hospitality. Later that night, when the celebrants returned to the houses for beer, these speeches were repeated. But this time they were made by minor officials, because by then the *gobernador* had passed out of the picture from his over-consumption of beer.

Everyone carried little earthen *ollas*, since stew, made from the slaughtered cattle, was to be served. The stew had been cooked without salt, but with this everyone had provided himself. *Tortillas* also were given out. Their number, corresponding to what the *fiestero* thought his guest's social status to be, varied from two to five. Bennett and I received two apiece. This warned us that we had dropped a little in the estimation of our hosts, a rebuff for which we were grateful, ungracious though it seemed. On reflection we decided that we should have fired off some rockets at each house. Even so, we did obtain a nice saucepanful of beef stew.

Toward evening everyone returned to the church. There the *matachines* again danced for a couple of hours. This terminated the sacred formalities of the ceremony, and led up to the beer-drinking orgy.

As before, a procession formed to follow the dancers to the houses of the *fiesteros*. Darkness had fallen over the sierra, and each had provided himself with a torch. It was a splendid spectacle. Two hundred Tarahumaras with flaring torches winding, in a long procession, over the hills that separated the houses of the *fiesteros* . . .

This time, and particularly as it was dark, Bennett and I did not fail the Indians. We shot off rockets at each house. The *matachines* danced. Generous quantities of beer were ladled out. Lorenzo got drunk at the first house and crawled in, along with several other drunken Indians. Inside, a riotous party was in progress. We watched from without with forlorn envy. Violin and guitar music was audible to us where we stood. Men and women were laughing, talking, dancing. But this was not for us, because we had to attend to those fire rockets. For this we had no recourse but to ape the Indians and put our faces close to the rockets to blow on the smouldering corncobs. Each of us thought, "Ah, the things I have done for science!"

The drinking and hilarity continued throughout the night. This made Bennett's second night on his feet, noble man. The *gobernador* succumbed to the effects of his beer fairly early; he dropped out at the second house, and we left him safely protected within. The number and vitality

of the dancers slowly diminished. At the last house only
four of the ten were still going through their sacred gyra-
tions. Four of the musicians remained, ludicrously sawing
at their violins and plucking their guitars. Behind us we
had left a mighty host of drunken Indians.

The night was cold and frosty. At each house the revel-
ers built fires with the pitch-pine torches they carried.
Soon every dancing-patio was dotted with dozens of little
blazing fires; and before these the men and women
squatted to absorb the heat. Even the dancers stopped
occasionally to warm their feet. The dogs, too, squatted
before the fires, as if in grave imitation of their masters.

Smaller each time by a few members, the procession
would form to go on to the next house. The remains of the
pitch-pine fires were picked up to serve as torches for the
continuation of the round. I shall never forget that long
queue of boisterous Indians following the *matachines*, who
continued dancing to the music of violins and guitars
even on the trail, while their way was lighted by the leaping flares of torches.

At the last house, at five-thirty in the morning, we sent
up our last rockets. As usual, we had to assure the *fiestero*
that we would not try to collect for them after the festivities were over. Since we had drunk very little beer, I felt
that this was the mere shank of the evening. Bennett, however, was tired from his vigil of the previous night.

The Indians were in various stages of happy, ebullient
intoxication. Some were dead drunk and had fallen to sleep
by the remains of their little fires. Others had been hauled
into the houses by those less drunk so that they wouldn't
freeze to death in the bitter cold. Some were violently sick.
I recall seeing one Tarahumara matron in very bad straits
retching repeatedly, while her husband looked on solicit-
ously, unable to do anything for her.

I was in no mood by this time for our cold *convento*

room, with its bloodless celibatarian and ecclesiastical associations. So I edged into the last house and found sitting-room among the Indians that jammed the place. I sat between two Tarahumara friends. Each would whisper confidentially to me at once. I would nod my head gravely, without, however, understanding a word uttered. Then I would whisper back at them, one at a time. They would gravely nod as I had done before. The scene was quite lively and animated. And I was a part of this primitive festivity. Indeed, I was so integrally a part of it that I could hardly crawl out of bed the next day. But that was a trifling forfeit.

The light of the roaring fire played throughout the room, revealing in bulking outline the forms of Indians in an interesting variety of postures. Here a wife watched over the recumbent body of her slumbering husband lest, in his drunken insensitivity, he might burn his feet in the fire. There a husband, his jealousy dulling the effects of the beer, crouched vigilantly beside his tipsy mate, as if afraid she might slip away from him in the hub-bub and join some waiting lover. At such brawls these little breaches of fidelity are not uncommon. I distinctly recall the hawk-like visage of one old fellow who scruitinized me alertly for fear I might offer attentions to his wife. Finally he keeled over and fell into a drunken sleep.

Even more vividly do I remember the dark, flashing eyes of a Tarahumara girl, who gazed haughtily at me from the door. In the inter-racial language of the eyes of youth they said, "No, I am not for you." And they seemed to really mean it— though I had no intentions of leaving my snug corner by the fire-place anyway. I had never seen her before, nor did I see her after; so I cannot imagine why I was made the recipient of such a brilliant but haughty glance which for an instant sparkled like a fire-opal in the lurid atmosphere.

Christmasing with the Tarahumaras

Others were still going strong. There was considerable laughter, for Tarahumaras surprisingly free and raucous. One woman got up and weaved through a slightly voluptuous dance for the special benefit of the violinist, for such men prove attractive figures to the belles of Samachique. He, however, paid no attention. Finally she gave him what she thought was a gentle, lover-like shove. But her efforts were too vigorous; her push sent him over on his back, and there he remained.

Happy Tarahumara nights, the drink, the warmth, the congeniality, the close contact with the Indians, the bright roaring fire casting a weird light on the equally weird scene! These occasions always gave me such a feeling of contentment and oneness with the Indians, that for once in my anthropological career I felt I was seeing what everyone in my profession should see — the real spirit of the people under observation. It was worth all the fantastic hardships, the isolation from accustomed life, family, friends, and the gnawing loneliness that work such as this entails.

Lumholtz, our predecessor among these Indians, knew primitive people well; and although he did not record all he knew, may have had similar experiences. He speaks of an "animal magnetism." From my own participation I experienced something that derived neither from actual contact with the lice-infested savages nor from the beer that I drank, straining it between my teeth before I gulped it down. It was a feeling of exhilaration and exaltation, similar to that felt by the Indians whenever they went out to hard, communal labor before a *tesgüinada*.

I had experienced the same feeling before, though in different situations of close social participation. As an undergraduate, I had had similar experiences at football rallies and the numerous, primitive displays that are staged during football games. Again, during the World War, particularly a time of exhilarating participation, I had had the same feeling while marching shoulder to shoulder with the men of my company in military reviews.

This feeling has passed from me since I have become partially civilized — its loss is one of the prices we pay for civilization. But when I go off to a primitive tribe, it returns to me, although with difficulty, because of my being insulated, as it were, by a vast difference in culture and custom.

Marihuana: A Story of Its Curse

By A. F. SCHARFF

I. "La Cucaracha" : Editorial Foreword

EVERYBODY—with the exception of a great many bodies — has been haunted by the words and music of "La Cucaracha," which Pancho Villa's men made their official anthem and which became one of the most popular musical compositions that Mexico ever transmitted to the United States. A *cucaracha* is, as many people know, a *cockroach*; but it is also a slang word for the *marihuanero*, the addict, or smoker, of marihuana — a drug that has come to be in America a problem nearly as serious as that of opium. There is little of the serious about "La Cucaracha," however, though the strains of its music are as alluring and into-the-blood running as the fumes of any opiate ever inhaled by either Oriental or Occidental.

As a prelude to the strange story involving marihuana that is to follow, it seems appropriate to give here the verses of "La Cucaracha," remembering that the "cockroach" of the song is a user of marihuana.[1]

La Cucaracha

La cucaracha, la cucaracha,	The cucaracha, the cucaracha,
Ya no puede caminar,	He can't travel any more,
Porque le falta, porque no tiene	Because he lacks, because he hasn't
Marihuana que fumar.	Marihuana for to smoke.

[1]The *versos* are endless. The first seven here printed are taken from a book little known but nevertheless easily.one of the half dozen best books that have been written in English about Mexico: *Bullets, Bottles and Gardenias*, by Timothy G. Turner, Southwest Press, Dallas, Texas, 1935, pp. 178-181. Mr. Turner says the song came originally from southern Mexico, where it was sung by the smokers of marihuana. He prints the tune. So does *Cancionero Mexicano*, edited and copyrighted by Frances Toor, Mexico, D. F., 1931, p. 33. Miss Toor's version contains four verses not given by Turner.

Coyote Wisdom

Un panadero fué a misa;
No encontrando que rezar,
Entonces le pidió a la Virgen pura
Marihuana pa' fumar.

A baker-man went to mass
But couldn't think what to pray
for;
So then he asked the Virgin pure
For marihuana for to smoke.

O, hermoso San José!
O, bonita Santa Ana!
Dale permiso a tu hijo
Que fume su marihuana.

Oh, handsome Saint Joseph!
Oh, Saint Anna so lovely,
Now give permission to your son
To smoke his marihuana.

De por allá abajo vengo
Cansado de caminar;
Me monté en un burro muerto
Y no me pudo tirar.

From down yonder I just came;
Tired from traveling along,
So I mounted a burro dead—
And he couldn't throw me off.

Tengo un amigo listo
Que está en el ayuntamiento
Y que tiene la exclusiva
Para un nuevo pavimento.

My friend's prepared for action,
He's fixed in the city council;
He's got exclusive concession
On a new paving job.

Una mujer fué la causa
De mi perdición primera,
Y también de la segunda,
Y también de la tercera.

A woman she was the cause
Of my downfall number one,
Also of my second perdition,
And also of number three.

De las barbas de Carranza
Voy hacer una toquilla,
Pa' ponerla en el sombrero
Del valiente Pancho Villa.

Out of Carranza's whiskers
I'm going to make a hatband
To put around the hat
Of valiant Pancho Villa.

Ya murió la cucaracha,
Ya la llevan a enterrar,
Entre cuatro zopilotes
Y un ratón de sacristán.

Now the cucaracha is dead
And they are taking her to the
grave,
Four buzzards for pall-bearers
And a bull rat for sacristan.

Necesito un automóvil
Para hacer la caminata
Al lugar donde mandó
A la Convención, Zapata.

I need an automobile
To make the journey
To the place where Zapata
Orders the convention.

Marihuana: A Story of Its Curse

Una cosa me da risa:	One thing sure makes me laugh:
Pancho Villa sin camisa;	Pancho Villa without a shirt.
Ya se van los Carranzistas	The Carranzistas pull out
Porque vienen los Villistas.	When the Villistas show up.
Para sarapes, Saltillo,	For sarapes, Saltillo;
Chihuahua para soldados;	Chihuahua for soldiers;
Para mujeres, Jalisco;	Jalisco for the woman, and
Para amar, toditos lados.	For loving, every old place.

II. *Mallihua*

Mazatlan, Sinaloa, Mexico,
April 18, 1938.

Yesterday one of the children of the *Sun* and the *Moon* spoke:

"Yes, my son, I am no longer young—I am old, very old, and I do not see too well. No, I am not of the low country; I belong in the high places. I was born among the rocks above Tenancingo — high, high up, near to the home of the Sun, my father. Yes, señor, to be sure I am Aztec —my fathers' fathers for many hundreds of years have sat here and looked into that canyon yonder, the canyon of Tonatico.

"The shadows creep slowly longer. Do you, too, feel the chill in the air?

"You remain sincerely interested, señor, in the history of my humble family? Or is your interest that of an idle person who approaches us with the slyness of one who wishes to purchase one or more of the articles our women make with their nimble hands? A sarape, perhaps, or a riata woven from the hair of the horse? The women have many things to sell to strangers, señor. We who were once the proud rulers of Tenochtitlan are now very poor, with only the rich memories and the glorious history of our forefathers left us.

Coyote Wisdom

"I am the *cacique* of this village. My father was also the *cacique*, and his father and his father's father before him were head men in their days. On back into the time of Popo were my noble fathers the heads of their families. We were once many, many souls, but not so now. I still wear the token of my rank — you will see it here, señor, this *chalchihuite* hanging about my neck. It was handed to me by my father when he returned to the Moon, many, many years ago! He received it from his father, and I will leave it to my oldest son when I join my fathers.

"The great and glorious Popo gave to my first father this token of rank, señor, gave it to him after a fierce battle with our hated enemies, the Tlaxcalans. For many seasons our tribes had been at war with those misbegotten creatures of the hot country.

"My first father was a very brave man, who, when all his older brothers had been killed, received from the great Popo this token which made him *Cacique of Tinaquis.*

"Many things did my father tell me when I was young that were told him by his father about our people.

"What did you ask, señor? Do my people know marihuana? They know it, yes, but it is forbidden. The gods have forbidden it. It means death — a horrible death — if not through madness, the ant hill. Did the señor ever see a person stripped naked, smeared with honey, and staked down near a bed of ants?

"No, señor, once in a great while one of our unruly young men becomes a victim of this unholy curse, but we remember the terrible destruction of our beautiful and good Queen, Ixtlatl, the happy wife of Popo! And it is the law that the spawn of the God of Mirthless Laughter be crushed into the ground whenever and wherever it is found.

"You do not know the beautiful and sad story of Popo and Ixtlatl, my good señor? Then if you will honor my humble *casa* with your elegance, I will retell to you what my father has told me. It grows cold outside now. The sun has gone westward from the cañon. It will be more comfortable inside, perhaps. Will you come?

"Sit there, señor, by the door where you can see the shadows. Those who have lived are happy again.

"My father said to me, and it was told to him by his father, that long, long years ago the great and *valiente* Popo was king of the Aztecs and much beloved by all the people. The people of the lake and the hills were all very happy when the great Popo fell in love with and married the beautiful Ixtlatl, whose family ruled the hills below Toluca. There was great joy and happiness for all the people when Ixtlatl came to live in the great palace on the Silver Blue Island in Lake Texcoco. All those in trouble and misery and sickness soon came to her and she helped them, and to her husband spoke kind words regarding some of them who were in trouble. Popo listened and, more often than not, did what the fair Queen Ixtlatl wished him to do. So Ixtlatl became as divine to my people and all worshipped her as one of the gods.

"Then came again the wars with the tribes of the *tierra caliente*, and our enemies, the Tlaxcalans, joined forces with them; and Popo went forth to battle with many, many Xiquipeles. He took with him my father's father's great grandsire and his seven brothers, and all the cousins and relations of each until an army of more than 100,000 brave men were at the great Popo's shoulder, seeking battle with the enemy.

"And thus it passed that in the State called Tlaxcala, not far from the village of Chignahuapan, our brave army under the daring Popo met the thousands who opposed him. For days they battled, one of my people against five of the enemy, until thousands upon thousands were dead

» 229 «

on both sides and the enemy remained without hope of victory.

"My father's father told him that at the moment when defeat was certain for the Tlaxcalans, a meeting of their *caciques* was called and a scheme was hatched. This terrible scheme was proposed by Chichimecatecle, the great, great grandsire of Xicotenga, of whom the Spaniards speak. Chichimecatecle had with him a bag of flowers. He called the flowers *mallihua*,[1] a weed that has been cursed by all the gods, but which grows straight and tall and flourishes over the face of the earth as does all the spawn of the wicked.

"Chichimecatecle, himself a miserable, diseased vermin to behold, stood up and spoke to the other *caciques*. Said he, 'I propose to steal into the city of Tenochtitlan and plead with the beautiful but foolish Queen Ixtlatl. I will tell her that we of the lowlands and of the hot countries desire peace, and wish to return to our homes. I will tell her that we fear to show our desires to her great master, the g-r-e-a-t and g-l-o-r-i-o-u-s General Popo, for fear he will pursue us and strike us down in our sleep, should we turn our faces toward our homes. I will humble myself! I will weep as do the women. The foolish queen will believe. She will order food and drink served to me. Then when the tea is mixed and ready, I will place in her cup some of the flowers from this bag. The curse of *mallihua* upon the House of Popo! The g-r-e-a-t General Popo will no longer

---

[1]Available records disclose that the word *marihuana* was derived by Spaniards early in the conquest of Mexico from an Indian word of similar sound. Francisco Fernandez de Castillo, writing to Ignacio Guzman in the sixteenth century, advised that during his campaign with Herman Cortez he had found a narcotic weed peculiar to New Spain. The Indians called the weed *mallihua* or *malihua*, which the Spaniards corrupted into *marihuana*.

The word *mallihuan* comes from the combination of the Aztec words *mallin* (which means prisoner), *hua* (which means property or substance), and the termination *ana* (which means to seize or take possession of). Therefore, it would seem that when the Indians called the weed *mallihuan*, or *malihuan*, they wished to impart the idea that the substance of the weed seized and took possession of and made a prisoner of the person using it.

war against us, for his gods will forsake him in his sorrow for his Queen.'

"Chichimecatecle's proposal was greeted by his scurvy *compadres* as a light in the darkness, and he was directed to depart on his mission before the rising of the next sun.

"With the wicked gods of his father guiding his footsteps, Chichimecatecle managed to evade the outer and the inner Aztec guards and came in a short time to the palace where Ixtlatl lived in prayer for the safe return of her beloved Popo. The guards at the palace gates did not recognize Chichimecatecle, and as their Queen received the sick and poor at all times, and it was her command that all such be brought forthwith into her presence, the guards, believing him to be an unfortunate subject of the Queen's from a distant land, brought him into her council chamber.

"The sly Chichimecatecle told his tale with the quick, double tongue of his natural father, and the poor Queen, believing that she saw an ending of the war that was keeping her beloved Popo away from her side, did as he said she would do. She believed him and she ordered food and drink served to the misshapen son of a dog. The food was of the best, and after it came the juices of all the berries that then grew, mixed with *miel de abejas*, fragrant honey gathered from the beautiful flowers that have always bloomed in our ancient mountains.

"Chichimecatecle, the sly one, spoke to Queen Ixtlatl in words of doubt. 'Will my glorious and good Queen seal her promise to me, her servant, with a cup of tea — tea made from the flowers of that rare plant known to no Aztec, and known only to those favored by the gods of my people?'

"The good Queen, not given to suspicion, wishing harm to no soul, living or dead, readily agreed. The tea urn of solid gold and cups of mother of pearl were fetched. Water from the garden spring was made to boil. Chichimecatecle placed a full potion of the accursed *mallihua* in the Queen's cup and bade her drink. At the same time he mixed for himself a brew much less potent.

"They both drained their cups and Chichimecatecle hastened his departure so as to be gone ere the effect of the *mallihua* was seen.

"The Queen retired to her chambers to paint a message to her beloved Popo, to tell him what had taken place in their palace that day, and to beg him to allow his enemies to return to their homes without further fighting and bloodshed.

"In the midst of her preparations the world crashed upon her beautiful head. Ten million demons sprang into her soul. She became at once a slavering, snapping beast, the like of which stalks the still night and feeds upon the rotting bodies of the dead.

"Alas, our beautiful Queen was no more. In her place was a stranger, a woman abandoned by all the gods except those of the regions of hell. This all could see. Messengers sprang swiftly to carry the terrible news to Popo. Fleet warriors dashed in pursuit to Chichimecatecle and took him prisoner before he could reach the safety of his own lands. His living heart was permitted to remain with his foul breast until he was brought before Popo, bound hand and foot like a mountain pig, strung on a pole.

"When the prisoner arrived before him, the horrified Popo had just been told by the messengers from his palace the story of his Queen. Popo asked no questions. The gods knew. He knew the creature before him had done that which no brave and honorable enemy would do.

"With fewer than few words, he ordered the beast staked upon the yellow mountain that then stood between the villages of Chignahuapan and Zacapoax, and that the mountain be set on fire. Soon the yellow mass was one searing

Marihuana: A Story of Its Curse

flame, reaching high into the blue heavens, sending its evil smell down to the sea so that all the Tlaxcalans and those of the *tierra caliente* might know forever and ever that Popo had avenged his Queen. Down through the ages, señor, the yellow mountain, now a deep, fiery pit, still burns the slimy soul of Chichimecatecle.

"With the firing of the yellow mountain well under way, Popo, his great and noble heart bursting with sorrow and anxiety for his Queen, handed the command of his army to his chieftains with orders to destroy the enemy. Then sorrowfully embracing his people, he bade them farewell and flew on wings of the hawk to Ixlatl. Never before or since has the journey from Chignahuapan to Tenochtitlan been made in such a short time. Popo slept not nor paused in his mad flight to reach his Queen. But he was too late. The horrible work of the *mallihua* was done, and our Queen was now mad, bereft of all the beauty of face and soul which the gods had given and which was now taken away. The great Popo was heart-broken, and hoping against hope, he picked his Queen up in his magnificent arms and carried her away into the mountains. When the night overtook him, he still walked on and on, hugging his Ixtlatl until at dawn he came to the top of a great mountain from whence he could see all the world. Here he laid his Queen. Soon she died, and the snow gently covered her. Popo, destitute in his grief, sat down near her to watch.

"There, señor, they are today. Look, you can see them — Ixtlaccihuatl and Popocateptl."[2]

---

[2] Ixtlaccihuatl and Popocatepetl are two extinct volcanoes near Mexico City. Upon the crest of Ixtlaccihuatl can be seen the form of a snow-draped sleeping woman. Beneath, there remains a burning pit of sulphur which is an interesting sight to behold.

Mexican Folk-Escapades and Tales

By MALNOR SHUMARD, JR.

THE Mexican people tell humorous stories as such. Sometimes religious strains are woven ironically into the humor, but among the *gente* — the common people — there will be found little conscious irony directed against anything sacred. A great many of us do not know what we ourselves believe; I would not undertake to say just how much Jesus believes of his own story about the four devils he saw on the Guadalupe River. He knows he had the experience, but there is a cast in the story not found in the sure belief in "The Sign of the Cross."

Here these Mexicans are in Texas by the hundred of thousands. Some of them are out of families that have lived in the land for more than a hundred years; others, almost pure Indian in blood, have but recently come from Mexico. Nearly all of them adapt themselves quickly to the changes of what is called progress; yet, without exception, all remain themselves. Always there will be the inevitable frijoles; the poorest man will never be without a hand-carved belt; and never among them will the stirring, romantic strains of La Golondrina be silenced.

I have written these tales down as they were told me by Mexicans living in Kendall County, Texas. Cruz and Jesus are real people; the stories are theirs.

The Four Devils of the Guadalupe

As a young man Jesus worked on my father's ranch. He had come from Mexico as a boy and had spent several years as a horse-breaker near Helotes, Texas. When the demand for horses lessened, he worked as a general ranch hand. Then as the section north of San Antonio became more thickly populated, he felt that the farm work required of him was too degrading, and once more he changed his profession. This time it was cedar chopping, out from the Guadalupe River.

In his rather varied career Jesus had left behind him a liberal quantity of knife scars and an enormous number of empty tequila bottles. Fiesta days were his only aim in life, but they were too few and far between. He had a way of settling the deficiency, however. So pleasing to him was the breath-taking passage of a pint of tequila down his throat that he needed only the price of a bottle to surround himself with all the glories of a three-day county fair. And, as you can imagine, it was his wife who suffered. She begged him to be temperate, but without result. Not being a tequila addict herself, she had no knowledge of that utopia in which he often strolled. But she was convinced that Jesus had to stop drinking so much, or — what amounted to the same thing — spending all his money on tequila.

Her problem was solved for her. One morning Jesus loaded his family into a rickety old buckboard and set out down the Guadalupe on a fishing trip. At noon their destination was reached, and he, with customary tactfulness, left the pitching of camp to his wife, and strolled down the river.

The hot sun beat down upon him as he walked. Birds twittered in the cedars, and an occasional turtle splashed into the water. A deer bounded off into the brush. All in all, the scene was quiet and beautiful, but Jesus was not concerned with the beauties of nature. A mile from camp he stopped before a large cedar and produced, from some hidden pocket, his bottle of tequila. He took a long drink, then paused with a happy benign smile to curse a large gray lizard that was sunning itself upon a rock before him. Once more he drank and reduced the contents of the bottle to the half way mark. He sat down suddenly and smiled to himself at the ease with which he had negotiated the difficult task of sitting down. The gray lizard was dancing a fandango. He drank the rest of the tequila and winked at the lizard.

Then a terrible thing happened. The lizard winked back at him and suddenly there appeared before Jesus the Devil himself. Tall and black, his tail waved cat-like behind him. His face was that of a true demon, while fire issued from his mouth and nostrils. The muscles of his body moved rhythmically as he approached Jesus and his claw-like hands were extended to seize his victim. Behind him appeared three smaller devils, all of the same character as the first.

Jesus fell upon his knees in terror. He prayed to the Virgin and all the Saints. He repented of all sins past and all to come and swore never to take a drink again. Then he fell asleep.

When he awoke the sun was setting. The gray lizard had disappeared, but the honeycomb rocks still spoke of the noonday heat. In a panic, Jesus rubbed his eyes, but the devils were gone. Then he fell upon his knees and thanked the Virgin for his deliverance.

Jesus returned to camp a changed man and it was many a moon before he looked again into the bottle.

The Sign of the Cross

In the spring of '34 we had a long rainy season. It rained for days and weeks with intermittent hail to emphasize the power of the storm. Cruz, the old Mexican woman, who worked in the kitchen, was visibly worried. She had been raised on the ranch and knew what such storms meant.

"Soon the fences will be washed out," she said.

"The Cibolo Creek fence is already gone," Jesus replied, "and the water is rising."

The wind outside roared in a dismal whine. Cruz said nothing for a moment. Then she rose quietly and went to the pantry. She returned with a sack of salt and made the sign of the cross in salt on the kitchen table.

"The rain will stop now," she said, "but we will have much dry weather."

Within the hour the rain had ceased. I laughed, "It was time for it to quit, anyway."

"No," Cruz replied, "the sign of the cross will stop the rain, but it must never be used except when a storm is dangerous. Even then there will be a drought afterwards. When I was a girl in Mexico we lived up in the mountains above Saltillo. Once there was a terrible storm. Many people were killed. Then an old man made the sign of the cross on the floor. He had nothing to use but salt. He lit a candle, one he had been saving to light for the soul of his wife, who had died. Then he prayed. He prayed as hard as the *padres* pray, and the storm ended. After that there was a terrible drought. It lasted for four years. We had to leave the mountains. The people in Saltillo were good to us, but many of our number never returned to their homes.

"That was when we came to Tejas," Cruz ended. "I was twelve years old."

I said no more to Cruz about the cross, but, if you will remember, we did have a drought in 1934.

The Nanny-Goat Treasure

One winter evening I found an old grave back in our pasture. It was marked by a small wooden cross, doubtless the resting place of some Mexican ranch hand. I was then about twelve years old, and, believing that I had made a real find, I bore the cross proudly home. On my arrival my ardor was quickly dampened by a terse command from my father. I was to take the cross back immediately and put it where I had found it. In spite of the cold mist and norther, Jesus announced he would accompany me. On the way we entered into a deep discussion of buried treasure. I was all for digging away that night, but Jesus was not so keen for it.

"I never heard," he said, "of but one treasure that was found. That was 'way back, when I was young. Then there were no banks, and you carried all your money with you. Bandits had an easy time in those days. They held up everything from the stage coach to a burro loaded with wood. If you were attacked, you hid your money. Most of the money was taken up, but some people did not live to find theirs.

"There was one old man who started out from San Antonio with a wagon train. He took his household belongings and his pets, one of which had been blessed by the priest. Somewhere near Elm Pass[1] they were set upon by Mexican outlaws. During the fight the old man was separated from the other wagons. He whipped his team into a run and by following a winding canyon managed to evade his pursuers for a long time. But the outlaws thought he had the money for the outfit; so they kept on following him. At last, when they overtook him, he raised his hands in fear and trembling.

"Spare her!" he cried. "Spare my treasure!"

The leader of the outlaws then dismounted and prepared to search the wagon. "Give us the treasure," he said, "and we won't harm you." Seeing that the old man was paralyzed with fear, the outlaw started for the wagon. Amid

[1] About twenty-five miles northwest of Boerne, near Bandera.

pleas and lamentations, he threw back the wagon-sheet. Out jumped an old milk goat. There was nothing else in the wagon.

"Is that all you have?" said the bandit in a rage. He drew his dagger and started for the old man. "I'll—"

"And is it not enough?" croaked the old man. "That is Niña, my pet, my treasure. She has been blessed by the *padre*."

"Madre de Dios!" retorted the bandit. "Let the old fool go."

The Stranger

Pedro was on old wizened Mexican. He was called "El Viejo," the Old One. No one remembered where he came from, but all knew him for his meanness. He had no friends and wanted none. Even the *padres* had long since ceased their efforts to bring him to church.

One day, at the beginning of Lent, he was working alone in his garden when an old man suddenly appeared.

"What are you planting, Pedro?" he asked.

"I am planting *piedras* (rocks)," replied El Viejo, angrily.

"PEDRO SAW ONLY ROCKS"

"It is well then," the old man replied. "As ye sow, so shall ye reap." Then he disappeared.

Pedro went on about his work grumbling at the intrusion. A few days later when everyone else was at church he returned to his garden to see if any sprouts had appeared. To his astonishment, in the rows where he had planted corn, there shone only the glittering surfaces of gray rocks. With mixed feelings of awe and fear, he threw the rocks from the garden. Several days later he returned to plant again. Once more the stranger appeared before him. It was Good Friday, the last day of Holy Week.

"Pedro," the stranger asked, "where are the others?"

"In church," El Viejo replied.

"And you?"

Then Pedro fell upon his knees, for he knew that the stranger was Christ. When he looked up to beg forgiveness, he was gone. Then he left his tools and went to join his people in prayer.

When he returned, his field was growing in lush green corn.

Cuerpo sin Alma
(Body without Soul)

By MILDRED COHEN

Felipe Paredes, Jr., a student in the School of Mines at El Paso, who related this tale to me, said his grandmother used to tell it in installments night after night in order to put him and his brother to sleep. He said he often wondered how Pedro when changed into an ant could still carry all the paraphernalia the animals had given him. Felipe is Americanized and speaks English fluently; his family, however, is one of the old aristocratic families of Mexico.

MANY years ago an evil trouble befell the usually happy people of a beautiful country in Mexico. The cause of this frightful state was a bad spirit named Cuerpo sin Alma, or Body without Soul. He took away young brides from their husbands on their wedding night, and that was the last anyone ever saw of the brides. So a bad time came to the land. Young people were afraid to marry because they knew Cuerpo sin Alma would seize the bride and disappear.

There was just one method of defeating the bad spirit, but as yet nobody had been able to break the evil spell. If the groom could stay awake until the dawn and not wink once, the spirit could not take the bride. But it is not possible for a person not to wink his eyes once; and in that short space of the wink the bride would disappear.

In the capital of the country lived a young man, Pedro, who was in love with a gracious senorita, Teresa. Pedro resolved that he was going to wed Teresa despite the bad spirit, Cuerpo sin Alma.

Coyote Wisdom

"*Ay*, Pedro, *mi hijo*, don't risk the perils of losing your Teresa," his mother said.

"*Sí*, Pedro, my son, listen to the little mother," urged the father.

Many others added their pleadings, but Pedro was undaunted by all that had gone before and said that he was not afraid.

"My Teresa, life of my life, has too good a heart to be taken from here or harmed by any evil genius," he said.

So matters went. Time passed and the arrangements for the wedding were being carried on.

Great was everyone's excitement the day of the wedding. All the people gathered around Pedro's house after the ceremony and eagerly awaited the dawn.

Inside a well-furnished room, Pedro looked at the beautiful Teresa in her wedding garments.

"Do not fear, loved one," he said; "I will never let you go from here."

"You are very brave and good," Teresa replied. "I hope you will be strong enough to keep me safe."

They continued talking the greater part of the night. Just before the first streaks of dawn arose, Pedro felt a fine grain of sand in his eyes. He determined not to wink, but this irritation became more pronounced. For one short second he winked his eyes to rid them of this foreign substance. When he looked up, Teresa was gone!

Wildly he looked around. No Teresa was anywhere in sight. Being a brave-hearted boy, Pedro resolved to go after his bride. He opened the windows and told the people assembled that Teresa was gone and he also told them of his plans to rescue her.

"I will catch this thief of brides and bring them all back in safety."

Pedro made himself ready for the journey. When he had completed his preparations, he bade his parents goodbye, and also comforted the tearful mother of Teresa. All the distance to the outskirts of the town Pedro was accompanied by prayers and good wishes of the populace.

Pedro left the farming land and walked through wild and desolate country which had not ever before been traveled by any of the townspeople. He walked through dense underbrush, rock-covered plains, and passed through slushy streams.

The next day as he was climbing a hill, sounds of growling and quarreling reached his ears. Looking down, Pedro saw a lion, an eagle, an antelope, and an ant arguing over the division of a deer they had murdered.

"Here comes a man," said the eagle; "let him divide it for us."

"I will be pleased to," responded Pedro, "if all of you will be satisfied."

"Oh, yes, señor, we will regard your decision," shouted the group.

Thereupon Pedro divided the meat in proportion to the size of the lion, the eagle, the antelope, and the ant. The four were well satisfied.

"You are a man of good soul," said the lion. "I should like to reward you for your good deed. Here is a claw. Should you ever need to be strong and powerful like me, just say, 'God and lion,' and you will be a lion. When you wish to become a man again, just say, 'God and man'."

Then the antelope spoke up. "For your kind deed I am also going to aid you. Here is a *peluche*, the tip part of my horn. Should it chance that you need to cover space quickly, just say, 'God and antelope,' and you will be an antelope. When you wish to become a man again, just say, 'God and man'."

Now the eagle handed Pedro a feather. "I am also going to help you, young man; to be a bird swift in flight and strong in battle, say, 'God and eagle,' and you will be an eagle. When you care to return to human state again, just say, 'God and man'."

"Don't forget, I'm grateful, too," said the ant, which had crawled up to Pedro's shoulder. "This leg will enable you to become tiny and unobserved. You can be an ant by saying, 'God and ant.' When you want to be yourself again, just say, 'God and man'."

"My dear friends," Pedro responded, "you are very kind. Please receive my thanks for your help. I will follow out your instructions. Now I must hurry on my way. *Adios, amigos,*" and Pedro turned to continue the ascent of the hill.

"*Adios* and good fortune," shouted his new friends.

Pedro continued his journey and wondered whether these gifts would really prove as helpful as they sounded. Soon he came to a jungle. He did not have to wait long for some proof of the power in the gifts. A tiger sprang at him.

With a prayer in his heart Pedro held up the lion claw, said, "God and lion," and at once he was a lion. With his superior strength he soon made an end of the tiger.

After he was safely away from the jungle, he said, "God and man," and became himself again. How Pedro rejoiced in his good fortune! To himself he thought, "Yes, it does pay to be good and kind with everybody, and also with animals who mean no harm."

During one part of his travels a vicious snake threatened him; thereupon he held up the eagle feather and said, "God and eagle." Upon becoming an eagle he killed the snake and ground it under his beak. He decided to remain in the shape of an eagle for a while, as he could thus cover the territory more quickly.

When night came, Pedro flew to a tree for safety. From that point he noticed a beautiful castle in the distance. Immediately his heart said to him that this was the home of the evil Cuerpo sin Alma.

Cuerpo sin Alma

He flew near the castle. Then he became an ant and crawled through the yard unobserved. He passed rows of guards, motionless, but with eyes gleaming wickedly on large swords of steel ready to cut down any creature who might think himself so bold as to pit his strength against Cuerpo sin Alma. He shivered as he thought how he would have been killed if he had attempted to come here as a man. He crawled up the steps of the castle, which shone like a diamond in the night.

Pedro, still in the form an ant, of course, passed through many rooms furnished in silver and in gold. In each room was a stolen bride, dressed in gorgeous raiment and adorned with diamonds, rubies, sapphires, and many other precious stones. However, no gems were brighter than the tears standing in the eyes of each bride as she grieved for her lost husband.

Pedro hurried on until he came to the last room, where to his great delight, he beheld his dear one. Teresa was garbed in a fine weave of cloud-like silk studded with rubies and emralds. On her head was a diadem of turquoise set in onyx. Her shapely arms and fingers were covered with well-hammered gold bracelets and rings of filigree. From beneath her gown peeped tiny feet encased in cloth of gold interwoven with topaz and amethyst. Despite all this finery, Teresa was sobbing her tender heart out.

"*Ay de mí,* I want my Pedro," she wept.

Pedro could not remain silent a moment longer. He said, "God and man," and there he was, well and safe, before the astonished eyes of Teresa.

"Why, it couldn't really be you," she joyfully said. "It must be a dream."

Pedro took her quickly in his arms and Teresa was happy that he was not an apparition.

"O my Pedro, you must take us all away. In the middle

of this castle is a tower where this demon lives; he treats us kindly, but he boasts that we can never depart because the wild beasts in the jungle will devour us, and, anyway, we don't know the way by ourselves. Besides, he has all those guards, yet they would be harmless if he were only dead."

"Teresa dear, you must find out where Cuerpo sin Alma keeps his power. Then I can do something," said Pedro.

"We know the secret, because he tells it to each bride he brings here, but there is an evil spell over us that we dare not tell anyone else the secret," sobbed Teresa.

"Do not weep, lovely one, for your Pedro is here. Just get this demon to tell you his secret again, and I'll hear it by being an ant on the floor near him. And another thing, don't tell any of the brides yet that I am here," answered Pedro.

Quickly the arrangements were made. Pedro became an ant again. Teresa and the other lovely brides flattered and admired Cuerpo sin Alma until he became quite boastful and gay.

"I can tell my power because it can never be reached," bragged Cuerpo sin Alma, dressed this day like a man. "In

"HE BECAME QUITE BOASTFUL AND GAY"

the middle of the stormy lake is a tiny island. There is a cave with a ferocious bear inside, the wildest of all bears; inside the bear is a rabbit that cannot be caught by human hands; inside the rabbit is a dove that flies the fastest of all birds; inside the dove is a white egg that contains my power and life. To capture that power the egg would have to be smashed against my forehead. Little chance there is of getting across the wild waves to the island, or even of getting past my guards at the palace. Ha! my power is safely guarded." And Cuerpo sin Alma laughed like ten demons.

"I will soon prove you wrong," vowed Pedro to himself.

As an ant, he crawled out into the great yard. Once outside the high walls, he turned into an eagle. With eagle eyes he noticed the tiny island in the middle of a lake whose waves were at least thirty feet high and were constantly tossing and churning. Pedro flew straight across the lake and landed on the island.

Suddenly frantic growls were heard and the great big bear threshed through the trees with his strong paws. Someone had disturbed his island and he was very angry.

Pedro spoke the magic words of "God and lion" and became a lion, the strongest of all animals. He was able to kill the bear. As he took the hide from the animal, a rabbit hopped out of the huge jaws.

Then Pedro uttered "God and antelope" and became the antelope, fleetest of all animals. He caught the rabbit after a wild run. He quickly stifled the rabbit and began to skin it. A black dove flew out of the dead animal's mouth.

Pedro changed himself back into the eagle, fastest and most powerful of all birds, and soon caught the dove. When he killed the dove, he carefully opened its body and removed the white egg.

Then Pedro was ready to leave the island. With the

egg firmly grasped in his beak, he flew back to the court-yard and right through the castle doors.

Safely inside the doors, Pedro became a man and hurried to the great tower. There he found the brides fluttering about excitedly. In the middle of the floor lay the demon, barely alive, in great agony.

Holding the egg over the demon's head, Pedro spoke in a loud and firm voice: "Cuerpo sin Alma, you will never again bring sorrow and grief to people, for I am going to kill you."

The demon, so strong when he was all-powerful, whimpered and begged for mercy.

Pedro spurned him with his foot, and with all his might and strength, he smashed the egg on the forehead of the demon, who quickly expired.

With the death of Cuerpo sin Alma, the evil spell was broken. All the brides called down upon Pedro the blessings of all the saints in the calendar.

After quiet was restored and order reigned once more, Pedro began to make plans for the return to their own land. First he went to the great treasure rooms and gathered the vast heaps of precious metals and jewels. He called the guards from the outside to carry the trunks laden with the valuables. Since the death of Cuerpo sin Alma, the guards obeyed faithfully the victor over their former master. As Pedro made a last survey through the castle, he found the map which gave easy directions for a safe and short way to his own country.

Finally the group were ready to leave. Pedro and Teresa walked together, arms linked. Then followed the guards with the treasures of Cuerpo sin Alma. Last came the brides, happily singing praises for their wonderful deliverance.

What a time of rejoicing, laughing, and singing began when Pedro led his procession into the city. Straight to the

Cuerpo sin Alma

capitol they marched, and there the many reunions took place. Bridegrooms and brides embraced each other, and there was so much confusion that nobody understood what anybody else said, but words were not necessary at that moment. With the great fortune each bride brought, all the couples were enabled to live comfortably and happily for all their lives.

Naturally, Pedro was the hero. How proud his parents were when they heard the cheers and shouts given for their son. He turned over the trunks of the demon's treasure for the use of the poor. He used the guards as defenders of the country, and their fame spread so rapidly that nobody attacked this country, which enjoyed peace and tranquility for a long time.

So everybody lived happily, thanks to the bravery and the goodness of Pedro.

(NOTE BY A. L. CAMPA)

Note on the tale of Cuerpo sin Alma: Many of the elements of the story are common enough in folk-tale tradition, but nowhere have I found a story exactly like the one related by Mildred Cohen. Maria Luz Morales has a translation from Grimm's collection entitled "La Dama y el León"[1] in which a young bride is seeking her enchanted husband. The moon, the sun, and the night wind provide her with similar magic objects that enable her to reach her goal, but that is the only point of resemblance.

On the Sonoran border there are two variants known respectively as "Malograda" and "Los Llanos de Berlín y las Cuevas de Quiquiriquí" that bear a close resemblance to *Cuerpo sin Alma*. Both stories are much longer and considerably more elaborate. Instead of the incident of the stolen bride they lead up to the killing of a giant in the following manner:

---

[1]Morales, Maria Luz, *Cuentos de Grimm*, Juventud, Barcelona, 1935.

Coyote Wisdom

A prince goes hunting one day and meets a coyote who promises him in exchange for his life to tell him where the beautiful Malograda and her two sisters bathe every afternoon. The prince consents and is led to the edge of a lake. Shortly afterwards three doves come flying and turn to princesses upon alighting on the shore. The prince takes the clothing of the youngest, Malograda, and does not return it until she promises to marry him.

The prince sets out to find "los llanos de Berlín y las Cuevas de Quiquiriquí," where the princesses live with a giant.

In the course of his travels this prince meets the sun, the moon, and the wind, who give him some information of the whereabouts of these famous *llanos*. He too meets the ant, the lion, the eagle and a greyhound instead of the antelope referred to in *Cuerpo sin Alma*. Upon arriving at the castle where the princess is to be married to the giant he makes himself disappear with a miraculous hat and takes counsel from Malograda, who asks the giant what makes him invulnerable. The case is identical from here on except that the prince becomes a shepherd in order to find out about a serpent that he is warned to avoid. In the end the prince kills the giant in the manner of Pedro.

The fact that all three stories are found in Mexico may be of some significance in establishing the origin of the tale. The coyote and the transformation of the prince into a shepherd are two additional characteristics that would support such a theory if we assume that the three tales are variants of a similar tale or from each other. In New Mexico I have found several variants under the name of "Las Tres Princesas" but the informant in each case came from Mexico or learned the story from someone coming from the southern republic. Frank Dobie informs me that he has heard the story both in Saltillo and in southern Texas.—A. L. Campa.]

Tales to Tell

The Miller and the Devil

By George C. Taylor

(A story for use by any political party against any other political party.)

The few folk-lore specialists whom I have consulted tell me they do not know the story of The Miller and the Devil. I am very sure no man, certainly not I, could make one up like this. It seems to me a fine example of folk accretion. After fifty years I remember it somewhat as follows as my uncle, Albert Rhett Taylor, of Columbia, South Carolina, told it to me, a bare-legged boy riding behind him on horseback down to the mill to grind corn, late one July afternoon.

ONCE there was a miller who could "toll 'em heavy" or "toll 'em light" as he ground corn for rich farmers, ordinary farmers, and farmers who made barely enough to eat. As he ground the corn, the miller always carried on a conversation with the devil, who stood behind his shoulder, as to whether or not he should play fair with his customers.

One day, a little before noon, there drove up to the mill a very rich farmer with fifty wagon loads of corn. The miller began to grind.

And as he ground, he turned his head over his shoulder and said, "Devil, he's rich. Must I toll him heavy or toll him light?"

And the devil said to the miller, "He probably got rich being hard on the poor. Toll him heavy."

And the miller tolled him heavy.

Coyote Wisdom

Early that afternoon came to the mill just an ordinary farmer with ten wagon loads of corn. And the miller put the corn into the mill and began to grind.

And as he ground, he turned to the devil and said, "This fellow is not poor, he is not rich. How must I toll him, heavy or light?"

And the devil said, "Oh, he'll get along all right. Certainly he will not starve. He is contented with his lot. He is healthy. He is happy. Toll him heavy."

So the miller tolled him heavy.

A little before sundown came to the mill another farmer. He had one sack of corn on his back, about a bushel perhaps. He was tired from walking a long way. He was hungry. And the miller put his corn into the mill and began to grind it.

And as he ground, he turned once more to the devil and said, "Devil, this fellow certainly is poor. He's tired. He's hungry. What must I do with him, toll him heavy or toll him light?

And the devil answered, "He's poor, damn him, keep him poor! Toll him heavy."

And the miller tolled him heavy.

The Poopampareno

By Julia Beazley

The story of the terrible and wonderful poopampareno I heard from the Reverend Mr. Werlein, rector of Eastwood Community Church in Houston, who told it at a children's story hour. As he told the story, with action finely suited, he gave the line, "Here Sambo! And Ringo!" a kind of "Old Black Joe" tune.

A man who was a great hunter got to thinking he could do without the faithful dogs that had always helped him. Their names were Sambo and Ringo, and one day he left them shut up behind a high picket fence and went off into the woods alone. Before he left, he put a pan of milk in the pen for the dogs, but they felt so bad about being left behind they didn't go near it for a long time. When they did try to drink the milk, they found that it had turned to blood.

Now, the hunter was walking boldly through the woods when suddenly he found himself face to face with the Poopampareno! There was only one place it could be hurt, and that was right under the chin. Anywhere else a bullet would bounce off from its skin like a rubber ball. So it's no wonder the hunter threw down his gun and ran for his life.

Just in time he reached a tall pine tree, the tallest in that section of the woods. He didn't stop climbing until he was at the tip-top. When he looked down, his blood ran cold. The Poopampareno's lips were drawn back from his terrible saw teeth and he was grinning at the hunter like this. (Register exultant malice.) Then he began to saw with his teeth. (Imitate sound of saw.) Through the bark he sawed, and into the wood. Then the hunter called to his dogs as loud as he could:

> Here, Sambo! And Ringo!
> Your master's almost gone!
> And a poo-pam and a poo,
> And a poo-pam and a po-o-o!

The dogs were far away. They thought they heard something but couldn't be sure. The milk in their bowl was blood. They feared their master was in danger. They looked at the high fence and wished they could jump over it.

When the hunter called, the Poopampareno looked up at the hunter and grinned like this. (Repeat exultant grin.) Then he began to saw harder than ever. (Repeat sawing sounds, turning head from side to side.) The tree began to tremble. Again the hunter called, louder than before:

H-e-r-e Sambo! A-n-d Ringo!
Your master's almost gone!
And a poo-pam and a poo,
And a poo-pam and a po-o-o!

This time the dogs barely heard him. They looked at the fence. It was too high to jump, and there was no hole anywhere. Far out in the woods the Poopampareno was taking his time, but the tree was now more than half cut through. It would soon fall. So the hunter called louder than ever:

H-e-r-e Sambo! A-n-d Ringo!
Your master's almost gone!
And a poo-pam and a poo,
And a poo-pam and a po-o-o!

This time the dogs heard their master plainly. They backed off as far as they could, and together they jumped. They cleared those high pickets by a scratch. Then neck and neck they raced into the woods. Just as the tree was about to fall, they tore up to the Poopampareno, and they had him by the throat before he could take his teeth out of the trunk.

Roy Bean as Coroner

By J. Marvin Hunter

This incident actually occurred in 1882, when the Galveston, Harrisburg and San Antonio, more generally known as the Southern Pacific railroad, was building west from San Antonio to El Paso. The building of that road in the exceedingly rough, canyon-cut country west of Del Rio called for great engineering skill. When the Pecos river was reached, it was spanned by a great cantilever bridge, 320 feet above the river bed. There were draws and canyons to cross, cuts and fills to make, and the construction of the road proved to be very expensive. A Philadelphia bridge company had the contract to put in all steel bridges, while another company erected the falseworks.

One day while the bridge carpenters were erecting the falsework for an iron span across a deep, rocky canyon, the structure fell. Seven men were killed outright, and three were injured fatally.

It was thirty miles over to Langtry, where Roy Bean was justice of the peace and saloon keeper. As the nearest coroner, he was summoned to hold an inquest. Mounted on a mule, he hastened to the scene of the accident. When he arrived, he found the seven dead men laid out side by side on the bottom of the canyon, and alongside the corpses lay the three injured men, so near to death that they were scarcely breathing.

Bean immediately selected a jury from the crew of workmen, and, calling them together, viewed the ten silent figures lying in the blistering sun of the hot afternoon. Then he proceeded to examine the bridge timbers, remarking on the size and length of the heavy beams.

Approaching the corpses once more, he examined each one, and remarked, "No doubt but that this man came to his death by them big timbers falling on him." When he came to the dying men, he made the same remark.

At this, one of the jurymen called Bean's attention to the fact that the last three men in the row were not dead.

Bean silenced him. "Say, you gander-eyed galoot," he said, "who's running this hyar inquest? Don't you see them three fellers is bound to die? Do you think I am damn fool enough to ride thirty miles on a sore-backed mule again to hold another inquest? Officially and legally them fellers is dead, and so I pronounce them dead, every mother's son of 'em, and you will accordingly render your verdict that they came to their deaths by them big bridge timbers a-falling on 'em."

The last of the injured men did not die for three days.

The Toe Wiggled

By Lynne Wooten Platter

Good story-tellers will surely inherit a part of that kingdom promised to blessed people. Among the story-tellers of the high plains no name stands higher than that of Judge J. C. Paul, of Amarillo. I wish I could reproduce his dramatic account of how he took his first bar examination under Temple Houston, who, like his father, Sam, has become a kind of folk character. Exemplifying a class of which there are many examples, this lawyer story of Judge Paul's has passed into the tradition of the Panhandle.

"Not guilty." The verdict of the jury rang out like a clap of thunder in the tense, sullen atmosphere of the stuffy courtroom. In the ensuing buzz and hum of the crowd that surged out towards the sun-baked open space that served as the courthouse square, one could catch here and there such remarks as: "Damn good speech of Lawyer Bickler"; "The jury was plum' wore out by that plea"; "Man alive, that sun-of-a-gun sure got off light." Zeke Traylor, the town wit and ne'er-do-well, drawled out his appraisal of the defending lawyer: "By heck, 'fore I plug a guy, I'm goin' to be sure Pinky Bickler will be my lawyer."

The five or six of us who made up the inner circle of Pinky's cronies singled him out from the throng of curious onlookers who were loitering around the railing that enclosed the tables and chairs below the jury's box. Pinky had gathered up his few papers and pads, and was stuffing them into the dingy leather pouch that served him as a brief-case.

"Here, Pinky, don't forget your bottle," and Abe Smith stuffed a small green bottle into Pinky's coat pocket.

Someone opened a side door at the back of the courtroom, and we hurried Pinky out into the glaring sunlight, across the side of the courthouse square, and over to the unpainted shack that served as Pinky's law-office, bedroom, and bar, as well as a sort of club-room for a few of us congenial and convivial souls—a kind of "lean-to" oasis in this West Texas desert of cactus and cattle, sunshine and sandstorms.

Pinky was feeling the effects of his two-hour speech to the jury. A choking gasp and wheezing cough warned us before he began to push us aside and stumble towards the cot. "Just one of his spells!" A hurried snatching of the bottle from his coat pocket, a few drops of chloroform sprinkled on his crumpled handkerchief, and Pinky fell back on the piled-up pillows that some one had thrust under his head.

We sat around and waited silently. For fifteen years we had watched Pinky in his spells. A law degree from the University of Virginia, a brilliant mind, a promising future in that Commonwealth that has furnished the law-givers of the nation—all had faded away before the attacks of spasmodic asthma that had driven him west, and farther west.

We could never quite figure him out. He was habitually taciturn, serious, non-committal, with a rather cynical smile on his "poker-face." At times he seemed to be about to give up and call off his part of the fight. Then, suddenly, he would come back with a show of the Irish in him. In his dry, precise way he would be old Dr. G— lecturing to aspiring law students, or an itinerant preacher harranguing a group on a street corner; then again, he would be Joseph Jefferson as Rip Van Winkle, or Booth as Hamlet. When he was in the mood for it, the fellow was a born actor. We never knew when he was in earnest or when he was having fun at our expense—putting something over on us who had never seen anything more dramatic than a round-up or a chuck wagon.

"Gentlemen, do you know how it feels to be a murderer?"

Pinky was sitting on the edge of the cot, looking at us with piercing eyes and tense features. We looked at each other searchingly, shook our heads, and waited.

"Well I do," said Pinky, in a choking whisper.

Now, at last, we were to hear the secret chapter in Pinky's life story. Not a soul stirred. We sat waiting for the dramatic disclosure. It was forthcoming in a tragic monotone.

"Do you remember when the Missus and I were living out in H— County? Well, we had a certain Gabe Miller working for us—a lousy, drunken rascal. We let him stay in the dugout under our one room. There was an outside door, and also stairsteps leading up to our room. One night, after we had gone to bed, we heard him come in drunk, kicking stuff around and making an awful clatter. I called to him to be quiet and go to bed, and he yelled back some oaths.

"He kept up the noise until I got sick of it; so I jumped out of bed, opened the door, and yelled down to him. Then he sailed a stick of wood at my head. That riled me. I grabbed up an iron poker and started down the steps—with Mary swinging on to me and telling me that he'd kill me if I went down there.

"Well, I got down the steps, and with one swing of the poker I knocked him cold.

"'My God, you've killed him,' Mary screamed.

"We picked him up and laid him on the bed, poured water on his head, rubbed his hands, called to him—but not a sign of life.

"'Mary,' I cried, 'I'm a murderer! I've killed him, I've

killed him! The world is better off without him, for he was a low, drunken brute, but he was one of God's creatures, and I've killed him in an angry fit. Yes, I've killed him!' I began to cry and wring my hands.

"By this time Mary had undressed him, and was rubbing his body to restore circulation. I knelt down too, and began to rub him.

" 'Get there, Mary, and rub his legs and feet while I rub his arms and chest. Rub hard Mary, and maybe he'll move a foot. Tell me, Mary, if he moves just one toe. Oh, if he'd just wiggle one toe! I'd give a section of land to see that one toe wiggle—I'd give two sections.'

"Mary stopped rubbing and looked at me in amazement.

" 'Two sections of land, that we've worked so hard to get! Why Pinky, he's not worth it. He'd probably die in jail, even if he had six sections!' and Mary began to cry.

" 'No matter, I know he's a worthless cuss, but I'd give six sections of land to see just one of his toes wiggle. Rub harder, Mary, rub harder! Don't you see just one of his toes wiggle?'

" 'Not a wiggle, Pinky!'

" 'Then rub harder,' and we rubbed harder.

" 'Rub harder, that toe must wiggle!' and we rubbed harder.

"And then, gentlemen"—

Pinky reached for the chloroform, poured some on his handkerchief, put it to his face, closed his eyes, and drew a long breath. We waited.

"And then, gentlemen—the toe wiggled!"

A True Story of Buried Gold

By Mrs. L. G. Smith

My great-grandfather, H. C. Routh, owned and lived on a ranch, identified by Tonkaway Springs, in Wise

Coyote Wisdom

County, Texas. His wife had died in 1855; his four sons had gone to the Civil War and then after the war the two survivors had left home. In the year 1870 or 1871 he was living alone, except for hired help, with his only daughter and youngest child, Mary Elizabeth. She was my grandmother, and I have heard her tell the story that follows many, many times.

One day, the housekeeper being absent, my great-grandfather Routh brought out from some hidden place several bags and poured the contents, gold coins, in a big dishpan. The coins mounded up in this pan like shelled corn, so grandmother said. Her father told her he wanted the bags mended. After she helped mend the bags, he told her he was going to bury the gold. Lawless men called bushwhackers were going about the country robbing people; under the reconstruction government, the native citizens had almost no legal protection.

Grandmother always remembered her father as saying: "I am going to bury the money between two trees on the bank of the creek just over that rise." And from the house he pointed out the rise to her. She knew the creek. One of the trees was supposed to be marked in some way, but I have forgotten how.

Some time passed after this episode, and then one day my great-grandfather told Mary Elizabeth he was going to Decatur, the county seat, to pay his taxes. She saw him ride over the hill towards the creek where he had told her he was burying the money. He was riding a very fine saddle mare that had a colt. This colt, however, was not allowed to follow the mare but was kept shut up in the horse lot. There was some sort of gathering in the country a few miles off, though nobody on the ranch had gone to it.

Along late in the afternoon grandmother and the people hired to keep house and keep the place up heard the mare nickering for her colt. There she was by the corral gate, trying to get in. The empty saddle on her back was splattered with blood. The housekeeper's husband mounted her and rushed to the place where he knew the country people were gathered. Among them were men who could follow tracks and cut for sign as well as any Comanche. They came to the ranch, took the mare's trail made that morning, and followed it until they came to a cross-road near Decatur.

Here they found the dead body of my great-grandfather. He had been shot from the mare. In his pockets were only his knife, tobacco and a little change. If he was carrying gold to pay taxes, the murderers took it. Who they were or why they killed him, whether for gold or out of hatred, was never determined. Until this day, so far as the descendants of Great-Grandfather Routh know, the gold has never been found. When a body remembers how it mounded up like shelled corn above the rim of that big dishpan, he can't help figuring how nice it would be to find it.

Paisano Tracks

He Belongs to The
Texas Folk-Lore Society

EDITORIAL NOTE.—Under this title has been initiated a department in which will be published items of folkish significance that are too brief for independent articles. This year the contributions run toward tall tales and folk cures. This results from the nature of the contributions and not from any preconceptions on the part of the editors, whose only requirements are that the items be brief and of the folk. Readers are invited to contribute. —M. C. B.

Hugo: The Giant Unkillable Bull Frog

By JIMMIE POUNDS III

HUGO, the king of all bull frogs, resides at Elberta Lake, a club lake situated in the woodlands seven miles south of Sulphur Springs, Texas. According to tradition, he has inhabited the lake since its construction some time in the late '90's. The old-timers say that Hugo will never be caught. They say his skin it too tough for a gig and that he is too clever for the many frog hunters who have attempted to catch him. Hugo learned his lesson when just a youngster. Somebody stuck a gig in him, but he managed to escape. Since that time, more than forty years ago, no one has touched Hugo with a gig.

Every night Hugo comes out and bellows defiance at the hunters by the hour. His voice is easily recognized, for he is by far the loudest bull frog that ever sang his song in East Texas. His booming has tolled many a man to the wilder part of the lake shore, a quarter of a mile directly across from the boathouse, in search of him. But no one has laid a gig on him since the first time. In fact, very few people have even caught a glimpse of this king of frogdom. People with powerful flashlights lie in wait for him, but he is too cunning to get in the light. As King of the frogs, Hugo lives and bellows alone. He has taught the other frogs in the lake their places; for, when he begins to chant, he is not bothered by competition. The other frogs, with no hope of outdoing him, occupy themselves in other ways. His voice is easily identified, and it is unforgettable. It has given Hugo a fame that will probably keep him alive long after he is dead.

Paul Bunyan: Oil Man

Miss Margarete Carpenter of Fort Worth takes issue with Mr. Brooks[1] and Mr. Garland[2] on one point concerning Paul Bunyan in the oil fields. She writes:

---

[1] John Lee Brooks, "Paul Bunyan: Oil Man," Texas Folklore Society Publications, VII (1928), pp. 45 ff.

[2] Acel Garland, "Pipeline Days with Paul Bunyan," *ibid.*, pp. 55 ff.

Coyote Wisdom

"The majority of Paul Bunyan's oil wells were drilled by digging a long ditch and shoving it into the ground. Also, one train load of post holes Paul shipped were exposed to a salt atmosphere and were so badly rusted as to be a dead loss when they arrived at the point of delivery. Since then he has been painting them and wrapping them in wax paper."

Windy Yesterdays

By SUE GATES

Once back in the days when hogs were hogs and ran wild, a sort of disease came through the country and blinded nearly all the hogs. That fall the acorn crop was good and the hogs got rolling fat. One old grandma sow, who could see, figured out a system for leading the hogs to water. She had them form in a line, each hog taking the tail of the hog in front of him. The first hog took hold of Grandma's tail, and she led the whole lot to water and to the places where the acorns were.

Now there was a young fellow living about who was just itching to steal a hog. One day he saw the old sow leading the string of hogs through the woods. He cut off her tail and held it in his hand. Well, the hogs followed him, and he led the whole bunch off and sold them for ten dollars apiece.

* * * *

A backwoodsman had a dog he claimed was the fastest runner alive. He could run for days and days and never get tired. Now, one day the dog was running and had to jump over a jagged stump. He didn't jump high enough and one jag ripped him clean in two from head to tail. His master came along, and when he found him, he just reached up and wiped a handful of turpentine tar from a nearby tree, rubbed the tar on the two dog halves, slapped them together, and the dog got well. The master was in such a hurry, though, that he did not notice that he had turned one-half of him upside down, the result being that the dog had two legs up in the air, no matter which way he stood. He could run longer than ever. He would run on one set of legs till he got tired and then he'd flip over and run on the other.

* * * *

"I ain't never seen much of this world," said an old-timer. "But I had some great times when I was younger. In them days I had the fastest horse in the country. I knowed I could outrun anything in that whole section. One time I was out scoutin' on a buffalo hunt and was takin' special notice of the country since it was new to me. To the right there was a sort of gully, and some piece down another gully forked into it. Suddenly I heard a noise. Looking around, I seen what I knowed must be a band of Comanche Indians headin' straight for me. But I didn't git scared, 'cause I knowed I had the best horse and could outrun any Indian.

"I picked up my speed, but they was a-gainin' on me. I looked up directly, and right there in front of me was a deep precipice where that other gully branched in formin' a V. I couldn't blame my horse, 'cause I still know he was the fastest horse in the country. So I got off and was tryin' to think of a way to escape from them Indians closin' down on me. Jest at the top of the hundred-foot precipice I noticed a spring of water all froze over. I seen there was icicles that ranged from big as a man's leg to the size of a barrel, and reached clean to the bottom. I locked my legs and arms around one and started slidin'. I slid so fast on that ice my britches caught fire. I was beatin' this fire when I heared a splash. I seen my pony had come down on that biggest icicle and had busted the water.

Coyote Wisdom

Sand Storm Yarns

Collected by HENRY W. BARTON

As Bill and I were working one hot afternoon, we saw a bank forming in the northwest. We could see a rolling cloud of dust below it, and we knew we were in for another "Panhandle rain." The wind caught us as we ran down the turn-row. Before the sun was shut out, we saw the birds were flying backwards to keep the sand out of their eyes. We also noticed a little flurry in the dirt, and there was a prairie dog, digging straight up, trying to get a breath of air.

We got to the house just before the storm settled down to real business. We ran in at the nearest door and managed to slam it shut, but the sand began to pour through the key hole like shelled corn out of a feed bin. Bill's wife brought her pots, and in the blast got them clean for the first time since they were new. The sand came in faster than we could shovel it out; and on the second day when the sand gave out and the wind started whipping gravel too big for the hole, we just barely had room to stand in the back door and swing our scoops.

We rested until middle afternoon, when the wind died down just before the gravel ran short and the rocks started flying. We went out to stretch our legs a bit and found the old rain barrel chuck full of sand. The barrel had been empty so long that both ends and the bung had fallen out, but the wind had blown dirt in at the bung hole faster than it could run out both ends. The sand blast had worn it down to the size of a pickle keg.

A neighbor came by on a dead run with his combine. I asked him where he was going so fast. He said he'd planted wheat and he was going to harvest it if he had to chase it to the Gulf. We had planted our north section in oats, but we found it covered with barley. During the week we located our oats five miles to the south, but we never did find out who the owner of the barley was.

Old-Time Remedies from Madison County

By Gabe Lewis

My grandmother recalls the following home remedies, current in Madison County fifty years ago.

For stomach-ache. Chew liveoak leaves.

For night-sweats. Place a pan of water under the bed.

For crick in the neck. Rub your neck against a post that hogs have rubbed against.

For infant colic. (1) Give nicotine from pipe stem in breast milk. (2) Give poke root tea in whisky. (3) Split an onion, put sugar in it, and roast; give the juice.

For sore throat. Wrap around the neck a stocking or sock that has been worn and is still damp with perspiration. Leave on all night.

To prevent lock-jaw. Place brown sugar on a shovel of coals; smoke the wound well with this; and then apply a poultice of turpentine and brown sugar.

To settle stomach. Give broth made from the lining of a chicken gizzard.

For caked breast. Apply hot molasses and cover with a flannel rag.

To remove splinters. Poultice with fat bacon or flax-seed meal.

To prevent rheumatism. Carry a buckeye in your pocket.

To prevent asthma. Wear amber beads.

For croup. Give ten drops of coal oil on a teaspoon of sugar.

For colds. (1) Give equal parts of hot vinegar and water, to which has been added sugar and butter to taste.

Coyote Wisdom

(2) Place on the chest a flannel rag soaked in equal parts of coal oil and turpentine.

To make a spring tonic. Boil the roots of queen's delight in water. Mix this tea with whiskey and take three big doses a day.

Home Remedies from Scurry County

By Leon Guinn

To stop hogs from eating chickens, put a horseshoe in the fire.

Some ranchers recommend for flu a quart of whisky and a dozen lemons. Throw the lemons at a fence post and drink the whisky.

Inhaling smoke from pine knots (taken from lumber) is one method of treating croup. A similar result is obtained by heating turpentine in a spoon and inhaling the fumes.

Warts are sometimes removed by the "Bible cure." One goes to a recognized curer, who recites a certain verse of scripture. The patient must keep the verse secret from members of his own sex, or the cure will not be effective.

Another way to remove a wart is to tie a horse-hair around it tightly without cutting the hair. The wart should disappear in a few days.

Other home remedies include chewing mesquite bark for cholic, taking hoarhound and honey for a cold, and watermelon seed for "kidney trouble." An ointment for wounds was sometimes made of gunpowder, lard, and eggs.

Note on Frontier Journalism

By Leon Guinn

Dick Lively, an Irishman, established a newspaper, which he called *The Coming West*, in Snyder, Scurry County,

Paisano Tracks

September 1, 1887. A rival boasted editorially of the productivity of Nolan County soil. Lively replied, saying:

That neighbor county's corn was nothing; a farmer in the Camp Spring community in Scurry County had raised a stalk of corn so high he was unable to count the number of ears upon it. His eldest son was sent up the stalk to ascertain the amount of corn. The stalk grew so fast that . . . the boy disappeared heavenward, the last report being that the boy had already thrown down three bushels of cobs and shucks.

An English Source of "The Trail to Mexico"

By J. W. HENDREN

IN an earlier volume of the Texas Folk-Lore Society's publications, Mr. Dobie has shown that the familiar cowboy song "Oh Bury Me Not on the Lone Prairie" derives from an old song "The Ocean Burial," first printed in 1850.[1] Not long ago I made a similar find while leafing through John A. Lomax's collection of cowboy songs.

---

[1] See "Ballads and Songs of the Frontier Folk," Vol. VI (1927), 121-183.

An English Source of "The Trail to Mexico"

"The Trail to Mexico,"[2] a very well known frontier ballad, is really an English folk-song in cowboy dress, having unmistakably been developed by traditional processes from the old ballad "Early, Early in the Spring." It is, in other words, a variant of that ballad. Resemblances in story and phrasing are too remarkably close and consistent to admit any doubt of the relationship. The reader may judge for himself from the two songs, which I am setting down below for side-by-side comparison. The cowboy composers who refashioned the English original have completely shifted the setting, omitted the girl's suicide[3], and added freely of local color and incident, but they have not changed the fundamental situation and story. Parallel phrasing in the two songs is of particular interest. Compare stanzas 2, 9, 10, and 14 of "The Trail" with stanzas 1, 2, 3, 4, and 8 of "Early, Early." The two texts, considered together with all their similarities and local differences, demonstrate once more what can happen to a product of folk tradition when transplanted into a new and wholly alien environment.

Of course, no general conclusions can be drawn from two such examples; nevertheless there may be some significance in the simple fact that two songs as famous in Western tradition as "The Trail" and "Oh Bury Me Not" should both derive from known originals, one of them British. It is at least possible that the songs represent, in their manner of development, what has been not an exceptional but a fairly common process. The examples we have may be the beginning of a growing list of similar discoveries, although it is well known that many cowboy songs are indigenous. The two examples cited at least make it clear that the tradition of cowboy singing has been by no means an isolated growth, but is linked to some extent

[2]See John A. Lomax, *Cowboy Songs and Other Frontier Ballads*, 132-135.
[3]Other American variants have done the same. See footnote 5.

Coyote Wisdom

with the older tradition of folk-singing brought over by the settlers from the British Isles, and carried in their memories to all parts of the American continent.

The Trail to Mexico

Lomax does not give the music to the song, but Carl Sandburg, in *The American Songbag*, does, having found it in Fort Worth. The song, he says, "is a cow trail classic. . . . 'Get the hang of the tune and all the lines are easy to pucker in'." In order that tunes as well as words may be compared, the tune recorded by Sandburg is here reproduced, (A). Following it is a tune (B) supplied by Frank Dobie, who heard his brother sing the song "maybe thirty years ago, down in Live Oak County." The verses that follow these tunes are those found in Lomax's *Cowboy Songs*. *Cowboy Lore*, by Jules Verne Allen, contains a shorter variant of the song, with music, also variant.[4]

It was in the mer-ry month of May When I started for Tex-as for a-way I left my darling girl be-hind, she said her heart was only mine

(1) I made up my mind to change my way
    And quit my crowd that was so gay,
    To leave my native home for a while
    And to travel west for many a mile.
    Whoo-a-whoo-a-whoo-a-whoo.

(2) 'Twas all in the merry month of May
    When I started for Texas far away,
    I left my darling girl behind,—
    She said her heart was only mine.
    Whoo-a-whoo-a-whoo-a-whoo.

---

[4] Allen, Jules Verne, *Cowboy Lore*, Naylor Printing Company, San Antonio, Texas, 1933, pp. 72-73.

An English Source of "The Trail to Mexico"

I made up my mi-n-d I'd change my way and
leave old Tex- is while she-uz gay I'd
tra-vel west for ma-n-y a mile and
live out there 'till the day I die

(3) Oh, it was when I embraced her in my arms
I thought she had ten thousand charms;
Her caresses were soft, her kisses were sweet,
Saying, "We will get married next time we meet."
Whoo-a-whoo-a-whoo-a-whoo.

(4) It was in the year of eighty-three
That A. J. Stinson hired me.
He says, "Young fellow, I want you to go
And drive this herd to Mexico."
Whoo-a-whoo-a-whoo-a-whoo.

(5) The first horse they gave me was an old black
With two big set-fasts on his back;
I padded him with gunny-sacks and my bedding all;
He went up, then down, and I got a fall.
Whoo-a-whoo-a-whoo-a-whoo.

(6) The next they gave me was an old gray,
I'll remember him till my dying day.
And if I had to swear to the fact,
I believe he was worse off than the black.
Whoo-a-whoo-a-whoo-a-whoo.

Coyote Wisdom

(7) Oh, it was early in the year
  When I went on trail to drive the steer.
  I stood my guard through sleet and snow
  While on the trail to Mexico.
  Whoo-a-whoo-a-whoo-a-whoo.

(8) Oh, it was a long and lonesome go
  As our herd rolled on to Mexico;
  With laughter light and the cowboy's song
  To Mexico we rolled along.
  Whoo-a-whoo-a-whoo-a-whoo.

(9) When I arrived in Mexico
  I wanted to see my love but could not go;
  So I wrote a letter, a letter to my dear,
  But not a word from her could I hear.
  Whoo-a-whoo-a-whoo-a-whoo.

(10) When I arrived at the once loved home
  I called for the darling of my own;
  They said she had married a richer life,
  Therefore, wild cowboy, seek another wife.
  Whoo-a-whoo-a-whoo-a-whoo.

(11) Oh, the girl she is married I do adore,
  And I cannot stay at home any more;
  I'll cut my way to a foreign land
  Or I'll go back west to my cowboy band.
  Whoo-a-whoo-a-whoo-a-whoo.

(12) I'll go back to the Western land,
  I'll hunt up my old cowboy band—
  Where the girls are few and the boys are true
  And a false-hearted love I never knew.
  Whoo-a-whoo-a-whoo-a-whoo.

(13) "O Buddie, O Buddie, please stay at home,
  Don't be forever on the roam.
  There is many a girl more true than I,
  So pray don't go where the bullets fly."
  Whoo-a-whoo-a-whoo-a-whoo.

An English Source of "The Trail to Mexico"

(14) I'll curse your gold and your silver too,
   God pity a girl that won't prove true;
   I'll travel West where bullets fly,
   I'll stay on the trail till the day I die."
   Whoo-a-whoo-a-whoo-a-whoo.

Early, Early in the Spring

And here is the text and music of one variation of "Early, Early in the Spring":

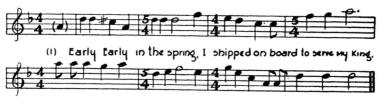

(1) Early Early in the spring, I shipped on board to serve my King.
Leaving my dear-est dear be-hind, Who oft-times told me her heart was mine.

(2) In writing letters to my dear
   And not one word from her could hear,
   Until I came to her father's hall,
   So loud did knock, so loud did call.

(3) My daughter is married, I suppose you know,
   My daughter is married long time ago;
   My daughter is married in the bloom of life,
   So young man seek another wife.

(4) Cursed be your gold and silver too,
   And curse the girl that won't prove true,
   And curse the girl that will forsake
   Her true love and marry for riches' sake.

(5) Turn back, turn back, my dearest one,
   If you've sent letters, I've had none;
   So come, don't blame the female kind,
   For it was Father's fault, it was not mine.

(6) Her father came home late in the night
And inquired for his daughter bright.
He went upstairs and the door he broke,
And found her hanging by a rope.

(7) He took his knife and he cut her down,
And in her bosom this note he found;
And in this note it was wrote down,
To a sailor's life her heart was bound.

(8) Cruel misfortunes around me frown,
I'll sail the seas all round and round;
I'll sail the seas until I die,
And watch the waves roll mountain high.

The above variant of "Early, Early" was sung to me in August of 1930 by Mr. Seth G. Stockbridge, of Swan's Island, Maine. Since it has not, so far as I know, been published in any collection, some remarks concerning it should be made here. This is one of the few traditional English ballads which somehow escaped Professor Child's vigilant search. Although variants have been collected within recent years both in Great Britain and in the United States, they are not numerous and, for the most part, not well preserved.[5]

[5]*Some notes on the variants:* I have not been able to make an exhaustive inspection of existing printed versions of the ballad, but the following comments will illustrate in a general way the present status of the song as it has fallen into the hands of collectors.

Of the four texts collected by Cecil Sharp in North Carolina (O. D. Campbell and C. J. Sharp, *English Folk-Songs from the Southern Appalachians,* 1917 edition, 232-234), two are mere fragments. In the other two the suicide incident is omitted, and the poetry is comparatively poor. Of the four tunes printed, none has the slightest resemblance to the melody scored above. All are phrased in a 3/2 time pattern which is a stock traditional formula in Southeastern United States.

Professor Cox has published (without music) three texts collected in West Virginia (J. H. Cox, *Folk-Songs of the South,* 358-361). Each of these ends in the daughter's announcement of her intention to drown herself. In two of them the lover, at the outset, is "pressed" on board to serve his king. These texts are relatively full and of good poetic quality.

The Somerset variant printed by Sharp and Marson (C. J. Sharp and C. L. Marson, *Folk-Songs from Somerset,* No. 70, Third Series, p. 44) is interesting (though the text is fragmentary) in that the melody (in the Dorian mode) shows a faint resemblance, especially in the concluding phrase, to the tune from Swan's Island. (In this connection it might be remarked that *close* melodic relationships between

An English Source of "The Trail to Mexico"

The one here given, considering the quality of both text and melody, is possibly the best so far committed to writing in this country. The singer admitted he had forgotten some of the stanzas; consequently, what we have does not represent the old ballad at its fullest; but the key situations are so retained that the essential story unfolds in the sharpest dramatic manner.

The melody, it will be seen, is cast in the Aeolian modal scale. The musical character of tunes so cast is generally melancholy, and often this quality is so haunting and palpable (as it is in the song above) that the singers themselves are keenly aware of it. Irregular time within the melody is a commonplace of English and American folk-song, though in this tune it assumes a rather curious alternating pattern.

Alternating rime is the general rule among English ballads, so that the couplet arrangement (aabb) of the rimes in this one must be regarded as unusual. This scheme, however, is standard among all the variants I have examined. It is perhaps noteworthy that the text is composed in the Long Meter stanza: a quatrain of four-stress lines. The fact

---

ballads recorded in this country and those recorded in Great Britain can sometimes be found, but they are rare).

Kidson once published, with music, a Lincolnshire variant in the *Journal of the Folk-Song Society* (Frank Kidson, *Journal of the Folk-Song Society*, II, 293-294). Here the story begins with the daughter in search of her lover on the high seas. Finally believing him drowned, she returns home to hang herself, though the father is not implicated in the situation.

In Belden's variant from Missouri (H. M. Belden, *Archiv fur das Studium der neueren Sprachen*, CXX, 69) there is no mention of suicide; at the conclusion of events the jilted lover leaves Scotland for America.

Recording the song under the title of "Early in the Spring," John Harrington Cox, *Folk-Songs of the South* (Harvard University Press, 1925, 358-361) gives three versions of it, besides noting a fourth. Each of his three versions contains a stanza, not given by my informant, adapted from "A Brisk Young Sailor."

The ballad was printed as early as 1869 in Logan's collection (W. H. Logan, *Pedlar's Pack of Ballads*, 29). Logan's text, evidently derived from a broadside, contains a possible historical reference to a naval event of the year 1740. While it is, of course, possible that this ballad was originally launched as a broadside, it has been in oral circulation for so many generations that its present claim to authenticity as a traditional product is beyond any question.

Coyote Wisdom

that this stanza pattern is extremely common in traditional balladry is recognized by few students of the subject.

Another fresh version of "Early, Early" was recently contributed to me by Mr. D. D. Kent, of Houston. Words and music follow:

For seven long years I sailed on the sea writing every op - por - tuni - ty; writing letters to my dear, but nothing from her could I hear.

> I rode up to her father's hall
> And for my true love loudly called;
> Her father came out and he replied,
> My daughter is married, and you denied.
>
> Your daughter is married; if that be true,
> I feel my sorrow much greater than you.
> I'll go to the sea and sail till I die,
> I'll seek those decks where the bullets fly.
>
> Oh Willie! Oh Willie! don't go to the sea;
> There are more pretty girls in town than me,
> With gold and silver, bright and fair;
> Oh! go no more where the bullets are.
>
> Curst be their gold and their silver too,
> And all pretty girls that don't prove true;
> I'll go to the sea and sail till I die,
> I'll seek those decks where the bullets fly.

This should, of course, be reckoned a Texas variant, though the singer's father, from whom he learned the ballad, was a native of Mississippi. It is becoming clear that this ballad has much wider currency in the United States than has hitherto appeared from the published collections. The text remembered by Mr. Kent is obviously fragmen-

An English Source of "The Trail to Mexico"

tary, but in this condition it serves to illustrate again the strong tendency of ballads in process of deterioration to hold fast to the stanzas revealing the central situation of the story. Those familiar with the characteristic tune of "Oh, Bury Me Not on the Lone Prairie" will doubtless agree with me that the pleasing melody of Mr. Kent's song is probably related somehow to it. The rhythmic pattern especially suggests a connection. The Texas variant, like the one from Maine, is cast in the Aeolian scale.

"There Were Three (Two) Crows"

In *Folk-Songs of the South*, collected and edited by John H. Cox (Harvard University Press, Cambridge, Mass., 1925, pages 31-32) may be found an extended history of this ancient English ballad known variously as "Twa Corbies," "The Two Crows," "The Three Crows," and "The Three Ravens." Cox regards the version now to follow, once sung on the stage and then adopted as a college song, as an American comic form of the tragic original.

I. *By* SAMUEL E. ASBURY

UNTIL recently I had never thought of this centuries-old ballad as anything else than a trick song to make people, when the raucous crow's cawing in it is reached, almost jump out of their skins. I don't know when or

"There Were Three (Two) Crows"

where I learned it—probably in my old North Carolina home. I have been singing it for forty years anyhow, startling in an unholy manner listeners not familiar with it, and giving a thrill to those familiar. The music bears a relation to the Civil War tune of "When Johnny Comes Marching Home." I sing it in minor, but I can't make out what the time is that I sing in. The 6/8 time of "When Johnny Comes Marching Home" is certainly not it.

Again we see how impossible it is for the printed page or merely a printed score to convey the tone, the flavor, the spirit, the personality of a song or story that is of the folk. No amount of explanation or musical notation will tell a person who has never heard my version of "There Were Three Crows" how to startle and astound his audience when he comes to the "Aouw! Aouw! Aouw!"—my attempt at spelling the crow's "caw."

There were three crows sat on a tree,
Sing Billy McGee, McGaw;
There were three crows sat on a tree,
Sing Billy McGee, McGaw;
There were three crows sat on a tree,

Coyote Wisdom

And they were black as they could be,
And they all flopped their wings and cried,
   Aouw! Aouw! Aouw!

Says one old crow unto his mate,
   "Oh, Billy McGee, McGaw."
Says one old crow unto his mate,
   "Oh, Billy McGee, McGaw."
Says one old crow unto his mate,
   "Oh, what shall we do for something to eat?"
And they all flopped their wings and cried,
   Aouw! Aouw! Aouw!

"There lies a horse on yonders plain,
   Oh, Billy McGee, McGaw;
"There lies a horse on yonders plain,
   Oh, Billy McGee, McGaw;
"There lies a horse on yonders plain,
   Who by some cruel butcher slain."
And they all flopped their wings and cried.
   Aouw! Aouw! Aouw!

"We'll perch ourselves on his backbone,
   Oh, Billy McGee, McGaw;
We'll perch ourselves on his backbone,
   Oh, Billy McGee, McGaw;
We'll perch ourselves on his backbone,
   And eat his eye-balls one by one."
And they all flopped their wings and cried,
   Aouw! Aouw! Aouw!

II. *By* ALICE ATKINSON NEIGHBORS

Our grandmother knew this song in Indiana, before
coming to Texas in 1843. It is still sung in the family.

There were two crows sat on a tree,
And they were black as crows could be.
Said one old crow to his mate,
"What shall we do for meat to eat?"

"There Were Three (Two) Crows"

"There lies a horse on yonder plain
Whose body has been but three days slain.
We'll perch ourselves on his backbone,
And pick his eyes out one by one."

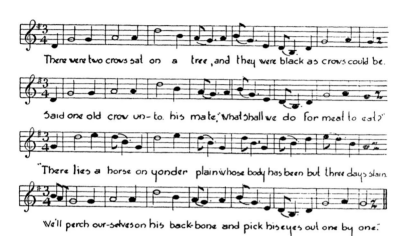

There were two crows sat on a tree, and they were black as crows could be.

Said one old crow un-to his mate, "What shall we do for meat to eat?"

"There lies a horse on yonder plain whose body has been but three days slain.

We'll perch our-selves on his back-bone and pick his eyes out one by one."

Contributors

SAMUEL E. ASBURY, State Chemist at Texas A. and M. College, lives alone—for he is a bachelor—in a house hidden by roses—plastered inside, ceilings as well as walls, with pictures, and filled with three pianos, phonograph records of virtually all the American folk songs that have been recorded, and books relating to Texas life and history. Years ago he started a magazine the nature of which can be deduced from its title, *The Nativist*. He designed and did much work on a grand opera meant to express the drama of the Texas Revolution. He contributed "Old Time Camp-Meeting Spirituals" to *Tone the Bell Easy* (Publications No. X of the Texas Folk-Lore Society). He can talk for ten hours by the clock and never run out of folk anecdotes.

LILLIAN ELIZABETH BARCLAY, who teaches English in a Waco High school, recently wrote a Master's thesis at the University of Texas on the coyote in American folk-lore and literature. Her important contribution to this book is a part of that thesis.

HENRY W. BARTON lives a Wichita Falls, where the wind blows either this way or that all the year round.

The first contribution that JULIA BEAZLEY, of Houston, made to the Texas Folk-Lore Society was a tale, "The Uneasy Ghost of Lafitte," in *Legends of Texas*, later appropriated by Frank Dobie for *Coronado's Children*. She is represented in *Texas and Southwestern Lore* (Texas Folk-Lore Society, 1927) by "The Ballad of Davy Crockett."

R. B. BLAKE, of Nacogdoches, is recognized as one of the most acute historians of Texas, his field being East Texas of Spanish and colonial times. He has just about vindicated the old story of Travis' having drawn a line across the floor of the Alamo. Some orthodox historians are offended at this kind of history. Look for his treatment of the subject in the next book issued by the Texas Folk-Lore Society.

Contributors

Tall Tales from Texas Cow Camps is well known, but many people who know it do not know that the author, MODY C. BOATRIGHT, has also published plays and is well recognized by historians of American scholarship. He is preparing a book to be called *Folk Laughter*, in which his treatment of Pulpit Anecdotes will appear. This is not his first appearance with the Texas Folk-Lore Society, of which he is one of the editors.

RALPH S. BOGGS teaches Spanish in the University of North Carolina and prepares annually a bibliography of contributions to American folk-lore. A. L. CAMPA teaches Spanish in the University of New Mexico and has made extensive studies, a number of which are published, of the Spanish-American folk-lore of his state. MARGARETE CARPENTER lives in Fort Worth. MILDRED COHEN was born in Iowa, but has lived in El Paso so long and so well that she comprehends Spanish-Mexican tales like one to the manner born, like her erstwhile mentor Charles L. Sonnichsen, of the El Paso School of Mines.

Taytay's Tales, Taytay's Memories, Swift Eagle of the Rio Grande and other books by ELIZABETH WILLIS DEHUFF have taken their place in the ever-growing volume of literature derived from the Pueblo Indians of New Mexico. Mrs. DeHuff has long been associated with these Indians. She lives at Santa Fé. In *Puro Mexicano* (published by the Texas Folk-Lore Society in 1935) she is represented by "The Metamorphosis of a Folk Tale."

MAE FEATHERSTONE, of Mills County, had a lengendary account in *Straight Texas* (the Texas Folk-Lore Society book for 1937). SUE GATES, of O'Donnel, in Lynn County, who was attending Southern Methodist University in 1935, entertained the Texas Folk-Lore Society with "Windy Yesterdays" when it met in Dallas that year.

JOHN GOULD, of the Wichita Falls *Daily Times*, writes something every day that is interesting, often educating the public on archaeology, public libraries, the history of Northwest Texas, and such subjects. LEON GUINN, another newspaper man, of the *Scurry County Times*, has made an extensive assemblage of

Coyote Wisdom

West Texas folk-lore. J. W. HENDREN teaches English in the Rice Institute, at Houston.

There are not many men in Texas adding more to the interest of the state than J. MARVIN HUNTER. His magazine, *Frontier Times,* published at Bandera, circulates all over the United States. He has built at Bandera a museum exhibiting pioneer life. On occasions he gets the people of the Hill Country together to fiddle, sing songs by organ music, pop whips, make shingles, spin on the spinning wheel, dance square dances and otherwise enjoy old-time folk practices and hand crafts. He compiled the monumental *Trail Drivers of Texas.* GABE W. LEWIS is connected with the John Tarleton Agricultural College at Stephenville.

As the world wags, more people in it are acquainted with the Tabasco sauce manufactured at Avery Island, Louisiana, than with the bird sanctuary at the same place. The "island" is an island of trees on the coastal plain. EDWARD A. McILHENNY is responsible for the marvelous bird sanctuary as well as for the sauce. He is one of the outstanding naturalists and wild life conservationists of the South. His published books include *The Wild Turkey and Its Hunting, The Alligator's Life History, Bird City* and *Befo' De War Spirituals.* He has in manuscript a wealth of Negro folk-lore not yet printed.

ALICE ATKINSON NEIGHBORS, of San Antonio, contributed a parcel of folk-songs to *Straight Texas* (1937). LYNNE WOOTEN PLATTER believes in mixing cowboys and the classics, which she has taught at Texas State College for Women, at Denton. JIMMIE POUNDS III, still an unlicked cub, has not heard the owl hoot in many places but he has heard Hugo, the legendary bull frog, bellow near Sulphur Springs, his home.

FANNIE E. RATCHFORD presides over the most beautiful rooms belonging to the public in the state of Texas—the Wrenn, Aitken and Stark collections in the Library of the University of Texas. Holder of both Guggenheim and Rockefeller fellowships, she is the author of a book on Emily Bronte and editor of two books (A. W. Terrell's *From Texas to Mexico* and *Camp d'Asile*) issued by the Book Club of Texas. She contributed to

Contributors

Legends of Texas, issued by the Texas Folk-Lore Society in 1924 and now long out of print.

A. F. SCHARFF, located at San Antonio with the United States Customs Service, is an authority on marihuana, opium, and such things. The strange and interesting tale he has contributed to this volume was written at Mazatlan, whither he had been taken by a job that had to do with leading squadrons of Mexican cavalry into the jungles and seeing that they destroyed extensive fields of opium-producing poppies. "It may surprise you," he says, "to know that in the states of Sinaloa and Sonora, Mexico, the culture of opium-producing poppies has become a menace to this continent." And marihuana, he adds, is becoming almost as menacing as opium.

MALNOR SHUMARD, JR. lives in Boerne, in the Hill Country he writes about. FRANK SIMMONS, Oglesby, in Coryell County, like many other writers for the Texas Folk-Lore Society, is not a professional man. He belongs to the folk himself. He gathered tunes and verses utilized in *Texas Play Party Songs and Games*, by W. A. Owens. MRS. L. G. SMITH, Dallas, sent in her "true story" of a buried legend because she had read some of the books issued by the Texas Folk-Lore Society and thought her story "might fit."

One of the two or three tales in *Puro Mexicano* (Texas Folk-Lore Society book for 1935) that have received most comment is "The Wonderful Chirrionera," by DAN STORM. He has lived in Mexico; his home is now in Austin, though he spends much time in New Mexico with Indians. He is storing away material for a book of tales.

GEORGE C. TAYLOR is a man who teaches Shakespeare. This means more than being merely a professor of English. The students in luck attend the University of North Carolina.

RADOSLAV A. TSANOFF is another professor who fulfills Emerson's ideal of the American scholar. He is a "man-thinking" instead of being merely an antiquarian. He expounds philosophy in The Rice Institute, is the author of various works on philosophy, and an authority on fairy tales. He is president of the Texas Folk-Lore Society.

Coyote Wisdom

ROBERT M. ZINGG, who teaches Anthropology in the University of Denver, spent a year among the Tarahumara Indians of Chihuahua, Mexico. His book, *The Tarahumara,* on these people was issued by the University of Chicago Press, 1935. He has also written on the Huichol Indians.

Proceedings of the Texas Folk-Lore Society

I. For 1936

The twenty-second annual meeting of the Texas Folk-Lore Society was held at the University of Texas, Austin, April 24 and 25. The following papers were read: *Negro Wisdom*, Martha Emmons, Waco; *Philosophy in Folk-Lore*, R. A. Tsanoff, Houston; *Tales of los Animalitos*, Dan Storm, Austin; *How Wildcat Creek and Wolf Creek, in Anderson County, Got Their Names*, Georgia McMeans, Palestine; *Mexican Lullabies*, Mrs. Raquel Rocha Wauls, Fort Worth; *Sacred Harp Singing in East Texas*, R. G. Upton, Nacogdoches; *Folk Ways of Pioneer Texans*, Afton Wynn, Austin; *Legend of the Treaty Stone of the Indians*, Adina De Zavala, San Antonio; *Spooks from El Paso*, Charles L. Sonnichsen, El Paso; *The Cristo of the Cactus*, Jovita Gonzáles de Mireles, Del Rio.

At the evening session of April 24, the Gant family, of Austin, sang popular ballads. On the afternoon of April 25, Esse Forrester O'Brien, of Waco, read original verses employing folk motives. At the dinner on April 25, Mrs. Morgan T. Smith presented some old time Texian sayings, and Trueman O'Quinn talked on *Colloquialisms of the Sabine Bottoms*. Various other attendants contributed folk sayings and brief folk anecdotes.

At the business meeting, the constitution was amended to provide for the office of Associate Editor, and it was voted to hold the 1937 session at Fort Worth.

The following officers were elected: President, Mabel Major, Fort Worth; Vice-Presidents, Charles L. Sonnichsen, El Paso; R. G. Upton, Nacogdoches; John Lee Brooks, Dallas; Councillors, Mrs. W. S. Randall, Dallas; David Donoghue, Fort Worth; George A. Hill, Jr., Houston; Secretary and Editor, J. Frank Dobie, Austin; Associate Editor, Mody C. Boatright, Austin; Treasurer, Marcelle Lively Hamer, Austin.

Coyote Wisdom

II. For 1937

The Society convened for the twenty-third annual round-up at Texas Christian University, Fort Worth, April 23 and 24. Papers read at the various sessions were as follows: President's *Address of Welcome*, Mabel Major, Fort Worth; *Syrup-Making Time in East Texas*, Guy Kirtley, Austin; *Kentucky Mountain Ballads* (with dulcimer accompaniment) Josiah Combs, Fort Worth; *Rattlesnake Oil*, Frost Woodhull, San Antonio; *Negro Superstitions on Duds and Grub*, J. Mason Brewer, Dallas; *Folk Heroes of America*, John Lee Brooks, Dallas; *Folk-Lore of the Tarascan Indians*, Eudora Garrett, Dallas, with guitar; *Texas Folk Tunes*, Mrs. Walter S. Robertson, Dallas, at piano; *The Federal Government Gathers Folk-Lore in Texas*, Harold Preece, Austin; *Old Pie-Biter: Camp Cook*, John Gould, Wichita Falls; *Folk-Lore in Names of Texas Flowers*, Mary Daggett Lake, Fort Worth; *Another Roy Bean Story*, J. Marvin Hunter, Bandera; *A Razorback Story*, G. T. Bludworth, Fort Worth.

The morning session on April 24 was given to various groups organized under Federal Recreational and Music Projects. At the dinner on April 24, the following Texas poets were presented, each reading briefly from his work: Hilton Ross Greer, Dallas; Lexie Dean Robertson, Rising Star; Stanley Babb, Galveston; Fania Kruger, Wichita Falls; Esse O'Brien, Waco; Ruth Averitte, Fort Worth; Patrick Moreland, Austin; Boyce House, Fort Worth.

The following officers were elected: President, Charles L. Sonnichsen, El Paso; Vice-Presidents, John Lee Brooks, Dallas; R. G. Upton, Nacogdoches; J. H. Farrell, Fort Worth; Councillors, Mrs. W. S. Randall, Dallas; George A. Hill, Jr., Houston; G. T. Bludworth, Fort Worth; Secretary and Editor, J. Frank Dobie, Austin; Associate Editor, Mody C. Boatright, Austin; Treasurer, Marcelle Lively Hamer, Austin.

It was voted to hold the 1938 at El Paso during the Easter holidays.

III. For 1938

The Society met in El Paso, in conjunction with the Hispanic Institute of New Mexico, April 15 and 16. The following con-

Proceedings of the Texas Folk•Lore Society

tributions were presented: *President's Greeting*, Charles L. Sonnichsen, El Paso; *Adventures of a Story Hunter*, J. Frank Dobie, Austin; *Indian Artists*, Ina Sizer Cassidy, Santa Fé; *Indian Dances*, Elizabeth Willis DeHuff, Santa Fe; *Santa Fé Fiesta*,* Ruth Laughlin, Santa Fé; *Folk Drama*, A. L. Campa, Albuquerque; *Cuentos del Diablo*, Margaret K. Kress, Austin; *Saints' Folk Tales*, Niña Otero-Warren, Santa Fé; *Folk-Lore and Fascism*, T. M. Pearce, Albuquerque; *Theology of the Pueblo Indians*, Reginald G. Fisher, Albuquerque; *Cuerpo sin Alma*, Mildred Cohen, El Paso; *Border Folk-Lore from the Big Bend*, Lutie Britt, Alpine; *Poetry and Pots*,* Jovita Gonzáles de Mireles, Del Rio; *Folk-lore from the Lower Rio Grande*, Frank Goodwyn, Sarita; *Native American Mother Goose Rhymes*,* Ray Wood, Austin; *Juicy Language from the Highlands*,* Josiah Combs, Fort Worth; *Rattlesnake Lore from the Witte Museum*,* Frost Woodhull, San Antonio; *Tales of Animalitos*, Dan Storm, Austin; *Humor in the Frontier Pulpit*, Mody C. Boatright, Austin; *Tales of the Chuck Wagon*,* Jack Thorpe, Albuquerque.

The following officers were elected: President, R. A. Tsanoff, Houston; Vice-Presidents, C. L. Sonnichsen, El Paso; Rabbi Henry Cohen, Galveston; Miss Ima Hogg, Houston; Councilors, Mrs. W. S. Randall, Dallas; John Lee Brooks, Dallas; Mabel Major, Fort Worth; Secretary and Editor, J. Frank Dobie, Austin; Associate Editor, Mody C. Boatright, Austin; Treasurer, Marcelle Lively Hamer, Austin.

The Secretary was authorized to confer with Harry Huntt Ransom, of the University of Texas, with a view of asking him to serve as associate editor. Mr. Ransom accepted the offer.

It was voted to hold the next meeting in Houston.

---

*Read by title only.

Index

A

Alamo, 185
Alexander, Bartley Burr, on coyote myths, 68
Allen, Jules Verne, 272
Americans, the first, 132, 133
Anderson, J. W., 157
Anecdotes of frontier preachers, 158 ff. See also Tales
Angel in Blue, legend of, 197
Angelina, missionary, 198
Animal People, 40, 66
Animals and Insects: Alligator, 135 ff.; ant, 243 ff.; antelope, 243 ff.; badger, 51-2, 129; bear, 121 ff., 247; bee, 79; buffalo, 70; bull frog, 262-3; burro, 28; coon, 80, 136, 137; Coyote (See separate entries); cricket, 78-80; deer, 74-6; dog, 8 ff., 50-51, 70, 136 ff., 252 ff., 264-5; elk, 70; fox, 29 ff., 32 ff., 121 ff., 128-9; gopher, 86-7; hog, 264; hornet 80; horse, 29, 70, 131, 265; lion, 27 ff., 243 ff.; locust, 85-9; mountain lion, 79, 128; 'possum, 136, 137; rabbit, 24 ff., 35, 44, 78, 118 ff., 247; rattlesnake, 24 ff., 29, 34-5; tiger, 244; sheep, 21 ff., 28, 131; snake, 82, 244; squirrel, 73; weasel, 129; wild cat, 79; wolf, 128; yellow jacket, 79
Apostolic succession, anecdote on, 166
"The Arkansas Traveler," 162, 187
Arnold, Oren, on coyote, 38, 43, 47, 56
Asbury, Francis, 155
Asbury, Samuel E., 284; "There Were Three Crows," variant of "Two Corbies," with music, 280-282
Atascosa County, 65
Austin, Mary, on coyote, 53, 55; on Cushing, 84; story by, 90-92; on folk-lore, 104
Austin's colony, religion in, 159
Aztec, articles of trade, 227

B

Baker, Jim (Pie Biter), 186
Ballads, texts of: "The Trail of Mexico," 272-5; "Early, Early in the Spring," 275-6, 278; "There Were Three Crows," 281-2; "There Were Two Crows," 282-3; discussion, 270-283
Banito, El, 196
Barclay, Lillian Elizabeth, 284; "The Coyote: Animal and Folk-Character," 36-103

Barton, A. S., on coyote, 61
Barton, Henry W., 284; "Sand Storm Yarns," 266-7
Bayliss, Clara Kern, story by, 76
Beazley, Julia, 284; "The Poopamareno," 252-4
Beechey, F. W., on coyote, 39-40
Begochidi the giant, 133-4
Belden, H. M., 277 n.
Bennett Creek, 200
Bennett, W. C., 207 ff.
"Bible Cure" for warts, 268
Bickler, Pinky, folk-character, 256-9
Biological Survey, 48, 63
Birds: blackbird, 80-81; bluebird, 44-5; buzzard 55-6, 177; chicken, 53, 54; cock, 82-3; crow, 27, 280 ff.; doves, 8 ff., 247; eagle, 243 ff.; owl, 129; paisano (chaparral bird, road-runner), 34-5; pigeon, 87-8; raven, 55-6; red bird, 197; turkey, 106
Blackman, Learner, 159
Black Mesa, 144 ff.
Blade, R. B., 284; "Traditional Nacogdoches," 195-9
Blue Beard, 109 ff.
Boatright, Mody C., 5, 285; "Comic Exempla of the Pioneer Pulpit," 155-168
Boggs, Ralph S., 285; "Running Down the Fool Killer," 169-173
Brazos de Dios, 198
Brinninstool, E. A., on coyote's song, 58
Brinton, Daniel G., on coyote, 39
Brooks, John Lee, 263
Burk Burnett Ranch, Pie Biter at, 189
Burr, Aaron, 198
Burton, Sir Richard, 149
Bustamente, 199
Byers, Texas, 200

C

Calvinism, 155
Campa, A. L., 285; "Note on 'Cuerpo sin Alma'," 249-250
Campbellism, 166
Cantina: "Mi novia, mi maguey," 18
Carpenter, Margarete, 285; "Paul Bunyan: Oil Man," 263-4
Car Snap, 205
Cartwright, Peter, 155-6, 157, 159, 163
Castañeda, 105-106
Cavens, William, 156, 160
Ceremony: Guadalupe Day, 210 ff.; Pueblo betrothal, 109; Twin War Gods, propitiation, 115-6; tea-drinking, 231-2

Index

Index

matachines, 214 ff.; of marriageable maidens, 90; in Mills County, 200-201
Deathbed stories, 168
Debates on doctrine, 166
Decatur, Texas, 259-260
DeHuff, Elizabeth Willis, 285; "Pueblo Versions of Old World Tales," 104-126; "Navajo Creation Myths," 127-134
De Soto, 197
Devil: in the churm, 194; Jesus the Mexican meets the d., 236; d. advises the miller, 251-2
Diction: "Canterbury move," 180; *chapeónes*, 215; "coyote giving," 91; "coyote song," 91; *cucaracha*, 225; *marihuana*, 230 n.; *marihuanero (cucaracha)*, 225; "Panhandle rain," 266; *prioste*, 218; "smarter than a steel trap," 52; "snap," 202; matachine, 214
Dobie, J. Frank, 250, 270, 272; "Pertinences and Patrons," 5-7; on coyote, 46, 53, 54 ff., 56
Dow, Lorenzo, 164
Dress: Taytay's costume, 105; Turkey Girl's magic costume, 107
Drouth, omens during, 177-8
Dupes: coyote dupes dove, 10; coyote dupes Juan, 21; sheep dupe coyote, 24; coyote dupes rattlesnake, 26-7; fox dupes coyote, 34; paisano dupes rattlesnake, 35; coon dupes coyote, 80; cricket dupes coyote, 80; deer dupes coyote, 75-6; turtle dupes coyote, 78; blackbirds dupe coyote, 80-1; frog dupes coyote, 81-2; cock dupes coyote, 82; locust dupes coyote, 89

E

Elberta Lake, 262
Elm Pass, 238
"Early, Early in the Spring," 271, 275 ff. (two variants)
Eclipse, the first, 128
"An English Source of the 'Trail to Mexico'," by J. W. Hendren, 270-279; (a) English sources of Texas ballads; (b) variants of "The Trail" and "Early, Early in the Spring," with music
Epiphany, feast of, 208
Espinosa, Aurelio M., 104
Evans, C. N. B., 169, 172

F

Faust-saga, 154
Featherstone, Mae, 285; "The Snap Party in Mills County," 200-206
Fiesteros, 210

Finley, Irene and William, on coyote, 43
Fire-boy, 114 ff., 128
First lines (including songs, ballads, and rhymes): "The blue sky is in the blue water," 45; "Early, early in the spring," 275; "For seven long years I sailed on the sea," 278; "Here, Sambo! And Ringo!" 253; "I am the Coyote that sings each night at dark," 59; "I made up my mind I'd change my way," 273; "I made up my mind to change my way," 272; "I have made the moon," 72-3; "It was in the merry month of May," 272; Keenah, o-la thay-lay!" 106; "Locust, locust, playing a flute," 85; "Mi novia, mi maguey," 18; "There were three crows sat on a tree," 281; "There were two crows sat on a tree," 282; "La cucaracha, la cucaracha," 225
First Man, 128, 132
Flint, Timothy, 159
Flood, Coyote causes, 128
Flower-petal, wife of Cliff-Dweller, 110
Folk idiom in frontier preaching, 157
Folk-lore, classification of, 104; philosophy in, 145-54
Folk-themes, 153-4
Folk-wisdom, 145 ff.
Food and drink: *agua miel*, 18 ff.; *pulque*, 18 ff.; *tortillas*, 80, 212; Tarahumara beer, 212; *tequila*, 235 ff.
Fool Killer, 169 ff.
"The Fox" (folk character), 121
Franciscans at Nacogdoches, 198
Fredonian Republic, 199
Frontier, preaching on the, 155 ff.

G

Games and sports: Coyote hunt, 64-5; hoop-and-pole game, 129; snap, 200-206
Garland, Acel, 263
Garrettson, Freeborn, 160
Gates, Sue, 285; "Windy Yesterdays," 264-5
Ghost legend, 179
Gobernador, 218
Goldthwaite, Texas, 200
Gould, John, 285; "Pie-Biter," 185-191
Grand Canyon, creation of, 128
Grass-on-the-Mountain, feast of, 91
Greeley, Horace, on coyote, 42-3
Grenade, John, 157
Grey, Viscount, of Fallodon, 5
Grinnell, George Bird, on coyote, 51-2, 54
Guadalupe, ceremony of, 210 ff.
Guadalupe, feast of Virgin of, 207 ff.

Index

Guadalupe Day, 210 ff.
Guadalupe Hidalgo, 209
Guadalupe River, 234
Guinn, Leon, 285; "Some Remedies from Scurry County," 268; "Note on Frontier Journalism," 268-9
Gustafson, Winfred, 5
Gutierrez, Bernardo, 198

H

Hamer, Marcelle Lively, 5
Harris, Mrs. Dilue, 159
Hearn, Lafcadio, 153
Hell, on the frontier, 160
Hendren, J. W., 286; "An English Source of the Trail to Mexico," 270-279
Holder, C. F., on coyote, 56-7
Holmes, Jesse, the Fool Killer, 169 ff.
Horn, Elder, 168
Hoop-and-pole game, 129
Hornaday, W. T., on coyote, 53
Houston, Sam, 158
Houston, Temple, 256
Hubbell, Jay B., on C. N. B. Evans, 172 n.
"Hugo: The Giant Unkillable Bull Frog," by Jimmie Pounds III, 262-3
Huichol Indians, 208, 215
Humphreys, Imogene, on coyote, 53
Hunter, J. Marvin, 286; "Roy Bean as Coroner," 254-6

I

Ifugao head-hunters, 212
Imperial, Texas, 200
Indians: attitude toward death, 125; Pie Biter's experience with, 187 ff. See Indian tribes
Indian tribes: Chochiti, 72, Comanches, 265; Huichol, 208, 215; Kutenai, 73-4; Maidu, 68; Mandan, 69; Miwok, 67; Navajo, 72, 74, 76, 127 ff.; Nahua, 67; Okanogan, 40, 66; Picuris, 78; Pima-Papagos, 44, 69, 72; Pueblo, 78, 104 ff., 132, 174; Shoshone, 68; Solian, 44; Tarahumara, 207 ff.; Wappo Shochamai, 68-9. See especially articles by DeHuff and Zingg
Ingersoll, Ernest, on coyote, 38. 46
Ingraham, J. H., 159
Inquest, anecdote on, 255-6
Ixtlaccihuatl, 233 and n.
Ixtlatl, 228 ff.

J

Jaurez, Benito, 208
Jesus Christ: appears to Pedro, 240; confused with Saint Joseph of Christ by Tarahumaras, 208

Jesuits, folk tales by, 37
Jewerta Maki (Earth Magician), 69
Jack the Giant-Killer, 114
James, W. S., 156
Job, 154
Juarez, Benito, 208

K

Kansas, frontier religion in, 159
Kendall County, Texas, 234
Kent, D. D., 278
Kentucky, frontier religion in, 159
Kidson, Frank, 277 n.
Kilpatricks, Texas desperadoes, 180 ff.
Kutenai Indians, 73-4

L

Landrum, Miriam, 5
Langtry, Texas, 255
Lantz, David E., on coyote, 40
Lee, Wilson, 163
Legend, interest in, 185
"Legend Making on the Concho," by Fannie E. Ratchford, 174-184; (a) the origin and nature of local legends, 174-5; (b) examples from the Paint Rock district, 175 ff.; (c) anecdotes concerning the Kilpatricks, 180 ff.
Legends: of Nacogdoches and Natchitoches, 195-7; of Red Feather, 197; of the Angel in Blue, 197-8; on Concho, 174 ff.
Leisy, E. E., on the Fool Killer, 169, 172-3
Lewis, Gabe W., 286; "Old-Time Remedies from Madison County," 267-9
"The Little Animals of Mexico," by Dan Storm, 8-35; (a) El Coyote, the Doves and the Dogs, 8-17; (b) The Coyote and Juan's Maguey, 18-21; (c) Mr. Coyote and the Two Sheep, 21-4; (d) Señor Coyote Acts as Judge, 24-7; (e) Judging Between Lions, 27-32; (f) Señor Coyote and Señor Fox, 32-4; (g) Paisano Saves Rabbit, 34-5
Lively, Dick, 268
Live Oak County, Texas, 272
"Los Llanos de Berlin y las Cuevas de Quiquiriqúi," 249-250
Logan, W. H., 277 n.
Lomax, John A., 270
Long's Republic, 199
Lumholtz, Carl, 207, 223
Lummis, Charles F., on coyote, 38, 42, 48, 49, 54, 57

M

McIlhenny, E. A., 286; "Trubble, Brudder Alligator, Trubble," 135-144

Index

Index

Pecan Bayou, 200
Pecos pueblo, 108
Pecos River, 200, 254
Penafiel, Antonio, on coyote, 39
Pence, Jack, 5
Peshlikai, story by, 74-6
"Philosophy in Folk-Lore," by Radoslav A. Tsanoff, 145-154; (a) folk-wisdom concerning problems of life and nature, (b) development of thought processes, (c) evolution of prayer, (d) folk-proverbs, (e) folk-themes
Picuris Indians, 78
Picuris River, 79
"Pie-Biter," by John Gould, 185-191; (a) in praise of legend, (b) Pie-Biter's identity, (c) his poker game, (d) his race with the Indians, (e) as camp cook, (f) how he got his name
Pima-Papagos Indians, 44, 69, 72
Piñon Harvest, 90
Pitner, Wilson, 156, 157
Plants and trees: buckeye, 267; chinquapin, 199; choke cherries, 121 ff.; maguey, 18 ff.; Jerusalem artichokes, 124; liveoak, 267; mesquite, 268; pine, 268; poke root, 267; queen's delight, 268; thorn, 35
Platter, Lynne, Wooten, 286; "The Toe Wiggled," 256-9
Play party, 201
Pojuaque pueblo, 114
Poker, Pie-Biter's game of, 186-7
"The Poopampareno," by Julia Beazley, 252-4; a story of the faithful hounds, Sambo and Ringo
Popo, 228 ff.
Popocateptl, 233 and n.
Potter, Jask, 156
Pounds, Jimmie III, 286; "Hugo: The Giant Unkillable Bull Frog," 262-3
Prairie fire, Pie-Biter cooks supper on, 189-190
Prayer, evolution of, 150; scepticism of, on frontier, 164-5
Prioste, 218
Prometheus, 154
Proverbs, 150; examples of Bulgarian folk wisdom, 151 ff.
Pueblo Indians, 78, 104 ff., 132, 174
"Pueblo Versions of Old World Tales," by Elizabeth Willis DeHuff, 104-126; (a) The Turkey Girl, 105-107; (b) Beauty and the Beast, 107-109; (c) Cliff-Dwellers, the Blue-Beard, 109-114; (d) The Giant-Killer Twins, 114-

118; (e) The Pueblo Tar-Baby Story, 118-120; (f) The Coyote Moon-Child, 120-121; (g) Fox-Woman and Bear-Woman, 121-124; (h) Observation on Indian Tales, 124-6

R

Rabbit, Br'er, compare with Coyote, 36
Race: Coyote and Dogs, 13 ff.; Fat Sheep and Thin Sheep, 22 ff.; Coyote and Turtle, 76-8; Cotton-tail and Coyote, 78; Coyote and Frog, 81-2; Pie Biter and the Indians, 188-9; Scout and Indians, 265
Rakes, L. W., on coyote, 43, 58
Ransbarger, David, 176
Ransom, Harry, 5
Ratchford, Fannie E., 286; "Legend Making on the Concho," 174-184
Red Feather, legend of, 196- 7
Red River, 196
Religion on the frontier, 158 ff.
Remedies, 267-8; liveoak leaves, nicotine, poke root tea, onion, molasses, buckeye, amber beads, coal oil, vinegar, flannel, queen's delight, horseshoe, pine knots, "Bible cure," horse-hair, mesquite bark, hoarhound and honey, gunpowder, lard, eggs; for warts, 193
Reynard the Fox, compared with Coyote, 6, 36, 37
Robelo, Cecelio A., on coyote, 38, 39
Robinson, W. H., on coyote, 62, 63, 69
Roman Catholicism, among Tarahumaras, 207 ff.
Romulus and Remus, 120
Roosevelt, Theodore, on coyote, 43, 64
Ross, James, 160
Routh, H. C., 259
"Roy Bean as Coroner," by J. Marvin Hunter, 254-6
Royce, Josiah, 153
Russell the Fox, 82-3
"Running Down the Fool Killer," by Ralph S. Boggs, 169-173; (a) quotations from the Fool Killer's columns, (b) identity and fame of the Fool Killer

S

Sabine River, 158, 198
St. Charles, Missouri, frontier religion in, 159
St. Denis, 198
Saint Joseph of Christ, 208
Saltillo, 237
Samachique, 208, 223
Sambo and Ringo, 252 ff.

Index

Index

CPSIA information can be obtained
at www.ICGtesting.com
Printed in the USA
FFOW03n1006161216
30392FF